A wave o
Shi

Please turn the page for more rave reviews!

Shinano!

The Sinking of Japan's Supership

Captain **Joseph F. Enright, USN**
with **James W. Ryan**

ST. MARTIN'S PRESS/NEW YORK

Front cover blueprint of *Shinano* is from *Battleships: Axis and Neutral Battleships in World War II* by Robert O. Dulin, Jr., and William Garzke, Jr. Copyright © 1985, U.S. Naval Institute, Annapolis, Maryland. Reprinted by permission.

SHINANO!

Library of Congress Catalog Card Number: 86–27927

ISBN: 0–312–90967–5   Can. ISBN: 0–312–90968–3

Printed in the United States of America

First St. Martin's Press mass market edition/April 1988

10 9 8 7 6 5 4 3 2 1

To my wife, Virginia, and the other wives and mothers who spent innumerable hours and sleepless nights praying that their husbands and sons on patrol in submarines would have successful missions and return home safely.

JFE

"The disaster of the *Shinano* is, I think, peculiarly symbolic of our war efforts. We built a fine ship and took much pride in her. She looked like a majestic and unperishable castle of the seas. But she was sunk before she fired a shot. There is more than a touch of irony in the fate of the *Shinano*."

—TOSHIKAZU KASE,
Journey to the Missouri (postscript)

"After the pyramids of Egypt and the Great Wall of China were the three ships of Yamato: wonders of the world yet, like the lofty pyramids and the long wall, great follies indeed."

—ANONYMOUS

"He who lived by the Samurai sword died by the air bomb and the submarine torpedo."

—THEODORE ROSCOE,
U.S. Submarine Operations in World War II

CONTENTS

Maps appear on pages 20, 161, and 203.

FOREWORD

Admiral Bernard A. Clarey, U.S. Navy[1]

The U.S. Navy fought the Pacific Ocean phase of World War II on a liquid chessboard with an area of more than 70 million square miles—the largest water mass on earth. In the maritime war, masses of men and ships of the United States and her allies were pitted against the modern fleet of Imperial Japan. The logistics involved were staggering and encompassed distances of thousands of miles in many of the campaigns.

Periodically, the opposing forces would clash in thunderous battles at Pearl Harbor, Coral Sea, Midway, the Solomons and Marianas, Leyte Gulf, and over the vast depths of the water surrounding the entrenched island bastions on the approaches to Japan itself. But on a day-to-day basis, it was the officers and men of the U.S. Navy's submarine fleet who kept up the pressure against the enemy's warships and merchant vessels.

By war's end, American submarines had sunk 201 Japanese naval ships with another 13 probables, and 1,113 merchant ships with another 65 probables.[2] In accomplishing this remarkable feat, 52 out of 288 U.S. submarines never returned from their final patrols. Approximately 374 officers and 3,131 men of the "Silent Service" descended forever with their submarines to the ocean's bottom and God's mercy.[3]

Usually operating alone, without recourse to assistance from their fellow warships and with only their relatively fragile submarine hulls to protect them from aerial bombs, surface ship guns, and depth charges, America's submariners wrote an unsurpassed chapter in the annals of the U.S. Navy's history for courage, dedication, and loyalty to their young country. No sailors were more worthy of the accolade "Well done."

On November 28, 1944, when I first heard of the events described in this narrative, I was a young submarine skipper on patrol in Luzon Strait, south of Taiwan. We submarines on patrol had our own separate communications—a very low-frequency (VLF) broadcast, which was copied by all submarines at sea. It was the practice of the submarine force commander in Pearl Harbor to immediately rebroadcast on this network important messages received from submarines, such as the contact reports of enemy ships. The purpose of this procedure was twofold. It confirmed for the transmitting submarine that her message had been received, and it enabled other submarines to assist, or take position to attack, if the contact was nearby.

It was via this broadcast that I learned that *Archer-Fish*[4] had made contact on a large aircraft carrier and three escorts a few miles south of the entrance to Tokyo Bay. The contact report stated that the range was too great to permit a prompt attack, and that the course and speed of the group prohibited *Archer-Fish* from getting into position. Nevertheless she would continue to track and pursue. I sympathized with my good friend Commander Joe Enright, skipper of *Archer-Fish;* about three weeks earlier, I had missed sinking an aircraft carrier under circumstances much more favorable than his.

Several hours later, early on November 29, another message from *Archer-Fish* appeared on the broadcast reporting that the carrier had been hit by four torpedoes from close range and had sunk. This was incredible—impossible and yet it had happened. I would have to wait several weeks, until I reached port, to find out how this magic was performed.

The saga of *Archer-Fish* and *Shinano* depicts a situation faced by many young submarine skippers in deciding strategy and tactics under the stress of combat operations, and it is one of the most fascinating stories of the Pacific war. His Imperial Japanese Majesty's Ship *Shinano* was designed to be one of a trio of the *Yamato*-class superbattleships laid down before the war. She had, however, been converted to an aircraft carrier after the battle of Midway and was on her maiden voyage when Commander Enright, skipper of *Archer-Fish,* sank her with only four torpedoes. Who would have believed this leviathan, an embodiment of Japan's aspirations to snatch victory from defeat, could be stopped in such a lethal fashion by a vessel less than a thirtieth her size, a 2,000-ton American submarine,[5] firing what the Japanese believed to be "inferior" torpedoes?[6]

In their six-and-one-half-hour confrontation during the evening of November 28 and the early morning hours of November 29, Captain Toshio Abe,[7] commander of *Shinano,* and Commander Joseph F. Enright of *Archer-Fish* played out a chess game of tremendous significance. For the Japanese, to be checkmated on their tiny segment of the Pacific, just south of the main island of Honshu, was to lose much more than a ship. It was to lose face and to suffer a shattering blow to the Imperial Japanese Navy's fighting spirit. It would serve, too, to quicken the Empire's slide into surrender.

Shinano was escorted by a trio of updated, battle-proven destroyers. The four Japanese warships had a total complement of some 4,000 men compared with the 82 aboard *Archer-Fish.* They held vast gun superiority over the U.S. submarine. Each of them was capable of greater speed than *Archer-Fish.* Captain Abe knew his destination after leaving Tokyo Bay, the seaport of Kure in the Inland Sea, while Commander Enright, not privy to this information, was under constant pressure to read Captain Abe's mind in order to gain a position ahead of the zigzagging *Shinano* and maneuver submerged into an elusive firing "window" measured narrowly in hundreds of yards and likely to be "open" only for seconds.

Unfortunately for Captain Abe, he assumed that his battle force was confronted by a wolf pack rather than by a lone opponent. As a result, his actions were defensive, designed to avoid combat. He was obsessed with the thought that his mission was to move *Shinano* safely to Kure. In failing to seize an excellent opportunity to destroy *Archer-Fish*, Captain Abe, a decorated combat officer, ultimately made a fatal move.

The Americans did hold several advantages. Commander Enright, his officers and men, and *Archer-Fish* itself were aggressive, determined, and tenacious—and, unlike Captain Abe, offensively minded as well as lucky. This book emphasizes the importance of good fortune in war, as well as the role played by past experience, the correctness of assumptions, the reliability of data, and the soundness of strategy and tactical analysis under stress.

Shinano! deserves to become a wartime naval classic for its gripping depiction of the way in which decisions were made by the captains of opposing men-of-war. The information on the construction of the huge and secret Japanese carrier, and the aura of mystery that enshrouded her brief, unhappy existence, makes compelling reading even forty years after her sinking. This firsthand account also conveys vividly a sense of how it was in an American submarine during those hectic days of 1941–45. Captain Enright's painstaking research has uncovered a number of valuable sources and revelations, including:

- The postwar report of the U.S. Technical Mission to Japan, the most authentic document available on the torpedo damage inflicted on the *Shinano* and why it proved sufficient to sink her.
- The conclusions and recommendations of the top-secret investigation conducted by a dozen Japanese officers into the cause of the catastrophe.
- Firsthand accounts of *Shinano* survivors, based on interviews conducted by trained Japanese navy veterans.
- Information that U.S. Naval Intelligence knew a third *Yamato*-class superbattleship was under construction but was unaware that *Shinano* had undergone conversion to an aircraft carrier. (For this reason, Commander Enright was initially denied credit for sinking an aircraft carrier.)

Shinano was the largest warship in history to be sunk by a submarine, a truly incredible exploit. In terms of tonnage, *Arch-*

er-Fish's sinking of *Shinano* was the most productive war patrol of the 1,682 undertaken by U.S. submarines during World War II.[8] In awarding the Navy Cross to Commander Enright, Secretary of the Navy James Forrestal credited *Archer-Fish* with the sinking of a 72,000-ton Japanese aircraft carrier.

An account of the duel between *Archer-Fish* and *Shinano* is long overdue. It has become a legend of naval warfare, but it needed to be told authoritatively. Captain Enright and James W. Ryan are to be commended for the fascinating, objective, and detailed way in which they have accomplished this task. Well done, indeed!

ACKNOWLEDGMENTS

First, I wish to thank Masataka Chihaya, a wartime combat commander in the Imperial Japanese Navy, for his generosity in providing access to many of the reports of *Shinano*'s survivors. Without these, this book would not contain the wealth of information about the activities of the crew during the pursuit and sinking of the giant carrier.

Similarly, I am grateful to Jo Toyoda of Yokohama, a carrier-based dive bomber pilot for the Imperial Japanese Navy during the war, for permission to use vital information he had gathered on *Shinano* since 1945. I consider both these gentlemen to be good friends.

I also wish to express my appreciation to many others who encouraged me to write this book in many different ways. They include: Professor P. Albert Duhamel, Admiral Arleigh Burke, Captain Edward L. Beach, Captain Roger Pineau, Captain David H. McClintock, Captain Paul R. Schratz, Rear Admiral Kemp Tolley, Rear Admiral John A. Scott, Rear Admiral Eugene B. McKinney, Captain W. J. "Jasper" Holmes, Vice Admiral James F. Calvert, Thomas P. McCann, Joseph C. Keeley, Richard H. O'Connell, Dr. D. C. Allard, Head, Operational Archives Branch of the Naval Historical Center, and Mr. Roger Chesneau.

A special word of thanks is also due Ms. Frances Chaikin for her typing and editing skills in the preparation of the initial manuscript; and to Mrs. Mieko Negishi Greene and Ms. Hatsue Akagi for their superb translation of Japanese sources. And also to Fred Freeman, Robert O. Dulin, Jr., Charles Haberlein of the Naval Historical Center, and Shizuo Fukui of the former Imperial Japanese Navy.

My gratitude has to be expressed to Admiral Bernard A. Clarey, who drew upon his Pacific war experiences as a submarine commander to prepare the incisive and informative foreword for this book. Now living in retirement in Hawaii Admiral "Chick" Clarey truly sets the fighting seascape for all that follows.

Boston writer-historian James W. Ryan and Senior Editor Jared Kieling of St. Martin's Press helped immeasurably with their professional writing and editing skills to produce the final version of the manuscript. To both of them, I am deeply grateful.

Finally, I want to express my heartfelt appreciation to my late wife of nearly 50 years, Virginia, who constantly encouraged and supported my efforts to write this book. Although she was left for countless lonely hours while I worked on the manuscript, she was always understanding and patient. God bless her.

—Captain Joseph F. Enright

Prologue

Once there were three awesome steel sisters, behemoths, conceived in cunning and secrecy to be implacable predators of the seas. Each was intended, in the beginning, to prowl the world's waters in search of prey to destroy with 18.1-inch guns firing 3,200-pound shells a distance of 22.5 miles.[1]

No warships of any other nation, including the United States, were to match their massive armaments, or their full-load displacement of 70,000 tons, or speed of 27 knots generated by 12 Kampon boilers. In comparison, the U.S.S. *Missouri* had a full-load displacement of 52,000 tons,[2] and Nazi Germany's famed battlewagons, *Tirpitz* and *Bismarck*, each totaled 51,000 tons.[3]

As a new class of superbattleships, the trio would be able to outrange and outgun any ship then in service or expected to be constructed by another naval power for at least a decade.[4] With the power, protection, and fearsome weapons of these dreadnoughts, Imperial Japan's hope of eleventh-hour victory in World War II could possibly become a reality.

They became known to history as His Imperial Japanese Majesty's ships—*Yamato, Musashi,* and *Shinano.* To this day their like has never been seen and is unlikely ever to be seen because of the incredible expense involved and the highly technical evolution of modern naval warfare.

The genesis of these sister ships came in October 1934, when

1

the Japanese Naval General Staff, planning for an inevitable confrontation with the United States, ordered the Imperial Naval Technical Bureau (Kampon) to report on the feasibility of building a new fleet of superbattleships.[5] At the time, the Staff chiefs were tightly bound to the conviction that the battleship was the key to naval dominance. They envisioned a fleet of battleships that would be vastly superior to any warships commissioned by the Americans in tonnage, speed, and armament.

While awaiting a response from the Kampon, Japan gave the world the required two years' notice on December 29, 1934 that after December 31, 1936 it would no longer be a party to the terms of the 1922 Washington and 1930 London naval limitation agreements. After all, who were these despised foreigners to dictate to Japan's military autocracy how many capital ships and auxiliary vessels they could maintain in their burgeoning navy? No longer would Japan's dreams of eventual control of the Pacific Basin be thwarted by a patronizing United States and an arrogant England. Even then Japanese troops controlled Manchuria, Korea, and huge areas of northern China; and its Imperial Army, supported by the modern Japanese Navy, sought to conquer all of the Chinese mainland. The year before, when the League of Nations condemned Japan for its unrelenting assaults upon China, Tokyo had canceled its membership —effective as of May 1935.

After the Kampon responded favorably on the feasibility of building the superbattleships, design began immediately under the direction of Vice Admiral Keiji Fukuda and Captain Kitaro Matsumoto. During a 29-month period, the tireless Kampon drafted 22 designs for the new battleships.[6] The final plan was approved in March 1937, and the General Staff placed an order at once for the initial pair of the new battleships under the Third Fleet Replenishment Program.[7]

The new class was designated *Yamato*-class battleships because the name Yamato was to be given to the first of the planned vessels. *Yamato*'s keel was laid down on November 4, 1937 at Kure Navy Yard; that of her sister ship, *Musashi,* was laid on March 29, 1938 at the Mitsubishi Yard in Nagasaki.[8]

Two more were ordered under the Fourth Fleet Replenishment Program of 1939, and the third keel, *Shinano,* was laid down as Ship Hull No. 110 in Drydock No. 6 at the Yokosuka Naval Shipyard on May 4, 1940. A fourth unnamed battleship of the same updated design of *Shinano* was laid later in the year at Kure. (Designated Ship Hull No. 111 she was never completed, and her hull steel was used during World War II for other ship-building projects of higher priority.) Moreover, the Kampon drew up plans for an additional trio of these hypothetically invincible dreadnoughts—two of them to bear even larger guns of 19.7 inches—but their keels were never laid.[9]

Following tradition, each of the three sister battleships then under construction had been named for an early prefecture (province) of old Japan. *Yamato* was given the name of the prefecture located on the main island of Honshu bordering the Pacific Ocean with Kii Suido to the west. The old Musashi prefecture ran along the shore of Tokyo Bay and contained the city of Tokyo. The prefecture for which *Shinano* was named was situated in the center and broadest part of Japan proper— northwest of Musashi. This same prefecture had given its name to Japan's principal river, the Shinano, which is 243 miles long. Admiral Isoroku Yamamoto, who was commander-in-chief of the Combined Japanese Fleet and top planner of the attack on Pearl Harbor, had grown up in a community along the Shinano River and would take every opportunity when home on leave to swim in the cool, crystal water fed by mountain streams.[10]

As the building of the superbattleships progressed (even with the tightest possible security precautions U.S. Navy Intelligence was still able to learn some details of their existence), Washington became increasingly exasperated over Japan's decade-old involvement in China. Tokyo's efforts to reach a settlement with Washington on this sensitive issue were consistently rebuffed. Washington's position was that there would be no reconciliation until the Japanese forces withdrew from China. With no such concession forthcoming, in July 1941 the United States placed an embargo on further shipments to Japan of scrap metal, iron ore, chemicals, and aviation fuel. In short order, Japanese shipping was denied passage through the Panama Canal and their assets in the United States were frozen.

In response to what they considered America's obtuseness, Japan's military leaders, with the reluctant acquiescence of Emperor Hirohito, decided to proceed with Plan Z—the surprise attack on Pearl Harbor.[11] With General Hideki Tojo, one of their "own," as the dictatorial prime minister, they saw no better option for achieving Japan's goal of a "Greater East Asia Co-Prosperity Sphere."

For an island nation with nowhere near the landmass of the United States or its resources in raw materials, minerals and production capability, and with a population of less than half the 145 million of the United States, the Japanese had achieved remarkable naval strength—in both numbers and level of technical proficiency—by December 7, 1941. Though Japan had only 10 battleships while the Americans had 17, four American battleships were destroyed and four others badly damaged in the Pearl Harbor attack. As for aircraft carriers, Japan had nine, versus seven for the United States. Moreover, Japan possessed nine auxiliary carriers (including seaplane carriers) while the United States had five. The Japanese also counted 22 heavy cruisers to 18 for the United States, and 23 light cruisers to 19 for the United States. However, Japan had only 124 destroyers and PT boats (170 for the United States), and 80 submarines (vis-à-vis 112 for the United States). The advantage in submarines was to be a key factor in America's favor during the Pacific war, and ultimately in the final defeat of Japan.[12]

In his definitive, unofficial operational history, *United States Submarine Operations in World War II*, Theodore Roscoe notes:

. . . the part played by the United States submarines in Japan's maritime demise is depicted with reasonable accuracy in the figures compiled after the war by the Joint Army-Navy Assessment Committee. According to this authority, United States submarines sank 1,113 Japanese merchant ships (of over 500 gross tons) for a tonnage total of 4,779,902 tons. They probably sank an additional 65 vessels, for an extra 225,872 tons. United

4

States submarines also sank 201 Japanese naval vessels—a total of 540,192 naval tons. Thirteen "probables" in this category added 37,434 tons to the naval score.

In the aftermath of Pearl Harbor and the devastation inflicted on the U.S. fleet, particularly on its battleships, the Japanese reexamined their naval shipbuilding program. They knew that they now held a commanding superiority in the battleship category. Moreover, *Yamato* was scheduled for completion on December 16, 1941; and *Musashi* on August 5, 1942. Requirements for a third battleship had obviously diminished sharply. As a result, orders were issued to slow work on *Shinano* and transfer many of her builders to more urgent projects.[13]

This temporary slowdown was abruptly reversed some six months later because of the beating Japan took in the battle of Midway. In that decisive June 1942 struggle, U.S. carrier-borne planes caught the Japanese carrier force rearming and refueling swarms of aircraft on its exposed flight decks. Four first-line Imperial carriers, *Akagi, Kaga, Soryu,* and *Hiryu*—all veterans of the attack on Pearl Harbor—were lost, along with their planes and veteran aviators. Only a month earlier, the Japanese light carrier *Shoho* had been sunk in the battle of the Coral Sea. Clearly, aircraft carriers had assumed a dominant role in the Pacific war. Japan's strategic planners pushed immediately for a sharp increase in the number of ships in this class, including conversion of *Shinano* from a superbattleship to the world's largest carrier.[14] At this time she was scheduled to be completed in January 1945.

It was at Midway that one of the two key figures involved in the ultimate fate of *Shinano*—the largest and most mysterious of the three sister superbattleships—first came to prominence. He was about to participate in the intriguing series of circumstances that led to one of the most memorable naval confrontations of the war—an event that would have a place in the *Guinness Book of World Records* nearly five decades later.[15] A graduate of the Japanese Naval Academy, married and the

5

father of a young son, he was Captain Toshio Abe, commander of Destroyer Division 10 and a veteran torpedo officer who two years later would be assigned skipper-designate of *Shinano*. A blunt, unsmiling man in the Bushido warrior tradition and ever conscious of his duty to the death for the Emperor and the Empire, Abe was once described by Lieutenant Commander Takamasa Yasuma, newly assigned medical officer aboard *Shinano:* "Expressing the flavor of an ancient samurai, he seemed to be a man of strong will and apparently was respected by his officers and men."[16]

The fatally stricken carrier *Hiryu* was dead in the water as night fell after the American aerial onslaught off Midway on June 4, 1942.[17] At 1703, thirteen American dive bombers had singled out *Hiryu,* flagship of Rear Admiral Tamon Yamaguchi, commander of Carrier Division 2, as their specific target. Four aerial bombs struck *Hiryu*'s deck adjacent to the bridge, engulfing the lines of loaded planes in flames and igniting a horrendous series of topside explosions the length of the carrier. By 2130, *Hiryu* had ceased all forward motion and listed some 15 degrees to starboard.[18]

Captain Abe fearlessly maneuvered his flagship destroyer *Kazagumo* alongside to help *Hiryu*'s crew fight the roaring flames and provide them with food and drink. But access to the engine rooms was cut off by the intense heat and acrid smoke, and the carrier continued to ship water. In the early hours of June 5, Admiral Yamaguchi notified his superiors that he was ordering the carrier's crew to abandon ship. No radio communications were permitted, so the message was carried to Vice Admiral Chuichi Nagumo, commander First Carrier Striking Force, by the destroyer *Kazagumo*.[19]

At 0230 Admiral Yamaguchi ordered Captain Tomeo Kaku, skipper of the *Hiryu,* to gather the surviving members of the crew topside. About 800 hands responded. Under the bright moonlit sky, Admiral Yamaguchi gave his farewell remarks: "As commanding officer of this carrier division, I am fully and solely responsible for the loss of *Hiryu* and *Soryu* [a sister carrier]. I shall remain on board to the end. I command all of you to leave the ship and continue your loyal service to His Majesty, the Emperor."[20]

Captain Kaku then ordered the flag of the Rising Sun lowered from the yardarm. Buglers played the national anthem, "Kimigayo." Upon the completion of this ceremony, Admiral Yamaguchi and Captain Kaku mutually agreed that Captain Abe's destroyers should torpedo *Hiryu* to prevent its capture by the Americans. They also decided that only they of all the officers aboard would go down with the carrier.

As the two commanders bade sad farewells to their staffs, the crew members began transferring to the destroyer *Kazagumo,* which had come alongside again. The remaining staff officers drank a final silent toast from a water cask sent over earlier by Captain Abe; then they too began to disembark.

Commander Ito, the senior staff officer, asked Admiral Yamaguchi whether he had a last message. The admiral replied: "I have no words to apologize for what has happened. I only wish for a stronger Japanese Navy—and revenge."[21] He handed over his black deck cap to Commander Ito as a memento. The staff officer in turn gave the admiral a length of sturdy cloth with which to bind himself to the bridge and fulfill his wish to go down with the ship.[22]

Upon learning of the decision of Admiral Yamaguchi and Captain Kaku to die with *Hiryu,* Captain Abe went aboard in a last effort to persuade them to leave. It was in vain. They thanked him politely and ordered him to return to *Kazagumo* to carry out his orders. When last seen, they were on the bridge waving good-bye to their crewmen aboard the destroyers.

As the sun thrust its first pink glow across the eastern horizon, Captain Abe prepared to carry out Admiral Yamaguchi's instructions. *Kazagumo* and *Yugumo* steamed away, circled, and headed directly for *Hiryu.* Within striking distance, Captain Abe unhesitatingly gave the order for torpedoes to be fired. The deadly fish sprang from the bows of the destroyers and rushed to the mark, scoring lethal hits against *Hiryu*'s tilted hull. A series of deafening explosions ripped the dawn sky as the coup de grace was administered.[23]

Captain Abe's torpedoes struck *Hiryu* at 0510 hours. Shortly afterward the large carrier started to go down at position 31 degrees, 38 minutes N, 178 degrees, 51 minutes W—a location at which the ocean bottom is marked by seamounts and valleys and the maximum water depth is some 2,800 fathoms.[24]

His mission accomplished, Captain Abe turned Destroyer Division 10 northwest to follow in the wake of the surviving Japanese fleet. He never looked back at the ship he had scuttled. He knew it was not one of his finest hours. Yet he had followed orders. He was full of admiration for Admiral Yamaguchi and Captain Kaku. He could still see them in his mind, braced bravely on the bridge in the face of death. It was how he would remember them—always. Yet he did not want to think about *Hiryu* plunging in her death throes to the ocean floor—smashing, grinding, sliding down the jagged slope of an underwater mount before coming to rest three miles below the surface, the lifeless bodies of Admiral Yamaguchi and Captain Kaku lashed to the bridge. . . .

He was keenly aware that Admiral Yamamoto, commander of the Combined Fleet aboard the superbattleship *Yamato*, would be very unhappy to learn of their beau geste. The admiral was adamantly opposed to the tradition of Japanese senior officers sacrificing themselves with their sinking ships. Ritual deaths no longer had a place in the modern Japanese Navy. The admiral desired his officers to live to fight another day. Their experience and expertise, acquired over so many years of service, were too valuable a resource to be lost in an act of penitence or propitiation.

As the new day broke serenely across the befogged expanse of the Pacific Ocean, Captain Abe wondered anew what decision he would have made in the same situation. Admiral Yamamoto was a man to be respected, feared, and obeyed. Even Rear Admiral Matome Ugaki, chief of staff of the Combined Fleet, was rumored to quake before his withering wrath. Still, Admiral Yamamoto could not be on the bridge of every warship in the fleet. Captain Abe left undecided how he would have resolved the conflict between duty and honor when and if this dilemma ever found him.

Two and a half weeks later, on June 22, 1942, some 7,000 miles away at the U.S. Submarine Base in New London, Connecticut, Lieutenant Joseph Francis Enright was ordered to his first command—the U.S.S. *O-10* (SS-71). Enright, a 1933 Annapolis graduate, had been a submarine officer for nearly six years and had been on five patrols aboard the U.S.S. *S-22,* which was deployed in the Pacific to guard against approaches to the Panama Canal by Japanese warships.

He was remembered among his classmates for his geniality, "lightly freckled countenance, and wide grin," and for the number of friends he made at the Academy. In the course of his first command, Enright, whose family's Irish crest bears a pair of dolphins similar to those in the submariner's emblem, became known as "Oh Boat Joe of the Oh-One-Oh." As skipper of the *O-10,* he later wrote: "We were fully employed as a training boat taking Submarine School students for training dives out in Long Island Sound. *O-10* was old—commissioned first in 1918 —and she was small, 480 tons and 172 feet in length. But I was proud to be her skipper."

As the war year of 1943 moved into its third month, Lieutenant Enright was just past his thirty-second birthday and expected to receive orders to the Pacific as an executive officer aboard a fighting submarine. Many of his classmates were already combat veterans—others had been killed or wounded— and he was eager to become active in the war against Japan. However, in mid-March 1943 he was designated the prospective commanding officer of U.S.S. *Dace* (SS-247), then being built as the first ship in the Electric Boat Company's new Victory Yard at Groton, Connecticut.

"I was elated," he later wrote. "It was another of my lucky breaks. I was one of the first in my class to get command of a new sub right from the building yard." A promotion to lieutenant commander soon followed.

U.S.S. *Dace* was launched on Easter Sunday, April 25, 1943.

She was assigned a complement of seven officers and 69 men. Executive Officer W. G. "Bill" Holman and a nucleus of the seamen had served aboard other subs on war patrols in the Pacific. *Dace*'s commissioning took place on July 23, 1943. In attendance were the new commanding officer's parents, Mr. and Mrs. John L. Enright, who had traveled by train from North Dakota to be present.

After a period of intensive training, test diving to a depth of 312 feet, and test firing of some 100 torpedoes, *Dace* departed New London on September 6, 1943 for a voyage to the Caribbean, through the Panama Canal, and on to Pearl Harbor, Hawaii, arriving on October 3. When she was successfully checked out and the crew brought up to fitness to conduct a war patrol, Lieutenant Commander Enright received orders to proceed 1,700 miles west-northwest to arrive at Midway on October 20. There *Dace*'s fuel and provisions were replenished, and she sailed on October 27 for the assigned patrol area—No. 5, in the so-called "Hit Parade" south of the major Japanese home island of Honshu. *Dace*'s skipper was convinced that his luck was holding. Area No. 5 was a veritable shooting gallery of plump Japanese naval and commercial shipping targets. Visions of victories swam before his pale blue eyes.

Area No. 5 lived up to its expectations—it was constantly crisscrossed by Japanese ships of all types—but Lieutenant Commander Enright's optimism was not rewarded. One target of opportunity after another was lost. Even after receiving a highly classified ULTRA[25] message giving the location, course, and speed of a large enemy carrier, Commander Enright went by the book instead of following his gut instincts and failed to maneuver *Dace* into the correct position for attack on the target. As a result, *Shokaku*, one of the surviving Japanese aircraft carriers of the Pearl Harbor attack, passed safely by *Dace* at a distance of some nine miles.

Dace returned to Midway from her first war patrol on December 11, 1943. The next day Lieutenant Commander Enright, convinced that he was a weak link, called on Captain J. B. Longstaff, the senior submarine officer on Midway and the local representative of the submarine force's admiral. In an almost unheard-of appeal for the wartime Navy, Lieutenant Commander Enright reported his disappointment in his first war patrol as a commanding officer. "I had an excellent submarine, fine officers, top-notch crew, and a patrol area with contacts," he told Captain Longstaff. "I feel I was responsible for the unproductive patrol and request to be relieved by an officer who can perform more satisfactorily."

On December 28, 1943, the Navy took him at his word and relieved him of command of *Dace*. He was ordered to report to the commander of Submarine Division 142 for duty with the submarine relief crews. On January 1, 1944, he was promoted to the rank of full commander and several months later assigned executive officer of the submarine base at Midway. At this post in the backwaters of the war, he learned in time that he was "no longer on the first team" in the eyes of his superior officers, and that, in retrospect, he should have followed his first judgment and responded to his gut instincts aboard *Dace* when confronted with targets like *Shokaku*.

Despite his self-criticism, the Navy never questioned Commander Enright about his abortive attack on *Shokaku*. He had been "the man on the spot," and if he had decided despite the ULTRA message to be nine miles distant in an effort to intercept *Shokaku*, Admiral Charles A. Lockwood, commander of the Pacific submarine fleet, would have backed him to the hilt. How many times had he heard fellow skippers repeat Admiral Lockwood's dictum: "The skipper has better information [in such situations] . . . he's the man on the spot . . . and can take more appropriate action than anyone at a desk hundreds of miles away." In other words, the admiral didn't want his deskbound staff second-guessing his fighting skippers after the fact.

The war, however, was far from over for the young officer; he was not to remain at the placid duty station at "Gooneyville" on Midway forever. In the next in a series of coincidences that would move him closer to his confrontation with *Shinano*, then undergoing rapid conversion from battleship to aircraft carrier, Commander Enright was about to sit down with some other

11

submarine officers for a game of stud poker for high stakes that might leave him with not only a winning hand but perhaps another command at sea.

Perhaps his luck was finally going to change. Perhaps the same qualities of dependability, unfailing good humor, and generosity that characterized him as a student were going to come together to make the "fine officer" envisioned in the 1933 Annapolis class annual's "Lucky Bag." Perhaps, too, he was finally going to receive a response to the hundreds of silent prayers he had murmured. He was aching to get back into the fight. His spirits were particularly low in that August of 1944. Back in the States his mother had died suddenly and without warning from a cerebral hemorrhage. He was painfully aware that she had died in the knowledge that her "Joe" was not performing the job for which he had been trained.

Meanwhile, within Drydock No. 6 at the Yokosuka Naval Shipyard on the western shore of the Bay of Tokyo, the conversion of *Shinano* to a carrier was progressing right on schedule for the completion date of February 1945. To conceal construction, a towering corrugated fence of galvanized steel had been erected on three sides of the graving dock. On the fourth side a tall, steep limestone cliff served as a natural barrier to curious eyes. In effect, *Shinano* and the drydock were sealed off from the rest of the sprawling base. Her thousands of builders were confined to the yard compound and lived under the threat of imprisonment or summary execution if they uttered so much as a word of her existence.[26]

These efforts to contain the secret construction of *Shinano* were virtually leak-proof. With the exception of a few inconclusive reports of her possible existence during the Pacific war, nothing was known of the warship even when she finally steamed out of Tokyo Bay. The U.S. Navy's *Recognition Manual* had no description of her. To reinforce their security endeavors, the Japanese secret police (kempei) had strictly prohibited even the possession of a camera within the shipyard

12

and anywhere near Drydock No. 6. No photographs were permitted for any reason.

As a result *Shinano* is the only major warship built in this century that was never officially photographed during construction.

The first photograph of *Shinano* was taken by a B-29 reconnaissance aircraft over the Tokyo area from 32,000 feet on November 1, 1944. It appears that this photo never reached Commander Submarines Pacific for distribution to the submarines. An entry in the patrol report submitted on December 15, 1944, suggested that the Army Air Corps Bomber Command planes whom Enright had seen flying toward Tokyo from *Archer-Fish*'s lifeguard station might be helpful in identifying the aircraft carrier victim. No help was forthcoming.

In 1983 when Enright learned that a Boston friend, Richard H. "Dick" O'Connell, had been on duty at the Joint Intelligence Center, Pacific Ocean Area, Enright attempted to get information on such data distribution. Dick said that the lack of photo interpreters precluded the service that should have been given.

It was in April 1986 that the picture appeared in *Battleships: Axis and Neutral Battleships in World War II* by William H. Garzke and Robert O. Dulin, Jr. With their helpful assistance Enright contacted the holder of the picture, Mr. W. G. Somerville of London. He kindly granted permission to include it in *Shinano!*

The second and only other picture taken of *Shinano* was also in the reference book. Again Dulin and Garzke aided in reaching the holder of the picture, Roger Chesneau of Essex, England. He also graciously granted permission to use the photograph.

This one was taken on November 11, 1944, when *Shinano* was in Tokyo Bay conducting builder's trials. A new tug owned by a large heavy industry company was also in the bay for the same purpose. A photographic technician, Mr. Hiroshi Arakawa, was aboard and surreptitiously took a picture of *Shinano* in the distance. He destroyed all but one print, which he gave to the president of the company, who in turn sent it to Shizuo Fukui. After the war it was given to Mr. Chesneau.

In the conversion plans for *Shinano,* Vice Admiral Keiji Fukuda of the Kampon and dean of Japan's naval architects, placed heavy emphasis on armor. Large bulges, or "blisters," below the waterline—like those on *Yamato* and *Musashi*—were provided to minimize the effect of torpedoes by causing them to detonate before they reached the main hull. However, unlike the 16-inch belt of armor provided for *Yamato* and *Musashi, Shinano* had only half that amount of anti-projectile protection. Her main deck, already armored with from 4 to 7.5 inches of steel, was retained as the hangar deck.[27]

The flight deck of the 839.6-foot warship and the two colossal elevators servicing it were designed to withstand 1,000-pound aerial bombs. A layer of 3.75 inches of steel covered the flight deck. Some 33 inches below this deck, another layer of .75-inch steel was placed. Box beams were sandwiched between the two layers, and the intervening space filled with a composition of cement, sawdust, and latex. All told, the flight deck had an area of approximately 12,000 square yards. With the deck only 48 feet above the waterline, or approximately 12 feet closer to the water's surface than that of the U.S.S. *Essex* class, *Shinano*'s metacentric height (a measure of stability) was an unusually large 11 feet.[28] The weight of the steel installed for defensive purposes totaled 17,700 tons—about one-quarter of *Shinano*'s displacement and equal to the tonnage of many light cruisers.

Shinano was exceptionally well outfitted to actively defend against air attacks. Her armaments consisted of 16 five-inch, high-angle guns, 145 twenty-five-mm rapid firing machine guns, and 12 multiple-rocket launchers in twin mounts—each capable of firing 4.7-inch rockets in a salvo of 28 or 30.

Midway had taught the Japanese many lessons, one of the most important being the need to improve their carriers' vulnerable ventilation systems. All ducts involved in the modification of *Shinano* were protected with one and a half inches of armor. Wherever possible, wood had been eliminated from her

14

construction. Fire-resistant paint was used throughout, and a Japanese-designed foam extinguisher system was introduced for added protection against fire.[29]

Shinano's four main steam turbines were capable of developing 150,000 shaft horsepower, providing a speed of 27 knots. She had more fuel tanks than were originally planned for her as a battleship, which gave her a cruising range of 10,000 miles. Tanks to hold aviation fuel were added, then surrounded by armor and by circumferential tanks filled with seawater for added protection. With all these modifications, *Shinano*'s full-load displacement of 71,890 tons topped by some 200 tons the original full-load displacements of her onetime sister ships, *Yamato* and *Musashi*. Later the battleships added 1,700 tons of armor. *Shinano* was therefore the largest aircraft carrier ever built, and she retained that distinction until the commissioning of the nuclear-powered aircraft carrier U.S.S. *Enterprise* in 1961.

On June 15, 1944 headquarters directed the Yokosuka Naval Shipyard to deliver *Shinano* four months earlier than had been scheduled. Yard officials were stunned by the command. There was still so much to be done to complete the carrier, and now there was even less time in which to do it. Captain Tatsuo Maeda, the engineering officer in charge of the construction crews, retained his positive outlook and used every means possible to get higher productivity from his workers. More people were desperately needed, but his efforts to recruit them were impeded by the strict security process new employees had to undergo.

When the authorities in effect placed this hurdle in the way of his efforts to hire more workers, Captain Maeda increased the working hours of his crews from 11.5 hours to 14 hours daily, seven days a week. The endeavor didn't work. After only a few days, most of the employees, exhausted, began to turn out unacceptable work. Captain Maeda realistically reverted to the old schedule, which was retained until *Shinano*'s completion.

By late 1944 the war was going badly for Japan. The carriers *Shokaku*, of Pearl Harbor notoriety, and *Taiho* were counted among the ships lost during the June 19 "Turkey Shoot" off the Mariana Islands. (American aircraft were to subject the Imperial Navy to another round of losses in October during the battle for Leyte Gulf. The victims would include one of the superbattleships—*Musashi.*) The depleted ranks of Japan's crumbling line of naval defense badly needed to be reinforced. Construction on *Shinano* was accelerated.

Under the new, compressed work schedule, the builders extended themselves to prepare *Shinano* for launching on October 5, 1944. At 0800 on that date, the flood valves in Drydock No. 6 were opened to complete the flooding of the dock and lift the new warship off the keel blocks on which she had been resting for the past four and a half years. Within an hour the water level inside the dock had risen to within four feet of the level of Tokyo Bay.[30]

Suddenly and without any warning, the 5,000-ton caisson serving as the drydock gate lurched with a mighty bellow from its sealed drydock seat. Almost instantly, the higher level of water from the bay rushed like a tidal wave into the dock, lifting *Shinano* and thrusting her forward. Some 140 mooring lines parted like so many elastics and flailed the vicinity of the ship in a deadly fashion, adding to the noise, confusion, and danger. Such was the power of the in-rushing sea that *Shinano*'s bow traveled the 100-foot distance to the dock's headwall within a few seconds and smashed into it at 15 miles per hour. The collision of the steel bow with the concrete wall made a frightful crash that was heard throughout the huge shipyard.[31]

The wave of water then reversed itself in a wild rush back through the drydock, and *Shinano* was swept along with it, her hull thrust out into the bay. When the level of the oscillating water within the drydock again fell below that of the bay, the in-flowing waters hurled the ship to a second grinding impact against the headwall. Three times *Shinano* rushed back and forth in her cement cradle before the waters within and without reached equilibrium and allowed her to come to an exhausted rest. No fatalities were reported, but scores of seamen and civilian workers aboard *Shinano* and on the drydock apron were injured.

In the investigation that followed, authorities were stunned to learn that the ballast tanks within the caisson, which served as the gate between the drydock and the bay, had never been flooded. In the years since the graving dock had been excavated, these tanks had remained empty of the water that should have been flooded into them to hold the caisson solidly in place at the sea end of the dock.[32] The usual procedure was to drop the caisson into position by filling its ballast tanks while the dock was flooded, then pump the drydock empty. During all those years of *Shinano*'s construction the caisson had been held fast against the foundation only by its own weight and by the pressure of the bay jamming it against the dock's sealing surfaces.

Despite this mishap *Shinano* was formally named during a ceremony on October 8. Then she was redocked for repairs of damages to her hull and to the sonar compartments in her bow, which had been crushed and flooded. The repairs were completed within three weeks, but what could not be so easily set right was the belief of the men in the ship's company that the launching misfortune was an ill omen—that the *Shinano* was a jinx ship and that only bad luck could now be anticipated.[33]

When the disastrous results of the battle for Leyte Gulf in late October became known and America's electronically equipped B-29 Superfortresses began their initial high-altitude reconnaissance flights over Tokyo during the first week of November,[34] Japan's warlords exerted increased pressure for completion of *Shinano*. It was decided that she would be deployed along with several other carriers, battleships, and cruisers still available in the Inland Sea. From that protected vantage, the fighting force could sortie for the showdown battle in defense of the home islands of Dai Nippon.[35]

Shinano left the shipyard for the first time on November 11 to conduct builder's trials in Tokyo Bay. Tests included aircraft recovery at ship speeds of up to 24 knots.[36] While they were being conducted in broad daylight on the broad expanse of the bay, another B-29 flew overhead at more than 30,000 feet.

Surely then, if not earlier, the Japanese believed that *Shinano* was spotted and photographed by the American flyers.

On November 19 *Shinano* was declared completed and the shipyard commander delivered the vessel to the Imperial Navy. The naval ensign was raised, and she was officially in commission. A gilt-framed portrait of Emperor Hirohito was presented to the ship and placed with great respect in the appropriate location on her bridge.

Intelligence officers briefed Captain Abe about the widescale bombing raids that were anticipated in Tokyo during daylight hours within the next few days. He was also informed that a U.S. submarine wolf pack had been deployed less than a week earlier to engage Japanese picket boats and patrol craft between the Bonin Islands and Honshu.[37] There was a report, too, of the departure of a fleet of American submarines from Saipan and Guam on November 10 and 11. Their probable destination was the waters off the home islands.[38]

The captain requested a delay in sailing for the Inland Sea on November 28; there were additional tests to be completed.[39] It was refused. Then, on November 24, the Americans unleashed their initial mass attack of B-29s on the Empire. Some 100 of the bombers assaulted the Nakajima aircraft engine factory on the outskirts of Tokyo. A similar raid followed three days later.

To avoid these aircraft and have a better chance of eluding the horde of U.S. submarines believed to be patrolling the waters off of Tokyo Bay, Captain Abe decided on a nighttime voyage to the Inland Sea. He was counting on his superior speed to help him outrace the U.S. subs. Then, of course, *Shinano* could take any number of torpedo hits without her performance being significantly affected. Her formidable construction, he believed, made her nearly unsinkable.

On Tuesday, November 28, the sun set at 1700. One hour later, right on schedule, *Shinano* steamed between Iro Saki and To Shima and into the open sea.[40] On board were a total of 2,515 people consisting of 2,176 officers and seamen, some

18

300 shipyard workers, and a group of 40 civilian employees, such as laundrymen and barbers.[41] Also aboard were 50 "Ohka" suicide planes and six "Shinyos" suicide speedboats. *Shinano*'s own complement of fighters and bombers would not come aboard until she was in the Inland Sea, so she had the space to transport these last-ditch suicide craft to the Philippines and Okinawa.

Her aircraft would consist of:[42]

20 fighters (two in dismantled condition) "modified Zeke" 17Shi "Reppu"
20 bombers (two in dismantled condition) "Grace" B7A1 "Ryusei"
7 scouts (one in dismantled condition) "Myrt" 6 N 1 "Saiun"

A trio of modern, battle-proven destroyers—*Isokaze, Yukikaze,* and *Hamakaze*—had been assigned as *Shinano*'s escorts. Their captains had argued vehemently in favor of a daylight passage close to the coastline. But *Shinano*'s captain directed an offshore track—which was about 25 miles longer—to give them an arrival time at the entrance to the Inland Sea of 1000 on Wednesday, November 29.

It was an almost perfect night for the ocean passage of more than 300 miles. The moon, bright and nearly full, was at an elevation of about 35 degrees. Light clouds drifted slowly across it. The weather was mild for late November. A moderate, northerly breeze broke the top of the waves into serried ranks of whitecaps. *Shinano* and her escorts steamed out between the offshore islands. Their course was adjusted when necessary to remain in the channel. The set speed held them to 20 knots. Clearing the islands, a southwesterly course of 210 degrees was ordered, and *Shinano* began zigzagging to throw off any enemy submarines that might be skulking about. Her speed varied as the engineers conducted various trials and tests. The feisty destroyers, two of them still unrepaired after being damaged in the battle for Leyte Gulf, cleaved the sea on their assigned patrol stations at about 25 knots.

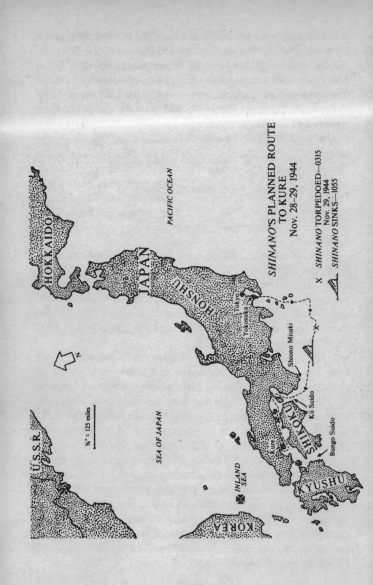

SHINANO'S PLANNED ROUTE
TO KURE
Nov. 28–29, 1944

X   SHINANO TORPEDOED—0315
     Nov. 29, 1944

△   SHINANO SINKS—1055

PACIFIC OCEAN

HOKKAIDO

JAPAN

HONSHU

Tokyo

Yokosuka

Shiono Misaki

SHIKOKU

Kii Suido

Bungo Suido

Kure

INLAND SEA

KYUSHU

SEA OF JAPAN

U.S.S.R.

KOREA

N

½" = 125 miles

At 2048 a lone American submarine's radar detected a target 12 miles to the northeast, bearing 030 degrees. Soon her lookouts could actually see "a small bump" on the horizon. Based upon the detection range, the target was assumed to be large. The tracking crew, with information compiled from radar ranges and bearings plotted and fed into the data computer, reported that the unidentified object was on a southwesterly course at a speed of 20 knots. Through their binoculars the submarine's skipper and the officer of the deck agreed that the "bump" was probably a Japanese oil tanker with a single escort.

Thus Captain and Admiral-Designate Toshio Abe of His Imperial Japanese Majesty's ship *Shinano* and Commander Joseph F. Enright of the U.S.S. fleet submarine *Archer-Fish* prepared for a confrontation that remains one of the legends of naval warfare to this day.

1. Contact

Earlier that Tuesday, November 28, 1944, at 1330 hours, the last lines had been slipped and *Shinano* and her trio of screening destroyers had maneuvered to leave the piers at Yokosuka Naval Shipyard. Reaching the open waters of Tokyo Wan (Bay), Captain Toshio Abe, trim and taut atop *Shinano*'s bridge in his tailored woolen uniform, implemented light signals to order the commencement of several hours of prearranged training exercises in local waters. As the quartet of warships steamed and zigzagged across the vast bay, *Shinano* appeared like a sleek, bulbous-nose whale alternately gathering in and shooing away three cavorting dolphins.

The innovative shape of *Shinano*'s bow, resembling the nose of a circus clown, was similar to those of the superbattleships *Yamato* and *Musashi* and was the design of Vice Admiral Keiji Fukuda and his Kampon architects. At 27 knots the bulbous nose reduced resistance through the water by 8.2 percent.[1] No other naval power had this type of bow construction. This was the original design and test for the bows of the post-war Japanese supertankers.

There was another remarkable thing about *Shinano*'s appearance as she churned about the bay. The upper section of the giant funnel enclosing her 12 smokestacks was angled to starboard 26 degrees from the vertical, so that stack gases were discharged overboard from the island superstructure, reducing the gases over the flight deck. As a result of her canted stacks, even Vice Admiral Fukuda conceded that *Shinano*'s appearance "seemed to be rather ugly."[2]

While all American and British aircraft carriers were constructed with funnels on the islands on their starboard sides, previous Japanese carriers had been built with side-lying funnels that jutted horizontally from the starboard beam directly below the flight deck. Such an arrangement was not feasible for *Shinano* because there was so little distance between the flight deck and the hangar deck immediately below it. Ship architects were reluctant to make room for horizontal funnels by raising the flight deck more than 48 feet above the waterline. If they had, *Shinano*'s heavy armored flight deck would have had an adverse effect on her stability. The alternative was to angle the smokestacks, and when wind tunnel tests established the feasibility of the canted funnel concept, the unusual design was implemented on three other carriers—*Taiho, Hiyo,* and *Junyo.*

The exercises had been completed at 1600 that afternoon, and Captain Abe had signaled again by flashing lights for the vessels to form up into cruising disposition with *Shinano,* as the guide, retaining the central position. The reliance on flashing lights was part of the pattern of secrecy that had grown up around *Shinano.* Neither then nor during her construction, builder's trials, and the planning for transit to the Inland Sea was any information about her transmitted by radio. Instead, all plans, orders, and reports regarding the warship had been distributed by messenger, mail, secure telephone, and telegraph —all of which were possible during the construction and testing phases because all interested parties were shore-based. Incidentally, this also helped reduce the load on Japan's radio message system.

As the group moved down the bay, the destroyers darted forward to patrol ahead and off either beam of the "mother ship." Captain Abe, as the senior officer, had been given the responsibility of selecting the exact hour of departure and the route to be followed on the ship's maiden voyage. His only specific orders from Japan's warlords were that *Shinano* be moved by November 28 from the vicinity of the Tokyo-Yokohama-Nagoya-Yokosuka industrial complex, which had recently been classified as a high risk area. The new designation resulted from the step-up of bombing raids on the harbor complex by B-29 Superfortresses of the 73rd Bomber Wing assigned to Isley Field on Saipan.

Captain Abe, with a respectful nod to the portrait of the Emperor on the after bulkhead of the bridge, was convinced, along with his ship's company, that *Shinano* almost certainly had been photographed during one of the reconnaissance flights conducted over Tokyo Bay since November 1. Certainly by November 11—the date *Shinano* had undertaken her first builder's trials in Tokyo Bay—the Americans would have photographed his ship.

During the forenoon of the day of departure, *Shinano*'s skipper had summoned the ship's company to the flight deck, where he delivered a brief address to put them into fighting spirits. Intense and direct, he ignored the buffeting of a chilly wind and informed the officers and seamen of his dedication to the Emperor, Japan, and to their "superb ship." He spoke of his determination to carry out his responsibilities to all three in a manner that would reflect the highest honor. In his summation he exhorted each officer and seaman in the ship's complement to respond in kind. The air rang with cheers as the crew quickly gave its collective pledge.[3]

Captain Abe did not, however, inform the ship's company of the formal request he had made to the Naval General Staff for a delay in the November 28 sailing date.[4] His petition had noted that due to a lack of parts, 4 of *Shinano*'s 12 boilers were still not functioning. With only eight boilers, her speed would be reduced. Further, he cited the fact that the majority of the ship's 1,147 compartments had not been airtight tested. The possibility of leaks around door gaskets and pipe flanges was most disturbing to him. Moreover, he argued that any delay granted to rectify these problems could also be used profitably to advance the training of the new crew.

The request had been denied almost out of hand. *Shinano*

would sail on November 28. The assessed risk of attack on the Japanese home islands by aircraft from a U.S. fast-carrier force had been ratcheted up from "possible" to "probable" after the battle of Leyte Gulf. Even with only eight operational boilers, Abe was reminded, *Shinano* was capable of speeds in excess of 24 knots. As for the watertight integrity of the ship, there should have been little cause for concern. Since 1933 Japanese warships were tested first by filling the underwater compartments with water, then, after the equipment was installed, by conducting air tests.[5] The compartments of *Shinano,* which had been tested hydrostatically, were structurally sound, and watertight doors had been installed.[6] Air tests to locate minor leaks around cables and door gaskets were not conducted because of the urgency to complete the carrier, but the Navy Ministry did consider the risk of sending the ship to sea without air testing and had accepted it.

The crew was another potential point of contention, but Abe had reason to be satisfied with the experience level of at least some of his officers and men. The younger ones were understandably green, but approximately 1,400 of his people had served on a seagoing ship.[7] This, at least, compared favorably with the training levels on new ships in the wartime U.S. Navy.

The Navy General Staff also informed Abe that friendly aircraft would not be available to help *Shinano* on the move to the Inland Sea. The absence of this key protection against submarine attack was an important consideration in the decision to make a nighttime transit. As a star graduate of the Imperial Japanese Naval Academy at Etajima in the 1920s and a veteran naval officer, Captain Abe had no difficulty understanding the finality with which his request had been denied. He accepted the decision obediently and without emotion. With it behind him and soon forgotten, he redoubled his evaluation of all factors involving *Shinano*'s sortie and passage to the Inland Sea.

Once there, he would complete the outfitting of his ship and the training of her crew, take on his complement of aircraft under Lieutenant Commander Shiga, and prepare to join the powerful fleet the Empire was marshaling to deal the enemy an overwhelming knockout blow. Then, with *Shinano* ready and eager for battle as the mother ship of the attack carriers (she not only carried her own fighters and bombers but had the space and equipment to give support to the planes of her sister carriers), she would demonstrate her prowess and invincibility. Then, too, he could officially assume the rear admiral's rank for which he had been designated. It would be a most auspicious day.

Darkness approached swiftly at about 1700 from the direction of the underwater Tokyo Canyon and the Sagami Bay as *Shinano* and the three destroyers steamed toward the lower end of Tokyo Bay. Bless whatever gods had stayed enemy bomber raids this day over Tokyo, Captain Abe intoned. A scrutiny of *Shinano* and her escorts showed no signs of any navigation lights. Throughout the carrier inspections were being carried out to ensure that no interior illumination could be seen from the outside. The brig and a court-martial awaited any man who failed to properly cloak even a single light.

Shinano was a beehive of activity. Every one of the more than 2,500 men on board was engaged in some shipboard routine. Officers made inspections to confirm that gun crews were at their stations and ammunition was handy for the 16 five-inch guns and the myriad batteries of antiaircraft weapons ringing the ship. Aboard each of the destroyers, men likewise checked the shell racks next to all four of the five-inch guns. Not to be overlooked were the full racks of 36 depth charges carried by the individual escorts, rigged for rapid release in the event of a submarine attack.

In the dying light of the late November day, Lieutenant Commander Takamasa Yasuma, *Shinano*'s chief medical officer, stood on the wind-whipped flight deck and watched the darkening hills and mountains recede far astern. He wondered whether it might be the last time he would see this beautiful landscape and the serene, snow-covered Mount Fuji where the ancient gods dwelled. These were trying times. What would be the ultimate fate of the Empire and his new ship?

26

His thoughts reached back to the autumn day several months earlier when he had first reported to the *Shinano*, which was still under construction in Yokosuka. By then, all crew members except the ship's flying officers had reported aboard. Recalling what seemed to be a moment buried in the distant past, he thought about his first meeting with Captain Abe. When he reported, the captain had told him rather bluntly: "You are responsible for the detailed fitting-out of the medical department. You are requested to fulfill your duties promptly and conscientiously so as not to discover discrepancies in your department after this ship makes a sortie. You are also requested to make every effort to complete the necessary loading of all your department's materials by the time of her sortie."[8]

Dr. Yasuma shook his head, later writing in his journal: "Captain Abe didn't show a sign of a smile while he received me. The Captain's decided coolness seemed to come less from his poor hospitality than from his hidden determination, and the obvious strain arising from his responsibility in taking command of our largest carrier manned by so many men at a time of grave importance to his motherland."

Meanwhile, *Shinano*, like her escorts, had set the highest standards of watertight integrity. Every watertight door and hatch below the main deck had been dogged shut. Ventilation ducts had been securely closed by valves and flappers between the compartments. Not even a cockroach could pass from one compartment to another. Battle damage, her officers believed, could now be localized.

On schedule, the four warships cleared the entrance to Tokyo Bay at 1700 and proceeded through Tokyo Canyon to enter the open sea at 1800. The destroyers took up their assigned patrol sectors, with Captain Shintani proceeding ahead of *Shinano* in flagship *Isokaze*. *Hamakaze* provided protection on the starboard flank of the carrier, and *Yukikaze* on the port side. *Shinano*'s skipper had set a course of 210 degrees true and a speed of 20 knots.

Ensign Singo Shoda, chief quartermaster on *Shinano*, later recalled how Ensign Tadashi Yasuda, the assistant to the navigator, had displayed the ship's course on bridge charts. "On the charts, the positions of recent enemy submarine sightings and the radio direction finder [RDF] network reports were indicated. I remember that many of those designated on the charts were off the entrance to Tokyo Bay. Near Izu Peninsula and Ensu Nada. Off the approach to Ise Bay, and near Cape Usino and Kii Strait."

To Ensign Shoda, who was making his inspection rounds, the sea appeared dark and rough, with a "fairly strong prevailing northwest wind." He did not find anything of beauty about the night passage. Yet the moon was within a few days of being full, displaying almost 97 percent of maximum brightness. A few flimsy clouds scudded before it. The wind, coming from a northerly direction, was measured at six meters per second, or slightly less than 15 miles per hour.

Shinano's base course was altered to 180, and the ships progressed to the south as the sum of their periodic zigzags. After an uneventful 25-mile passage through waters considered, on the basis of past torpedoings, the most inviting for an attack by enemy submarine, the highest degree of damage control security was relaxed to the second degree. At about 1900 a series of watertight doors were opened to permit easier access to many compartments housing the ship's various machinery. As commanding officer, Captain Abe was aware of this action.

Lieutenant Commander Osamu Miura, chief officer in charge of the machinery division, was the engineering watch officer on duty. He had only one major concern: keeping the propulsion plant functioning properly. It served no purpose to think about the four boilers that were out of service. If he had to power *Shinano* with just two-thirds of her boilers, so be it. He was getting better than 20 knots—2 to 3 knots better than the enemy submarines' top speed of 18 to 19 knots. Still, he was acutely aware that *Shinano*'s safe passage depended on the smooth operation of her power plant. As he later noted: "The steaming plan was based on the assumption that by implementing a speed of 20 knots and zigzag maneuvers at night, suspected enemy submarines infesting the area might be evaded.

By a night passage, the enemy's B-29 bombers, hopefully, could also be evaded."

On the lookout platform, officers on deck watch cautioned the 25 lookouts to be vigilant. The few islands still visible on the horizon, the unbroken lines of whitecaps, and the occasional low hanging clouds were good camouflage for hostile submarines. They could be circling already, stalking the big ship, waiting to ambush *Shinano* on her maiden cruise.

Disdaining his prominent, elevated chair on the starboard side of the bridge far above the flight deck, Captain Abe remained on his feet, aloof from his staff, to listen to the report of officer of the deck (OOD), Lieutenant Nobuo Yoshioka.

"Sir, the operator of our radar detector reports the signature of an enemy radar. The frequency and the pulse rate indicate that it originated from an American submarine radar. No bearing."[10]

"Time?" Captain Abe snapped.

"Nineteen-fifteen, sir."

Then, as though talking to himself, Captain Abe observed: "Sometimes I can't believe the stupidity of these Americans. Do they really believe they can use their radar—even in short spurts—without our being warned of their presence?"

No staff member responded. Unless they were addressed directly, they knew enough to keep their opinions to themselves. The captain did not suffer needless small talk. Captain Abe turned his head, bringing the front of his peaked black cap, embroidered with gold braid, to bear on his navigator. "Captain Nakamura, the report of this detection is an example of why I directed that no ship in our group use active radar or sonar during the transit to the Inland Sea. Radar signals travel for 100 kilometers or more. Every enemy ship within that area would be alerted that we are at sea."

"*Shoji itashimash'ta,*" the navigator replied. "I understand, sir."

After a few moments of silence, Captain Abe gave an order. "Navigator, inform the ship's company over the public address system that we have intercepted an electronic signal from an enemy submarine. Obviously it is proceeding on the surface. All hands topside should keep a sharp lookout for it. Any sightings are to be reported to the bridge immediately."

The officer relayed the order to Ensign Yasuda, who then turned to implement it.

Captain Abe continued a solitary vigil next to his chair on the bridge. Shortly after, he again turned to Captain Nakamura. With a jerk of his head, he signaled for the navigator to approach.

"Captain Nakamura, it is my conviction that we have an enemy wolf pack deployed against *Shinano*. Possibly as many as seven submarines. Certainly more than the one whose radar we detected. Undoubtedly it is the same group who surfaced and attacked our patrol boats to the north of the Bonin Islands on November 15. Agree?"

"*Yosoro*," came the quick reply. "Yes, sir."

"Then again, our intelligence reports that enemy submarines sailed four or five days ago from Guam and Saipan. Whatever, their commander obviously seeks to mislead us as to the size of the pack by using only his own radar. He makes the contact and then relays the information to the others. No doubt he intends to act as a decoy at some point to lure away our screening destroyers. That accomplished, his comrades can approach *Shinano* unopposed. We must guard against any such ploy."

Nodding his agreement Captain Nakamura murmured, "Understood, sir." As he stepped away to his duty station, the captain's announcement about the detection of the enemy submarine's radar signal went out over the ship's public address system. Staff officers glanced furtively at each other, but Captain Abe's features remained impassive.

Standing alone, he was thinking anew that *Shinano* was a great fortress of the sea, sweeping majestically across her water kingdom. To him she was indeed a fabled castle out of Japan's shogunate past—perhaps the fifteenth century, when the sublime poetry of the No drama was at its peak. Her progress through the waves, regal and stately, put him in mind of the tanka form of Japanese poetry, written in ornate court language. She was as heavily armed and garrisoned as the castles in those times of ageless landscapes, venerable structures, and ancient customs. And, as befitted a great redoubt, she was surrounded by a moat of incomparable grandeur and magnitude. Upon it, he believed, *Shinano* would display her aristocratic valor, and he would achieve unforgettable victories in the name of the Emperor and Dai Nippon.

Captain Abe peered from the bridge into the darkness, first to the flight deck below and to the left, then past the bulbous bow to the sparkling sea. Though he could not see them without binoculars, he was conscious of the attendance upon *Shinano* of her knightly triad of destroyers.

Isokaze (strand wind), *Yukikaze* (snow wind), and *Hamakaze* (beach wind) were three of the best. Fighters all. No captain could request finer escorts for such a dangerous passage. His only regret was the lack of more like them. Though modern, they were already veterans, as so often happened in this war year of 1944. Each displaced 2,000 tons and could dash about *Shinano* at 35 knots. They were capable of a radius of action of 5,000 miles at an average speed of 18 knots.

Captain Abe recalled that all three belonged to the *Kagero* class, which was similar in design to the enemy's U.S.S. *Fletcher*-class destroyers. They had been completed in 1940, then recently equipped with additional batteries of rapid-fire antiaircraft guns. Their depth-charge load had been augmented to the present 36. One escort, *Hamakaze,* had been the first Japanese destroyer to be fitted with radar. She and *Isokaze* had operated together since the outbreak of hostilities. They had served with the elite Pearl Harbor attack force, in the assault on Rabaul, with Admiral Nagumo's fleet as it swept across the Indian Ocean and fell upon Colombo and Trincomalee, and with the ill-fated Midway Strike Force.

Captain Abe shrugged imperceptibly, a thin smile creasing his clamped lips, when his thoughts turned to *Yukikaze.* Under Commander Tochigi Terauchi, she was a particularly tough ship. Her battle record was impeccable. She had participated in the memorable battles of the Java Sea, Kula Gulf, Santa Cruz

31

Islands, Guadalcanal, and the disaster in the Marianas. Only the month before, Abe knew, his accompanying destroyers had been in the thick of one of the greatest naval battles of the war, Leyte Gulf. Their spurs had been honed as members of the strongest of the three Japanese fleets involved, the Central Force of Admiral Kurita. In that struggle with the Yankee juggernaut, nine Japanese destroyers were sunk. Many more, including *Hamakaze* and *Isokaze*, had suffered damages of varying degrees. Among the more than 30 destroyers, only *Yukikaze*, the toughest of the trio, had emerged unscathed. Captain Abe sighed. As a veteran destroyer officer himself, he wondered where Japan was to find enough men and ships of this caliber. *Shinano*'s large crew still had a way to go before they could be considered the equal of these veterans. Yet Japan must find them. The struggle would go on. There could be no thought of defeat. Death was more endurable.

Thankfully, with men like Captain K. Shintani, Japan would never know defeat. The three screening destroyers were under his jurisdiction as commander of Destroyer Division 17, with his flag in *Isokaze*. Captain Shintani was regarded as one of the Empire's outstanding destroyer veterans. Most recently, he had been senior instructor at the Yokosuka Anti-Submarine School. He was a tough man to argue with. Thoughts of the destroyers aggressively patrolling the waters to keep *Shinano* secure in the darkness turned Captain Abe's mind to a haiku poem by Sempei Sawa. He repeated the few lines to himself:

> With the full tide's wind
> they are going out
> the flock of wild geese.

Yes, that's what they are, he decided. Wild geese. Always in motion. Perpetually on clamorous wing, ready to raise the alarm to battle. It's no wonder the Romans enlisted geese to guard their gateways at night. They are so steadfast and true.

2. Target

Confidential
Subject: U.S.S. *Archer-Fish* (SS-311)--Report of
Fifth War Patrol

(B) Narrative*

October 30, 1944
1330 (VW) Departed Submarine Base [Pearl Harbor]
           for patrol in accordance with Comsub-
           pac secret operation order 364-44 as
           modified by Comsubpac mailgram 302125.
           . . .

November 14, 1944
0543   Trim dive
0555   Surfaced
2200   Received message to take lifeguard
           station in Hit parade area [waters off
           south coast of main Japanese island of
           Honshu]. . . .

November 28, 1944
0556   Submerged. No [B-29 bomber] raid today.
1718   Surfaced.
2034   Sighted Inamba Shima [Island], distance
           about 12 miles, but no radar contact.

---

*Excerpts only.—Author's note.

Few radio messages were more welcome to my ears than the one *Archer-Fish* had received the day before—Monday, November 27. No B-29 bombers were scheduled to raid the Tokyo-Yokosaka industrial area for 48 hours. *Archer-Fish* was also informed that there were no other American submarines in the patrol areas east and west of us. In effect, we had authorization to roam at will over a vast expanse of enemy water, without any competition from our hot-to-get 'em brothers-in-arms. The message had concluded: "Good hunting!"

It was a lucky break in a rather routine patrol. For days we had been on station without sighting any torpedo targets. Our primary responsibility was to provide lifeguard service. That is, to rescue downed crew members from any B-29s hit by Japanese fire and to send weather reports by radio for the B-29 bombers. This hiatus in the raids, which had been building up since mid-November, meant that *Archer-Fish* could hunt the prey for which she was designed. I yearned for a target—especially anything over 500 tons.

On this patrol we were assigned to the Empire sector, or the "Hit Parade," as it was designated in the Submarine Patrol instructions. The nickname came from a popular radio program back in the States that played the top songs of the week. This sector covered the waters south and east of the Japanese home islands and was divided into seven patrol areas, ours being No. 5. It was above 33 degrees, ten minutes north and extended to the coast of the major island of Honshu. The western boundary was Shiono Misaki, the cape on the eastern promontory of Kii Suido (Strait), which led into the Inland Sea. The eastern boundary was 139 degrees, 15 minutes east. In effect we had the best shot at any shipping departing or entering Tokyo Bay.

From my post on the bridge, forward of the periscopes, I pressed my shoulder against the iron railing to steady myself and maintained a constant watch on the sea. The deck officer and the three crewmen on watch as lookouts with binoculars aided me. All of us were determined to win the combat insignia for *Archer-Fish*'s fifth patrol. Mostly me. Second chances are seldom given in the submarine force. I was extremely lucky to be getting this one. A third chance was not in the book. It had been one helluva gift to receive orders as the sub's skipper back on my thirty-fourth birthday, September 18.

Forward, *Archer-Fish*'s beautifully shaped bow cut cleanly through the fast-running sea. It was as though her 27-foot, 3 inch-wide hull was challenging the waves to slow her progress. Happily, the ocean was not in a mood to argue, and it permitted us to glide swiftly along on our foray. Even so, *Archer-Fish*'s passage tossed up a mighty plume of spray at the bow and left a frothy, glistening white wake aft. They were seductively beautiful to behold in the early darkness, but they were telltale signs that an alert enemy could read at a distance in the moonlight.

Below, *Archer-Fish*'s quartet of top-performing Fairbanks, Morse engines throbbed faithfully in the forward and after engine rooms, powering her at about 15 knots through the home waters off Tokyo, the heart and nerve center of the Japanese Empire. The engines' sounds reverberated throughout the confines of the submarine's 311-foot, 9-inch hull, their steady, synchronized beat imbuing the watch crew on the bridge with a sense of well-being and needed confidence. With dependable engines and unflagging power, submariners believe they can lick anyone who elbows up to them.

While peering intently forward, I became aware once again that I was unconsciously fingering the old black rosary beads in the left-hand pocket of my damp, wrinkled khaki trousers. I smiled sadly, remembering that they were a boyhood gift from my mother. She was Minnie Olson, born in 1885 as the fourth child of Norwegian emigrants. The Olsons had gotten their start homesteading on 160 acres near Berthold, North Dakota. Later, as a young woman, my mother was also able "to prove up" 160 acres near there.

I was trying not to think about her too much just then. I didn't want to dwell on her death the previous August, when I was a member of the relief crews at Midway. This duty required me to act as the commanding officer of any submarine back from a war patrol for a refit or to undergo any repairs, while the regularly assigned officers and men unwound at a recuperation center. The relief-crew work was an important assignment, and I was never embarrassed about performing it. Yet at the time I hadn't been exactly proud of myself either. It just wasn't the same as taking a fighting submarine into enemy waters.

Enough of these thoughts, I told myself. There'd be time later to come back to them in the solitude of my cabin. There would be moments, too, to think about my wife, Virginia, and my young son, Joe, Jr. I flicked my mind to another setting and fixed it for a few moments on my boat, *Archer-Fish*. Her crew was the best, a combination difficult to beat anywhere in the Silent Service. Strange name, though, for an American submarine. I had never heard of the archerfish in connection with American waters. But I later learned that this small fish *(Toxotes jaculator)* indigeneous to the East Indies was the warship's namesake. By ejecting drops of water at high speed from its mouth at insects resting on objects over the water, the archerfish knocks them from their perch and into the water where it quickly gulps them down.

From the little I knew (and believed) about astrology, I thought it was probably a favorable sign that we had been cut loose for two days on *Archer-Fish*'s fifth war patrol late in November. The date coincided with the movement of the sun into the zodiacal sign of Sagittarius—the Archer. It was, of course, just a fleeting thought. As a lifelong Roman Catholic who had been an altar boy for four years and who wore a scapular about his neck into the early years of high school, I was little given to reading my horoscope or regarding heavenly symbols other than for nautical purposes. I knew that Father James O'Neill, my father's cousin, would look askance at such activity. As a boy I had been one of his great admirers, and I always strove for his approval. My latest news of him was that he was an Army chaplain assigned to General George Patton's staff somewhere in Europe.[1] I prayed for his safe return.

Actually, I was staying on the bridge for two reasons—one minor, the other major. The routine reason was that I wanted to protect my night vision. After 20 minutes or more in darkness the eyes adapt to low-light conditions, and one can then see amazingly well in the dark. Dim red lights or red goggles can be used when going below, with only a slight degradation of night vision, but even a flicker of white light quickly cancels this capability.

During the night it was routine for submarines to "rig for dark." This called for all white lights to be extinguished in the conning tower below the bridge and in the adjacent compartments. Red lights were turned on only when needed. An officer working below in the conning tower or in these red-rigged compartments could go up to the bridge "chop-chop" with his vision already adapted to the darkness.

My more significant reason for being on the bridge when I could just as well have been below, had to do with an event that occurred at dawn that day after we dove for a submerged patrol. It had put me in an Irish vexation for some hours, and I was just beginning to cool off in the brisk night air and the chilling spray being whipped back from the bow. We had settled into the normal routine when I was approached by Lieutenant (j.g.) Joseph J. Bosza, *Archer-Fish*'s radar officer, a fine, young man from Pittsburgh.

"I'd like permission, Captain Enright, to put the SJ radar out of commission for repairs."

"How's that, Joe?" I replied. "I haven't noticed any malfunctioning."

Frankly, I was reluctant to leave the ship vulnerable by disabling such a valuable aid. Since the development and installation of radar aboard submarines, officers and seamen had come to depend on the device as they would on an old buddy. It was, indeed, a formidable Cyclops that could penetrate the shades of fog and nightfall and uncannily pinpoint perils invisible to us mortals. To return to the surface in the black hours without radar was to be exposed, blindfolded, to the enemy.

"Just a few minor problems, skipper. It'll also give us a chance to adjust the set for even better performance. I'll have it back in operation at 1700."

"All right, permission granted, Joe. But I want it working then—when we'll be surfacing again."

The day passed uneventfully. We ran east about 50 miles and conducted a submerged periscope watch off the entrances to Tokyo Bay. Mount Fuji loomed large above the littoral vista. No contacts were recorded. As the hours went by, I made periodic checks on the progress of the repairs on the radar. I was assured they were progressing on schedule. Still, as the sun dipped low in the western sky, my concern and ire began to rise as melded twins.

"When will the radar be operating?"

"Soon."

The lieutenant and I began to sound like a broken record. At 1718 I gave orders for *Archer-Fish* to surface. We still had no radar. The hours of darkness quickly enshrouded us. The watch section scanned the sea to every point of the compass. To my unending requests about the status of the radar repairs, Lieutenant Bosza only replied that "it will be ready soon." I was not convinced. I decided to remain on the bridge as an extra lookout.

Progress on the radar was reported at 1930. It was good and bad. The radar technicians had reassembled the set, but they would need about another hour to adjust, tune, and test it. During this operation I had to assume that some signals would of necessity be sent out, exposing us to detection. The thought did not sweeten my composure.

At 2030 Lieutenant Bosza called up through the open hatch to the bridge.

"Cap'n, SJ radar repairs are completed and the normal routine search has commenced."

I responded with a crisp acknowledgment and returned to my self-imposed watch duty. Within moments the deck watch had sighted Inamba Shima, an island near the entrance to Tokyo Bay. The sighting was called down to Mr. Bosza in the conning tower, but he reported back that the "repaired" radar was not able to detect it. I shook my head and thought fleetingly of chewing on my crumpled cap.

38

My impatience and exasperation increased when he reported a contact at 030 degrees. In rebuttal, I informed him harshly that the island was at 060 degrees and apparently the radar's bearing circle had been replaced improperly.

"Fix it!" I growled.

"Aye, aye, sir," floated halfheartedly up the hatch.

Undogged, Lieutenant Bosza called up almost immediately to report. "Captain, your island is moving. At 2048 the SJ radar detected a target at 24,700 yards, bearing 028 true."

It was no time for confusion. Ensign Justin "Judd" Dygert, on watch as the officer of the deck, and I swung our binoculars to that sector of the horizon and stared into the intervening darkness.

Within seconds, Torpedoman Third Class "Bob" Fuller, a new man aboard and stationed on the periscope support platform a few feet above the deck of the bridge, cried, "Contact! Dark shape on the horizon two points off the starboard bow!"

Fuller was one of the youngest men on board, and he probably had better eyesight than most. He was under eighteen when he signed up; his father had ridden double with him on his motorcycle to the recruiting office to give the necessary approval.

Elated, Judd and I fixed our binoculars on the contact. It resembled a long, low bump on the horizon. It was coming our way. I issued two quick orders almost automatically: "Station the tracking party. Start tracking from ahead."

Judd in turn ordered the helm over and *Archer-Fish* responded readily, swinging to the new course and putting the approaching target directly astern. He also called below to the telephone talker to have the maneuvering watch put "all engines on the line." *Archer-Fish* pulsated with the added power and surged ahead on the new course.

The crew jumped to their assigned tasks. Lieutenant (j.g.) John Andrews rushed to the bridge immediately to relieve Judd as the officer of the deck. Judd in turn disappeared down the hatch into the conning tower, where he began to plot our course

39

and speed, and the position of the target as provided by the ranges and bearings from the bridge and radar.

He was joined by Daniel W. Ellzey, warrant boatswain. The submarine's complement usually didn't include a warrant officer, but Dan had been the chief quartermaster aboard *Archer-Fish* on earlier patrols and had asked to remain aboard after his promotion.

By then, Lieutenant Davis Bunting had the Torpedo Data Computer (TDC) functioning and was entering data. At his shoulder was Ensign Gordon Crosby, the communications officer. Ensign Crosby hurried back and forth from the TDC to the radio room to draft, encode, and oversee the transmission of outgoing messages. Even before *Archer-Fish* had completed her turn to the course of 208 degrees, Radar Technician 3/c Earl Myers had assumed the duty of SJ surface-search radar operator.

By using the "tracking from ahead" procedures, I could get a rough fix on the track of the target, adjust our course, and speed to it. Personnel at the TDC and plot, using ranges from the radar, and bearings taken visually on the bridge, could then solve more accurately the contact's speed and course. These were the procedures preparatory to carrying out a torpedo attack.

The time we gained by remaining ahead of the target, with the distance between us closing slowly, would also provide us with a picture of any zigzag plan it was on. A good estimate of the target's base course—the real heading behind the zigzagging—could be obtained too. I was anxious to identify the large ship and determine the number of escorts, if any, and their position in relation to the main, high-value target. Time had to be used to our advantage. The plot maintained by Judd and Dan provided a record of the tracks of the target and of *Archer-Fish* from the moment we received the initial range and bearing. This compilation assisted me in projecting the probable future course of the enemy vessel and its destination.

The course and speed of the target were measured from the plot and were also obtained from the TDC by Lieutenant Bunting. Comparisons of these numbers, which were needed for a fire control solution, were made continuously. The TDC provided a real-time schematic diagram of the relative positions of the "hunter" and the "hunted," with a pointer displaying the attack angle of the torpedoes. The ready light on the face of the TDC would indicate when the optimum torpedo range had been reached. Ideally, our torpedoes would be fired from the beam (side) of the target, at a range of anywhere from 1,000 to 2,000 yards.

The conning tower TDC was used to compute the gyro angles, which were necessary to direct the torpedoes to the target. The angles were then transmitted electrically to the torpedo rooms, where they were indicated by a moveable pointer on a compass rose. A second moveable pointer on another compass rose indicated the gyro angle, which was automatically set on the gyroscope in the torpedo. This was accomplished by means of a steel rod, looking something like a socket wrench, that passed through the torpedo tube to a female socket in the torpedo. The rod was withdrawn automatically upon firing.

In the forward torpedo room, Torpedoman Petty Officer 2/c Edward Zielinski was stationed between the two triple banks of tubes. From there he could see the two pointers. If they fell out of synchronization he would manually set the gyros of the torpedoes in the tubes, as directed by the TDC or the fire-control party in the conning tower.[2]

Ed's station was also equipped with a manually operated button that he could push to eject the torpedoes by air pressure in the event of an electrical malfunction between the conning tower and the torpedo tubes.

Elsewhere aboard *Archer-Fish,* Lieutenant Romolo Cousins was maintaining a close check on our engineering requirements. During "battle stations" he assumed the responsibilities of the diving officer in the control room directly below the conning tower. Chief Yeoman Eugene Carnahan was set up as the telephone talker in the conning tower. With his telephone headset, the chief was connected to similarly equipped operators located in compartments throughout the submarine.

On the bridge, I was satisfied with the way the tracking stations had been manned. I turned to Lieutenant Andrews.

"John, stop the engines and use them only to keep the target astern. It will help plot and the TDC to get the most exact course and speed of the target."

"Aye, aye, skipper." The order was quickly relayed below. Like a long-distance runner, *Archer-Fish* wound down slowly, finally coming to a hushed halt in the darkness. Our wake subsided until the only sound that could be heard was that of the Pacific lapping unceasingly against the hull. Within about eight minutes we determined the enemy's course to be southwesterly at 210 degrees, at a speed of twenty knots. Now we were getting somewhere. Course and speed were being checked closely from both plot and TDC.

"John, steer course 210 degrees. Flank speed!" It would get us up to about 18 knots—usually *Archer-Fish*'s best speed. Lieutenant Andrews repeated the order down the open hatch to be telephoned by Chief Carnahan to the maneuvering room. The chief soon would be relaying requests for additional speed from our four 9-cylinder engines. Each was capable of delivering 1535 horsepower to drive the four 1100-KW Elliot generators. The maneuvering watch controlled the electrical power from the generators and could use it to drive either or both propellor shafts. When needed, the power also could be used to charge the 252 cells of the forward and after storage batteries used for *Archer-Fish*'s main propulsion when submerged.

As the submarine came to flank speed on the new course my mind was a whirlwind. What action to take? What *correct* action to take? I contemplated submerging to periscope depth, because we were in a prime attack position. That is, if the target continued on its present course. But this was no time to go by the book. To submerge prematurely was to commit *Archer-Fish* to the slower speed generated by our forward and after batteries.

There was still too much we didn't know about the target.

What type of ship was it exactly? Just an old tubby maru, or a real warship? Was 210 degrees its base course? Or was it merely a long zigzag leg? How about escorts? Were there any? The identification of a target by specific class of ship was of great value because it helped us obtain the range we needed for fire control purposes. Several pieces of data had to be put together. Our *Recognition Manual* provided line drawings of enemy ships that noted the height of principal features above the waterline, including the tallest mast, bridge structure, and funnels. Our periscopes contained movable prisms that provided us with a split image of a target. For example, by setting the listed height of a known ship's forward mast in feet on a dial near the scope handle, and rotating the handle, one of the mast's images would be displaced down to the waterline. The angle of the displacement could then be read from the dial as the range in yards.

In any attack situation, the number and whereabouts of escorts also provided valuable data. Screening destroyers, the scourge of all in my profession, usually moved about unpredictably while searching for enemy submarines. The movements of the destroyers could be compared to those of a hunting dog seeking a scent to flush an upland bird for its master. If the skipper of an attacking submarine could detect any pattern at all in a destroyer's maneuvers, it greatly aided him in his efforts to reach a firing position without being detected.

My mind felt like a kaleidoscope of conflicting thoughts—in turn selecting, mulling, and discarding—as I raced from one end of the spectrum of attack possibilities to the other. I'm certain I appeared imperturbable to the crew. And well I should. During the early stalking stages, most of my orders were routine and required no Olympian contemplation. I reminded myself that I had been in submarines for more than seven years. I had participated in hundreds of practice attacks. And most of the officers and crew were old hands at torpedo attacks. They knew their jobs and did them exceptionally well. *Archer-Fish* was also an old salt. Before I assumed command she had completed four war patrols under other skippers. The bottom line was that crew and ship were battleworthy and well aware of how they were expected to perform. Together, we were eager to get on with the job.

Engrossed, I watched the small dark dot on the horizon slowly burgeon and assume a more distinct shape. Who was she? How I wanted her to be a big warship. With the course the war was taking, there weren't too many of them still afloat. She just might be one. The target had been large enough to be detected by radar and sighted at a range of more than 12 miles.

I sifted through my mental file cards in search of a clue to her identity. I thought of the huge battleships that had first come to the attention of U.S. Naval Intelligence in mid-1938. By then the Japanese had commenced construction on the first of four of this new type. The size and power of those superbattleships were mind-boggling. At 70,000 tons they would be twice as heavy as our battleships then in commission. They would have a speed of 27 knots versus our 21 knots . . . projectiles 18 inches in diameter compared with our largest of 16 inches . . . and each projectile would carry appreciably more explosive. I frequently dreamt of seeing one of these ships.

I recalled that by late 1942 two of the leviathans—*Yamato* and *Musashi*—had been completed and dispatched on operations with the Imperial Japanese Navy. *Yamato* had been attacked on Christmas Day, 1943 by Commander Gene McKinney in the U.S. submarine *Skate*. She had suffered a torpedo hit on her bow but had managed to steam back to the Inland Sea. Both battleships were subsequently assigned to Admiral Kurita's Central Force at the battle of Leyte Gulf. *Yamato* had been damaged by several bombs and her speed was slightly reduced, but she had still managed to return to the Inland Sea safely for repairs. *Musashi*, however, received 10 certain torpedo hits, 5 on each side, and perhaps as many as 17 bomb hits—sinking her. All told, six U.S. aircraft carriers of Task Force 38 had launched more planes to mark "finish" to *Musashi* than the Japanese had used to attack Pearl Harbor.

My mind unaccountably jumped to the possibility of this contact being the third battleship. I tried to remember what intelligence had been made available about her. Information was scant, nothing that rang a bell. If this third ship existed at all, the Japanese had accomplished the near impossible and had kept a veil of secrecy over her construction. Still, I knew there was a major shipyard located at Yokosuka, on Tokyo Bay. Maybe they had built her there. Maybe she was coming out. . . .

Lieutenant Commander Sigmund Bobczynski, my executive officer from Portsmouth, New Hampshire—where *Archer-Fish* had been built and launched in 1943—had joined me on the bridge. In addition to his responsibilities as the submarine's second-in-command, I had assigned "Bob" Bobczynski the duty of coordinator during battle stations. This was not a customary role for an XO, but it made the best sense to me. I had seen too many instances in which coordination involving the bridge, conning tower, plot, and TDC broke down in tense moments.

Bob was referred to as "Mr. Bob" with respect and affection by the crew. He was a crackerjack executive officer, the most experienced man aboard in terms of war patrols. He had participated in one of the first patrols after the Pearl Harbor attack. His boat had gone a-hunting right off the approaches to Tokyo Bay during the first month of the war. I valued Bob's experience and his resolute support. As coordinator, he was the ideal officer to roam *Archer-Fish* at will during battle stations and serve as the catalyst who kept all the various operations functioning and synchronized. No one questioned his advice and recommendations.

Archer-Fish continued to stay ahead and on the same course as the mysterious enemy ship while attempting to gather as much information about her as possible. So far we knew her course and speed, but we needed a lot more data than that before we could contemplate an attack. Meanwhile, the shape Bob and I were watching loomed long and low on the horizon. No bridge, masts, or superstructure were discernible yet, despite the nearly cloudless sky and the illumination of an almost full moon.

I finally hazarded my best guess. "I think it's an oil tanker, Bob. At least that's what the shape indicates right now. What do you think?"

"I agree, cap'n. Tentatively anyway. At this point."

From the conning tower, just below, Mr. Bosza called up to tell us that his radar team had picked up a small pip to the left of the large target.

"It's moving faster and at less range," he reported. "Probably an escort on the target's starboard bow."

"Very good, Joe," I called down. "Stay with it." With the advent of our unknown target, my irritation over the earlier radar repairs had been forgotten.

It was then that the XO and I discussed the chances of a surface attack. Bob and I had agreed that the target was probably a solitary tanker with a single escort. Night visibility was good. Perhaps this was the time to conduct a surface attack on an unsuspecting enemy ship.

My mind went back to New London, where I had been in command of O-10. In October 1942 I received orders for temporary duty to attend the Prospective Commanding Officers School held locally. Its purpose was to provide a cram course in conducting submarine war patrols. There were ten of us in the class, all experienced submarine officers scheduled to take command of submarines conducting war patrols in the Pacific. The instructors were former commanding officers who had completed a series of successful war patrols. Our textbooks were the official patrol reports submitted by commanding officers on returning from enemy waters. They were as current as duplicating machines and air mail could make them. Our classes were conducted ashore and afloat. We analyzed the reports, discussing the skipper's actions and how we would have handled each combat situation. The instructor then gave his critique. His audience was always attentive.

The classes afloat were conducted aboard either U.S.S. *Mackerel* or *Marlin,* new submarines with modern equipment. Too small to conduct patrols in the Pacific, these boats were ideal for training. Our exercise areas were in Long Island

Sound; destroyers based at Newport served as targets. Our practice surface approaches took place both during daylight and at night. Several Japanese ships had been sunk by skippers using this method, and it was becoming popular under conditions similar to those in which *Archer-Fish* now found herself.

"Okay, Bob," I said. "We'll make a surface attack. I'll run through the details of how I expect to conduct it so that we understand each other."

He nodded his understanding.

"First, we'll pull off the track, to the west. That will place the target down moon from us. And those dark clouds over the land to the northwest will tend to hide our dark hull from their lookouts."

I explained my estimate that at a distance of five miles we should be reasonably safe from being sighted—that is, if we kept our bow pointed at the nearest ship. That way our silhouette would be smallest. We would stop at that five-mile position and observe the escort and the target as the range decreased. They could also zig. We'd been expecting that they would have done so by now.

"When the escort goes by," I continued, "we'll speed up and maintain our distance from him. Hopefully he'll be well ahead of the target, or, even better, over on the far bow as he patrols from side to side. When we're clear of the escort, we'll put on maximum speed and dash in on the target. We'll be abaft his beam. Usually the merchant-ship lookouts are least alert in the sectors from beam through stern to the other beam."

I told Bob that circumstances would dictate how close we would come to the tanker before firing our bow torpedoes. I hoped to get inside 3,000 yards. After he sighted us it would probably take him some time to start shooting. By then, I hoped, we could be heading away at high speed and watching our torpedoes exploding.

Exultant that the attack decision had been made, I turned to Lieutenant Andrews and ordered: "Officer of the deck, turn right to course 270 and stop when our distance to the target's track is five miles. Man torpedo stations."

The OOD sounded the general alarm. Instantly, the public address system resounded with the clanging of the sub's gong. I was struck once more with the responsibility I had as captain of *Archer-Fish*, especially for the lives of my 8 officers and 72 crewmen. Heady stuff. But we were all in this together. I knew that their hopes for victory were as high as mine. I'd go by the book, sure, but I'd also respond to my gut instincts. Once again I was the man on the spot. Unlike *Shokaku*, this enemy vessel would not escape.

I listened to Lieutenant Andrews's command echo the length of *Archer-Fish:* "All hands to battle stations! Torpedo!"

3. Evasion

Ensign Shoda, chief quartermaster of the *Shinano*, drained the last swallow of his bowl of tea, adjusted his cap and the final buttons of his all-weather jacket, and prepared to go topside to stand his watch from 2000 to 2200. It was about one-half hour after the enemy's radar signal had been reported to Captain Abe. Ensign Shoda announced his departure to several other young officers in the wardroom and went out to make his way through several corridors in the labyrinthine upper decks of the carrier. Finally he began his ascent to the lookout platform directly above the navigating bridge, where he would be in charge of the next watch of lookouts.

Beneath his feet *Shinano*'s huge steel hull cruised imperturbably through the Pacific. The only motion, he noticed, was a gentle, lulling pitch from bow to stern; the ship demonstrated no perceptible rolling. She might still be cradled in her drydock for all the awareness she gave of being at sea.

Ensign Shoda relieved his predecessor and was pleased to see that the moon still hung above the sea, sending its benevolent light in all directions. The moonlight, though, was a double-edged sword. Certainly it helped the watch in their efforts to detect any enemy ship, but in turnabout fashion it also made *Shinano* very visible to the enemy. Ensign Shoda was reassured by the presence of a screen of battle-hardened destroyers he knew were ready to pounce on any submarine rash enough even to approach *Shinano*.

Ensign Shoda checked the watch detail to ascertain the alertness of every lookout. They were spaced only a few feet apart on the lookout station, which measured some 10 feet by 24 feet. More than 30 pairs of binoculars of various sizes were available to the watch. The lookout detail had already selected the binoculars of their choice and were scanning the sectors of the sea assigned to them. The young watch officer took up a familiar pair and joined the lookouts along the railing as *Shinano* plowed through the ocean.

The night was warmer than usual for late November. Off the bow and on the starboard and port beams, *Isokaze, Yukikaze*, and *Hamakaze* plied the relatively warm waters of the Kuroshio Stream in a protective shield. Not a light was to be seen on any of the ships, and the only sound was that of the spume from the bow wave and the roiling wake of the newest warship in the Emperor's fleet as a moderate sea kicked against her side.

One hour passed. The watch detail were silent, absorbed in their task. Now and then, a lookout would step back and stretch his arms and shoulders to counteract the stiffness that built up during a stressful watch. Several rubbed their eyes softly to relieve the discomfort of binoculars pressed to their faces too tightly.

Standing in the buffeting wind, the lookouts gradually became chilled; they began to shift from foot to foot and flap their elbows at their sides. Ensign Shoda had to order them to settle down and be mindful of their responsibility.

"Not much longer, men," he repeated, walking about behind them. "It's almost 2200. No time to become lax."

It was then that one of the lookouts called out, "*Ugen ni, sensuikan hakken*. Periscope, sir! Starboard bow!" His voice was loud and shrill.

Ensign Shoda rushed to his side to aim his binoculars in the direction pointed out by the lookout. "Where? I can't see it."

"Broad on the starboard bow, sir. About half a mile."

Ensign Shoda's binoculars swept the area in that direction.

He was joined by several other lookouts. None of them found any sign of a periscope on the moonlit sea.

"I don't see anything, Kubonta. Are you sure?"

"Not absolutely, sir. For a moment there, though, I could've sworn I saw a periscope. Nothing now. Perhaps it was a wave breaking."

"I think so, Kubonta. I can see why you would think so. Some of the waves colliding with each other . . . breaking up against one another . . . almost give the appearance of a periscope rippling through the water."

Ensign Shoda wondered whether he should report the possible sighting to the captain on the bridge anyway. Better to be safe than sorry. He turned away to call to the bridge, one deck below on the carrier's steel island. His call was duly noted by Ensign Yasuda, the assistant navigator, who told him to stand by.

Presently Ensign Yasuda came back on the line. "We've checked it here and with other watches. Nothing. Captain Mikami, the XO, says, 'Keep the men at it.' "

Ensign Shoda replaced the telephone and returned to the railing next to Seaman Kubonta. "Captain's bridge can't confirm your sighting. That's all right. Anything else?"

"No, sir," Kobonta replied. The watch detail, however, were now more alert. Their bodies now braced to their duty as though a surge of electricity had passed around the reinforced railing.

At 2200 a new lookout section assumed the duty station, and Ensign Shoda and his watch went below. He commended his men as they passed in single file; he then made his way below to the officers' wardroom. The room was deserted and looked a little depressing in the dim illumination given off by the low-powered fluorescent lamps. The bulkheads, which had been painted throughout *Shinano* with gray, nonflammable paint, provided little welcome or cheer.

Ensign Shoda withdrew without partaking of any of the hot tea and snacks left by the messmen for the crew members on duty throughout the night. Weary and chilled after the strain of the two-hour watch, he went to his cabin to take a nap. Drifting off, he saw flickering visions of periscopes cutting through dark Pacific water. They were everywhere, circling *Shinano* like the fins of sharks.

Several decks below within the citadel of *Shinano*—the huge, heavily protected heart of the carrier that had begun as a battle-ship—Lieutenant Commander Yasuma, the senior medical officer, prowled restlessly through his extensive medical department. At his approach, his assistants and orderlies snapped to attention. Doctor Yasuma quickly motioned for them to be at ease. Rest while you can, he always believed. In an action situation, doctors and orderlies could be on their feet around the clock, tending to the dying and the wounded. This well-ordered antiseptic silence could, Yasuma knew, give way to bedlam in seconds.

He roamed the numerous spaces of his department, dis-creetly stifling the inclination to yawn after spending so many hours on duty, performing so many inspections since *Shinano* had sailed from Yokosuka. He thought again about Captain Abe's policy of simplicity. It was a principle reflected in almost every facet of *Shinano*'s fitting-out, even within the medical department. There was no escaping the skipper's intention to keep every accommodation and accouterment to the most un-complicated design. The beds were little more than canvas cots, with only a few high steel models in evidence. Rubber mats, which could be quickly changed and washed of blood, covered most of them. Few chairs of any type were found in the spacious wards, whose furniture, apart from the beds, was limited to small steel tables attached to the deck. The bulkheads held no artwork to cheer the casualties.

Captain Abe's was a fighting ship, and she was fitted out accordingly. Yet the department had an air of quiet efficiency because of the very simplicity of its design and furnishings. There were no unnecessary appointments to create roadblocks for corpsmen rushing the maimed to the triage area where the decision had to be made almost instantly: Who would go under the surgeon's knife? Who could wait a bit, probably with the assistance of a blood transfusion? Who would be shuffled off into an unlit corner to die alone because their injuries were beyond the capabilities of the ship's medical staff.

Even the bulkheads in the medical department—constructed as they were of steel and layered with heavy brown paint—were unappealing and bereft of any hint that the healing art was practiced there. The decks also were fashioned of steel and coated with a thick brown mortar. Because there were no portholes to admit natural light, the only illumination came from rows of dull fluorescent lamps. The dim light, lack of white paint on the bulkheads and deck, and the absence of the usual bedding associated with a hospital gave no assurance that the space was a modern medical facility.

Yet Dr. Yasuma was of a mind that the naval architects had provided ample space for his requirements. There were a series of operating rooms, warrens of sick bays, myriad examination rooms, storage chambers, and supply alcoves. The key medical areas had been solicitously soundproofed and equipped with an excellent ventilation system. Overall, the ship's doctor was convinced that his department was adequately fitted out and compared favorably with any modern hospital ashore—not so much in the appearance it offered but in the skilled staff and equipment provided by the Naval Ministry.

As he continued his informal inspection, Commander Yasuma smiled to himself as he thought of an incident involving Captain Abe. He had learned about it through the officers' grapevine. It went back to a time before he had come aboard the carrier. Captain Abe, with the ship's delivery date close at hand, had asked the Naval Ministry who would be assigned as his senior medical officer. He was informed that it would be a Lieutenant Commander Yasuma. This had come as a surprise to the skipper. In truth, it was also a surprise to the Navy physician, because both he and Captain Abe knew that such a senior billet was usually filled by a medical officer with the rank of captain. Though it was never mentioned, Commander

Yasuma sensed that Captain Abe was offended that a lower-ranking officer had been assigned to his ship.

Shortly after 2200, his rounds completed, Dr. Yasuma returned to his cabin, where he was in the habit of writing his daily observations in a journal he kept. This evening, as on many occasions, one of his main concerns was the readiness of Shinano's crew, including the officers and men assigned to the medical department.

"Generally speaking," he had noted in the journal, "the bigger the warship and the more modern her equipment, the greater is the time it takes for the crew to become familiar with her. This being so, a ship of Shinano's huge size needs at least three years of training to put her at top fighting strength, and to get the crew to take prompt and appropriate control measures when she is damaged in battle."

He noted in the journal his conviction that Japan's naval leaders had been unreasonable in their demand that Shinano sortie from Tokyo Bay so soon after being commissioned. Still, he realized that what appeared unreasonable to him was reasonable to higher authority in light of the massive bombing raids being carried out by the Americans over the Tokyo-Yokahama industrial sector during the past days. If Shinano had remained at Yokosuka, all too soon she would have been pinpointed as a prime target by the B-29s. The alternative, of course, was not much better—a nighttime dash to the Inland Sea through waters infested, from everything he had heard, by enemy submarines.

With Shinano's predicament in mind, he had written in his journal: "In order to overcome the tremendous odds, needless to say, it was required that the crew's skill and morale be of the highest quality. But for myself, who witnessed firsthand the superior seamen of the Imperial Japanese Navy at the outbreak of the war, it seems to me that many of Shinano's crew are rather inferior in skills and morale. I can't help feeling a sense of apprehension as to how they will demonstrate their ability in the event of a fierce battle."

Wearily, he laid the journal aside and stretched out on his

bunk without taking off his uniform. With the specter of enemy submarines behind his lowered eyelids, it took the ship's doctor a long while to get to sleep.

On the captain's bridge, on the steel island high above *Shinano*'s flight deck, the navigator, Captain Nakamura[1], and his assistant, Ensign Yasuda, were duly marking the ship's course changes on the bridge chart and plotting her position every 15 minutes. All required notations were made in the ship's log.

Captain Mikami, the executive officer, nodded quiet approval. There were more than a score of officers and seamen on the bridge carrying out various functions, but conversation was held to a minimum and only an occasional low voice could be heard. Captain Abe did not appreciate being disturbed from his solitary musings by loud or superfluous talk.

Although he was outwardly serene, Captain Mikami felt pressing concern about the ship's watertight compartments. The air pressure tests that would have confirmed his hope that the compartments were watertight had been canceled in the rush to move *Shinano* to the Inland Sea. He could not keep his mind off the issue because he was the officer in charge of the watertight doors and of damage control. Would they stand up in combat? What most concerned him was the cancellation of the air tests. The next matter had to do with the novel construction of the passageways running the length of the ship. Instead of the usual single, major lengthwise passageway on each side of the vessel, with narrow athwartship passageways connecting them at right angles, *Shinano* had been designed with *two* major passageways on each side, with the athwartship connecting passageways as large as the two main ones. Captain Mikami blamed this unusual construction for the fact that he often got lost in the ship. Because this confusion about directions in the passageway was rife among the officers and men, the XO worried that in the event of a disaster *Shinano*'s personnel might be slow in reaching their battle stations. He knew also that Captain Abe was unhappy because so many of his seamen had received only minimal training before going to sea for the first time. The skipper had approached him about running emergency drills to train the crew, but the XO had pointed out that with the ship still under construction, the myriad exposed pipes and wires would make full-scale exercises dangerous.

Inwardly, Captain Mikami sensed that Captain Abe well knew his ship was not safe and believed that their worst enemy was not the Americans but the headquarters bureaucrats focusing forever on their dream of victory. He thought back to November 11, when *Shinano* had conducted a limited shakedown cruise of 20 kilometers within Tokyo Bay to determine her top speed on eight boilers. The best she could make had been 21 knots—a speed insufficient for launching her combat aircraft in the absence of a headwind. Captain Abe's face had worn a black scowl throughout the exercise.

Incredibly, however, despite the severe limitations, the shipyard had insisted on performing the delivery ceremony on November 18, when *Shinano* was officially presented to the Imperial Navy. Captain Mikami cringed, recalling how the ceremony had been plagued with problems and breakdowns. An elevator carrying a top administrative headquarters officer became stuck due to burnt wiring, hardly acceptable on a brand-new ship. The ship's officers had begun to labor under a sense of foreboding.

And how could he forget noticing how Captain Abe's hands had shook with anger when he accepted the delivery certificate from the director of the shipyard. Seeing Captain Abe's reaction, everyone present knew he wanted to reject the certificate for cause. But all realized that it was unthinkable for a Japanese officer to oppose the will of headquarters.

As Captain Mikami reflected on these recent events, Captain Nakamura, short and stolid in his winter gear and with the unruffled demeanor of a seasoned sailor, leaned over the huge chart like a shaggy bear who had never known the serenity of periodic hibernations. War was unmistakably his calling. Like his captain, Navigator Nakamura was nearly indefatigable and alert every moment to the hazards of a passage like this.

While his eyes scrutinized the chart he already knew by heart, Captain Nakamura let his mind slip back to the Monday —November 20, eight days earlier—when he had accompanied Captain Abe ashore for a briefing by the Operations and Intelligence Section of Yokosuka Naval Shipyard. The captain had requested the briefing in order to put to sea with all available intelligence on the route of his scheduled sortie.

The briefing officer, constantly pointing to his own large chart of the waters off the main island of Honshu, had informed his visitors of the rapid buildup of the B-29 bomber force on Saipan and Tinian. Large-scale bombing attacks on the home islands, particularly in the Tokyo-Yokohama area, were certain to commence shortly. It was anticipated that these raids would come during daylight hours. The B-29s, flying at an altitude beyond the reach of Japanese fighters and accurate antiaircraft fire, could obtain a clear view of their designated targets. They virtually owned the high sky.

As for submarines, they definitely would be present along *Shinano*'s track, and in great numbers. During the past week there had been several surface gun battles between Yankee submarines and Japanese picket boats and patrol craft in the waters off the Bonin Islands and Honshu. At 0330 on November 16 a friendly cargo ship had been torpedoed and sunk some 350 miles southeast of Tokyo Bay.[2] Just a few hours later, some 50 miles north of that attack, Japanese radio direction-finding equipment (RDF) had detected the transmission of a long coded message—apparently from the victorious submarine skipper.

The briefing officer told Captain Abe and Navigator Nakamura about the detection of several other enemy submarine transmissions since November 16. In one case an effort had been made to get the enemy to retransmit his entire message in the hope of confirming his compass bearing. Though Japanese Intelligence knew U.S. procedures for making such a request it failed, because the enemy radioman apparently spotted the deception. The signal requesting the repeat was probably too strong to have come from anywhere but a nearby transmitter.[3] Moreover, the Japanese submarine I-365 had recently conducted a 50-day patrol in the Marianas area and reported by radio the sightings of a steady stream of U.S. submarines.[4] On November 10 and 11, reports had been received of the sailing of at least 13 American submarines from Saipan and Guam. A number of these, it was believed, had been among those observed by the I-365.

Captain Nakamura recalled that the briefing officer was unable to provide Captain Abe with any explanation for this unsettling flurry of activity by the Americans. When asked to express an opinion, he ventured that the hostile submarines could be concentrating in the waters south of Honshu in anticipation of *Shinano*'s sortie. Japanese Intelligence was convinced, he said, that B-29 photo reconnaissance planes had detected *Shinano* during a series of flights over Tokyo Bay in the past few weeks. On November 11, for example, *Shinano* had been under way and conspicuously exposed in Tokyo Bay when a B-29 aircraft passed overhead. The carrier was making good headway into the wind to recover aircraft, leaving a large, white arrow-shaped wake astern. How could the Americans help not seeing her?

Captain Abe had requested intelligence data detailing the specific areas of the home waters where submarines had been most active in recent days. The briefer quickly got the current status chart and submarine log maintained by the operations staff responsible for the stipulated area. The two officers' eyes swept over the chart, neither of them giving any outward sign of his dismay at the appalling chain of meticulously drawn "Xs." Each "X" designated the site where a Japanese ship had been sunk by the enemy—all of them by submarines. The "Xs" appeared singly and in groups on many areas of the chart.

Navigator Nakamura's stomach tightened. He felt his anger gathering as he considered that the crosshatches set down in such a detached manner symbolized the loss of so many fine ships. Having served aboard them, the names of quite a few were familiar to him. Even more gut-wrenching was the awareness that the "Xs" symbolized the death of so many old comrades. Is this what an era of dedicated service to the Empire came down to: an "X" on an intelligence chart? Though a believer in Buddhism, like most religious Japanese, he thought the "Xs" curiously resembled so many Latin crosses, tilting in the waves.

After that briefing Captain Abe had ordered Navigator Nakamura to transfer the Operations and Intelligence data to one of his bridge charts. With the information available to him back on the bridge of *Shinano*, Captain Abe would be able to study and evaluate the data circumspectly. And on November 27, a week later, he used this data to quash the energetic arguments of Captain Shintani, commander of Destroyer Division 17, and his three destroyer captains, for a daylight passage to Kure. Captain Nakamura, who had been present at what he later described to Captain Mikami as a "heated discussion," recalled that the destroyer officers were vociferously opposed to Captain Abe's new plan to sail far out to sea at dusk.[5]

Captain Shintani had noted pointedly that *Hamakaze, Yukikaze,* and *Isokaze,* his flagship, had arrived at Yokosuda only two days earlier. Their officers and crew were battle-weary and exhausted from the lengthy and punishing tour of combat they had just finished. They had been in the battle for Leyte Gulf and had seen havoc unleashed on a large segment of the Japanese fleet. A request for even brief leave had been rejected. Captain Shintani had emphasized the damage sustained by *Hamakaze* and *Isokaze,* which included the loss of radar equipment. In addition, the ships required vital repairs to sonar and other electronic systems. Only *Yukikaze* had emerged unscathed from the decisive engagement at Leyte. With *Shinano* under orders to sail on November 28, the destroyers would have to go to sea without undergoing any of the required repairs.

Captain Shintani emphasized that "there were too many mechanical problems on the ships" and expressed his concern that the destroyers "would not be able to prevent a night attack by enemy submarines." He argued again for a daylight passage along the Honshu coast, saying that he was confident *Shinano*'s heavy antiaircraft batteries and armored deck would "safely resist any attack by American carrier planes." Then, too, it would be easier for the Coast Guard and other defense forces ashore to dispatch assistance to a ship just off the coast. In the light of day, the American submarines would have to operate at lower speeds, underwater, to avoid being spotted, and would have no chance to pursue and intercept *Shinano* unless they were simply lucky enough to be patroling along her track. Finally, he pointed out that if *Shinano* sailed at 0600 from Tokyo Bay and took the shorter, coast-wise route, she could arrive at Kii Suido, the guarded entrance to the Inland Sea, at 2100 the same day; any nighttime passage farther out to sea would entail more time during which *Shinano* would be vulnerable to attack.

Captain Nakamura recollected how Captain Abe had listened without response while the four destroyer officers argued as one voice for the daylight passage. When they began to repeat themselves, however, *Shinano*'s skipper suddenly signaled for silence. They had made their views known; the formalities and protocol had been observed. Ultimately, as provided by the Naval General Staff, the decision regarding the route to be followed was his alone, and he knew what it was.

Captain Abe gave the destroyer officers the reason for his decision in favor of the nighttime passage. Upon first receiving his orders to move *Shinano* to the Inland Sea, he too had planned to move quickly during daylight hours along the Honshu coast with air cover. Shortly afterward, however, headquarters had informed him that all available Japanese aircraft squadrons were engaged in active combat duty. There would be no air cover available for the nation's most valuable carrier!

In Abe's opinion, to undertake a daylight passage bereft of air cover would be insane. This was compounded by the fact that *Shinano* itself would be putting to sea without its own complement of planes. There would not be a single friendly aircraft to scout the waters ahead of the carrier, much less any to help her fend off an actual attack. Yankee scout planes could find *Shinano*, approach her at will, and radio for hordes of torpedo planes to come and overwhelm her. The anticipated raid on the Japanese home islands by the powerful U.S. fleet under Admiral Halsey must be taken into account.

The daylight passage was not possible, Captain Abe had said bluntly. Rather, *Shinano* would sortie south at dusk on the twenty-eighth and run for deep water. Some distance out, she would change course to the southeast as if headed for Taiwan, then finally run west to Kii Suido. In stating his decision, he, as Captain Nakamura remembered it, had taken into account that the moon would be nearly full during the nighttime passage. However, the moon's illumination could work in *Shinano*'s favor, at least against enemy submarines that were on the surface. With a multitude of lookouts on the carrier and the destroyers, a sighting could be expected at a distance of several thousand meters.

The main threat to *Shinano*'s passage was indeed torpedo attack from American submarines, but Captain Abe had reasoned that *Shinano*'s speed of up to 21 knots would permit her to outrace any submarine proceeding at the relatively low speed they could make underwater. A submerged submarine could only menace *Shinano* if by sheer luck it happened to be within a few thousand meters of her projected track.

As for U.S. torpedoes, Captain Abe held a decidedly contemptuous view of them. One of Japan's top experts in torpedo warfare, he had detailed knowledge of the range and speed of the U.S. submarine service's Mark 14 and Mark 10 torpedoes. The information had come readily available as a result of General Douglas MacArthur's precipitous declaration on Christmas Day, 1941 that Manila in the Philippines was to be an open city.[6,7] The announcement had permitted American submariners only 24 hours to remove their prepositioned stockpile of torpedoes from Manila and its environs. Despite their best efforts, many Mark 14s—the basic U.S. submarine weapon— as well as dozens of the older Mark 10s were abandoned to the approaching enemy. The fall of Manila thus handed the Japanese invaluable details about the capabilities and limitations of American torpedoes.

Captain Abe had been presented with information that the

Americans had kept closely guarded. He was surprised to learn that the U.S. fleet submarine torpedo had a range of only 4,500 yards at a speed of 46 knots. To obtain a range of 9,000 yards, the speed had to be dropped to 31.5 knots. *Shinano*'s skipper had found these facts to be incredible. Dai Nippon's oxygen-and-alcohol-powered submarine torpedo not only carried a much larger warhead than the American Mark 14 but had a range of 13,000 yards at 45 knots. Once again he was reminded that the Americans' vaunted technical superiority was just mythmaking in so many ways.

Captain Abe had assured his destroyer escort officers that submarines would in any case be avoided by *Shinano*'s superior speed and by the course changes he would order. The offshore track would permit her greater flexibility in zigzagging; their option of altering course to starboard would have been severely curtailed by a passage close to shore.

The sound of Captain Abe's voice hardening as he concluded his soliloquy remained in Captain Nakamura's mind. Captain Abe had pointed out that it was his intention, and therefore their primary mission, to deliver *Shinano* safely to Kure: "Our objective is not to sink enemy submarines unless they threaten our passage. I want to make that very clear, and I want each of you to adhere absolutely to this order. I say again, the escort ships are to remain on guard in close proximity to *Shinano* and are not to be diverted, by any ruse, beyond the submarines' lethal torpedo range. It is imperative that you prevent any hostile submarine from slipping inside the screen undetected."

The navigator could almost remember word for word how Captain Abe had added: "If I believe an escort has left her assigned station . . . permitting such a possibility . . . I will call for her immediate return. The signal will be made by *Shinano*'s red truck light, which will be turned on and off for about ten seconds. I strongly suggest that you do not make this signal necessary." The meeting had concluded with Captain Abe directing that neither *Shinano* nor any escort that still had the capability to do so was to use her active sonar or radar equipment. As an alternative, they would operate their electronic equipment in the passive mode to detect any enemy transmissions. . . .

Straightening up before the chart, Captain Nakamura rubbed his big chin and stretched his back muscles under the heavy woolen jacket. Yes, indeed, the skipper had made it quite clear what their priority was, what the course was to be, and how the destroyer officers were to conduct themselves. He smiled to himself, remembering their discomfited expressions as Captain Abe had imposed his will upon them. Those wild-eyed samurai destroyer types had been put in their place for once. He almost chuckled aloud.

At Captain Nakamura's side, Ensign Yasuda remained hunched over the bridge chart, unobtrusively trying to become as familiar with all its marking and place names as the senior navigator. As his eyes roamed over the numerous notations, he recalled that shortly after the presailing conference the Direction Finding (DF) Network had reported the detection of an enemy submarine just off *Shinano*'s proposed track.[8] The detection, in the form of a lengthy transmission, had been DF'd the evening before, about 70 miles due east of Shiono Misaki, the prominent cape marking the entrance to Kii Suido.

Within an hour after the detection, the operations staff officer at the combined fleet headquarters—secretly located in a nondescript, two-story concrete structure at Hiyosi, a small city situated halfway between Tokyo and Yokohama—had inserted a blue pin into the flag-plot chart to indicate the position of the enemy submarine. During the night this new intelligence had been distributed to all interested commands. *Shinano* was informed by telegram.

Ensign Yasuda had carefully plotted this location on the bridge chart. It was prominently labeled because of its proximity to Captain Abe's choice of passage. Ensign Yasuda recalled that it had been the topic of some hushed conversations between the skipper and the executive officer, Captain Mikami, who had just stepped over and was standing behind the young officer and Navigator Nakamura.

63

Captain Mikami's presence in no way intimidated Ensign Yasuda, an engaging and remarkably self-possessed young officer who had graduated from the Japanese Naval Academy in the spring of 1944. Because of Ensign Yasuda's top standing in the class, his professionalism, and his quick mind, Captain Abe had immediately assigned him to the very sensitive position of *Shinano*'s assistant navigator. Captain Abe's assessment of Ensign Yasuda's capabilities and talents had thus far been on the mark. From the very beginning of his assignment, the young officer had carried out his duties with zeal and commendable judgment.

In the past few months, a special professional relationship had developed between the commanding officer and Ensign Yasuda. The skipper had in effect assumed the role of the junior officer's mentor. It had been done discreetly in order to avoid an appearance of favoritism and to spare Yasuda harassment by his peers. Still, when the occasion permitted, Captain Abe gave the ensign useful tidbits of information to help him in discharging his responsibilities. Occasionally the captain even said something that afforded a glimpse into his complex personality.

Ensign Yasuda doubted whether any officer aboard *Shinano* had the slightest inkling, for example, of the captain's love for traditional Japanese literature. The knowledge had come as a surprise to the ensign. Who would have believed it about the old man? So cold and withdrawn, so much the samurai in his bearing and demeanor, he had only to raise his eyebrows in a signal of disapproval for his officers to feel sharply rebuked.

Captain Abe had the reputation of being a hard man—stone-faced, unbending, certainly unforgiving. A thorough professional, he was also unswervingly loyal and dedicated to his country's cause. It had not occurred to anyone to try to see behind this rigid facade, to seek the human being behind it. Yet Ensign Yasuda well remembered a singular time when he had been returning with Captain Abe from a briefing ashore. Approaching *Shinano* in her drydock, the captain had gone to the end of a nearby pier and stared far across the bay to the far side.

"Shall we open fire, sir?" the communications officer inquired.

"Hold fire! Not a shot!" Captain Abe replied. "It will just confirm that we're a big warship. She may not even have seen us."

Silence again enveloped the lookout bridge as *Shinano* plowed through the ocean on a course that would take her to the left of the mysterious vessel at a distance of some three miles in about 20 minutes. The men awaited Captain Abe's further orders.

Then came a shocking announcement from a lookout. "Captain Abe, *Isokaze!* She's left formation. She's running at full speed for the unidentified ship!"

All binoculars swung in the direction of the bow. *Isokaze* was no longer in her correct screen position dead ahead of *Shinano.* Rather, she was slashing across the water, sending up a boiling wake, closing on the intruder. Less than four miles intervened. Her five-inch guns could fire twice that distance. At her top speed of 35 knots, she would be on top of her prey in less than seven minutes.

4. Frustration

Confidential
Subject: U.S.S. *Archer-Fish* (SS-311)--Report of
Fifth War Patrol

(B) Narrative

November 28, 1944

2140 It appeared [target] only had one escort.
With sky overcast, and dark horizon to the
north, started surface approach on starboard flank.

2230 Escort on starboard beam sighted. Not possible to make surface approach on this side.
Changed course back to his base course.

2250 Target group closing and we are off the
track too far to submerge . . .

Even before the gong sounded throughout *Archer-Fish* and
the word was passed—"All hands to battle stations, torpedo!"
—the crew had anticipated the order, hearing about the contact
by word of mouth inside their tubular steel world. Most of them
had already started for their assigned posts.

While I remained topside on the bridge—with my XO, Bob
Bobczynski; the OOD, Lieutenant Andrews; and the lookouts
—Chief Carnahan, an ex-steel mill worker and a descendant of
Daniel Boone, spoke quietly into the mouthpiece of his headset.
"All stations report when manned."

The responses came almost immediately: "Forward torpedo room, manned and ready!" "Forward battery compartment, manned and ready!" In precision sequence, the compartments throughout *Archer-Fish* reported their readiness for action. The voices Chief Carnahan heard were brimming with confidence and the desire to achieve something big. Within only moments, he was able to report: "Captain, the ship is at battle stations."

A key component of the ship's preparation for battle was the damage-control repair party. For the time being, it consisted solely of Motor Machinist Mate Second Class Carl Wilken. He had been a student at the University of Illinois when he decided to enlist for the duration of the war. He had a reputation for being unflappable, and at the sound of the general alarm he climbed into his bunk, knowing that if he were needed he could be readily found there. Then he promptly went to sleep. Close at hand was his canvas bag stuffed with assorted pipe patches, wooden plugs, mauls, and other leak-stopping tools.

With the bridge as my personal general-quarters station, I could easily make frequent trips down into the conning tower. Directly below the bridge, the conning tower in effect was the nerve center of the ship, particularly during the attack process. It contained the electronic equipment needed to help us obtain an identification and a location fix on a target. But on the bridge then under the night sky, at what I considered an observation post, I could *see* the enemy ships. There, simply by looking at them, I was in the best position to anticipate their course changes and other responses.

Periodically I dropped down the hatch ladder to the conning tower to study the radar screen and the pips it displayed— indications that we were receiving echoes from the enemy ships. In doing so, I conversed frequently with the radar operator, Radar Technician Third Class "Bud" Myers, and the radar officer, Lieutenant Bosza, to see if they had any information that I didn't. I also checked with the plot to determine from Judd and Dan the enemy group's track and speed. Our problem was that it was next to impossible to predict the destination of the enemy group. Lacking that capability, it was very difficult to get ahead of the zigzagging target. I went to the TDC to talk with Dave Bunting, who was an expert operator, capable of detecting almost instantly even a slight change in the enemy's course and speed.

Invariably, I noted that the plot and TDC solutions agreed. The officers and men assigned to the conning tower operations knew exactly what to do and were carrying out their complicated functions with a deceptive quiet. My visits there usually lasted only three or four minutes. While on the bridge, it became routine for me to speak down through the hatch to Chief Carnahan in the conning tower to inquire whether he was receiving enough information and sending it down to all compartments to keep our people informed. I wanted the men below to understand what was happening. His response was always: "Yes, sir."

Below the conning tower Lieutenant Rom Cousins, *Archer-Fish*'s engineering officer, was standing by in the control room in case I gave the order for a fast dive. Now and then Rom conversed with the chief of the "black gangs"—the men in the engine rooms—whenever the chief came forward to update him on their efforts to coax a few more turns from the four main diesel engines. Seeing all this coordination and esprit de corps boosted my determination to sink the target.

Actually, no one's spirits were keener than those of my officer of the deck, Lieutenant Andrews, who circled the bridge restlessly to check on the lookouts. It was his responsibility to ensure that all sectors were under close observation, every pair of binoculars was clean, and the lookouts were comfortable and were relieved at appropriate times. All of us on the bridge were heartened by his frequent exhortations: "We can do it! *Archer-Fish* needs this one! Stay with it, men." His cheerleading was infectious and even got us smiling as we went about our duties.

Every few minutes Lieutenant Bosza would quietly have the radar operator, "Bud" Myers, make a 360-degree search around us to confirm that no enemy was coming up on our disengaged side for a surprise attack. There was a complete absence of confusion and unnecessary noise below.

Lieutenant Bunting and Ensign Crosby were working together as a close-knit team at the TDC. Gordon Crosby, as communications officer, was also maintaining a close liaison with the radio room to be apprised of any incoming messages. Both the movements of *Archer-Fish* and those of the target continued to be plotted by Ensign Dygert and Boatswain Dan Ellzey.

I had some qualms about permitting such freewheeling use of the radar so close to the enemy, as I was well aware that to do so was contrary to Navy doctrine. But I was the man on the spot, and I said the hell with it. I wanted to see what was out there. I had the equipment, and I used it. We were all in a do-or-die frame of mind, and the devil take the hindmost. I figured that the Japanese ships had probably detected the unintentional emissions from our radar anyway, while it was being reassembled after the repair work. And surely they knew that there were hostile submarines in the "Hit Parade" sector off Honshu. It had been a fabled shooting gallery for American submarines since the early days of the Pacific war.

Meanwhile, *Archer-Fish* was running on a westerly course to take a position on the down-moon side of the tanker. It was my intention, in taking the offensive, to maneuver so that the target, rather than my ship, was silhouetted. Once in position, I intended to stop all engines and point the ship's bow directly at the target to decrease to a minimum his chance of seeing us. After the single escort had passed, it was my plan to rush the tanker at flank speed. *Archer-Fish* would pass astern of the escort, come in on the tanker's starboard beam or quarter, and fire a salvo of torpedoes. Then we would immediately withdraw to a point that would provide us with an excellent view of the results. It was to be a great pyrotechnics display!

That was the initial plan, as Bob and I conceived it. How could it fail? But we knew that our plan was just that—a scheme, a design, a concept. It mostly took into consideration our own thinking. What about the enemy and *his* plan? What about the captain of the Japanese tanker, and the captain of his escort? It was like a chess match. Neither of us was privy to the other's strategy. However one moved, the other had a counter move, or several moves. Check. Checkmate. In war against a skilled enemy, by definition nothing ever truly goes "as planned."

We were prepared to begin our approach. Once again I dropped below into the conning tower to inform the fire-control party of the minutest details of the plan of attack.

"We'll open out to westward from the target's track and then slow while waiting for the group to zig. Which direction? We'll have to wait and see. When we reach a position abaft the beam of the ship, we'll go to flank speed, cut behind the escort, and dash forward into torpedo range. Then we'll fire. Torpedoes away, we cut around, put the escort astern, and escape the usual depth-charge punishment. Once away, we'll all enjoy watching the explosions when our warheads hit the enemy ship."

Smartly said, I thought. I went up to the bridge. My target was still there. The plan was operational. Ah, what fools these mortals be.

Within a few minutes, at approximately 2140, Seaman Irwin "Stew" Stewart, a novice crewman with exceptionally keen night vision, called down from his raised lookout station on the bridge: "Mr. Andrews, that ship looks like an aircraft carrier."

Before I could even swing my binoculars onto the target, Lieutenant Andrews, who had been staring intently through his glasses, said, "Cap'n, I think Stewart is right."

Lieutenant Commander Bobczynski chimed in almost immediately: "Captain, it is a carrier—no question about it."

Slowpoke that I was compared to them, I finally got my binoculars on the target. "Look at that—a carrier," I exclaimed. "A big one at last!" I called down the conning tower hatch to the telephone talker: "Chief, we have an aircraft carrier as the target. Right now, we only see one escort. Pass the word!"

I fixed my binoculars back on the target. What luck! Instead of a piece of cake—a crummy tanker of probably no more than 5,000 tons—we now had a capital ship coming at us. I was still trying to make myself believe it. I felt so exhilarated. What an opportunity to make up for all the past lost opportunities. We just *had* to get this one.

"She's a carrier, sir. She's a carrier," Lieutenant Andrews repeated to himself quietly. "We can do it, sir. *Archer-Fish* needs this one."

How true, I thought. *Archer-Fish* does, and I personally need it too. For myself, for the crew, for Sam Dealey and all the submarine officers and seamen the Japanese had sent to the bottom of the sea. Memories of my days as skipper of *Dace* the year before came flooding back. There was one more ghost I still had to confront, deal with, and dissipate forever. . . .

It had been in the same "Hit Parade" area off Tokyo Bay. Commander Submarines Pacific (COMSUBPAC) had sent a message to *Dace* to intercept an aircraft carrier escorted by three destroyers. The ULTRA communiqué, for my eyes only, provided the longitude and latitude positions of the carrier group—not only for 2000 that day but also for 0800 the next day. Our intelligence people certainly had the goods on the enemy's intentions this time. Throughout the war, only the skipper on a submarine was privy to ULTRA information and to the knowledge that the United States was able to decode and read Japanese top-secret communications at will. (Upon receiving their commands, captains had to sign a statement that they would never in their lifetimes divulge any information about ULTRA and never discuss its existence with any unauthorized personnel. My ULTRA security restriction was not terminated until 35 years after the end of the war.)

I decided that *Dace* would ambush and torpedo the carrier at the position she would reach at 0600 the next day. At the time, we were running along the coast of Honshu, the main Japanese island, and we could be comfortably situated in our attack site by then. Landmarks along the coastline helped us to navigate precisely. I told my key officers that we had intelligence on a carrier's expected position, but I was not able to explain to them about the particular reliability—and sensitivity —of the ULTRA information on which I knew the COMSUB-PAC prediction to be based.

As *Dace* headed for the designated position, my XO and my navigator informed me that the Kuroshio, or Japanese Current, was not running at the normal speed of one and a half knots but at half that pace. After checking their computations, I had to agree with their finding. Now I had two problems to resolve. The first was mine alone, and it made the stakes even higher than my fellow officers guessed. There was always some risk that in acting on ULTRA information, we might provoke the enemy to wonder how a U.S. submarine had managed to be at the right place and time to intercept one of their ships. Higher authority had obviously weighed this and decided to accept this marginal risk of letting me use ULTRA information, because it would put *Dace* into position to sink the carrier. But to be spotted waiting in ambush at the Japanese carrier's supposedly top-secret position, yet *fail* to sink her, would be to have exposed ULTRA for nothing. I could not allow that to happen. And that brought me to the second problem, which I was able to discuss. It centered on one big question: Did the Japanese navigator aboard the carrier also know that the Kuroshio was only running at half its normally predicted speed of one and a half knots? I had to assume that the enemy navigator, though out of sight of land, had obtained a good star fix earlier at dusk, around 1800, just as we had aboard *Dace*. It was pro forma for any navigator to obtain star fixes at evening dusk and morning twilight—clouds permitting.

Then I had to wonder whether the Japanese navigator on his run during the next 12 hours to his 0600 position would compensate for the current at the expected rate of one and a half knots or at the unusual—and actual—rate of three-fourths knot. If the enemy had knowledge of the slower rate, the carrier group would indeed be on the track predicted by U.S. Intelligence. But if the enemy had no awareness that the Kuroshio was running at a lower rate of speed, he would overcompensate for it and be nine miles off the predicted track.

Talk about opening a can of worms—we had uncovered a pit of vipers! For the next several hours the three of us—my XO, the navigator, and myself—pored over the charts and discussed the problem from every possible angle. Not one was left undiscussed and undebated, except the extreme sensitivity of the intelligence I had been given. Finally the XO and the navigator took their stand. They contended that the Japanese navigator "doesn't know as much about the current as we do, skipper. Those people have been in the open sea for a long time. They're anxious to get back to Tokyo. They haven't had our advantage of piloting along the coast to measure the current. We say *Dace* should go to this other position—even though it's nine miles from where COMSUBPAC predicts the carrier will be at 0600."

I absorbed their argument and chewed it over in my mind. Yet I couldn't digest it. "I think you're right, but if we guess wrong, I'm the one who'll have to deliver the bad news to the admiral," I said carefully. "And you know what happens to the messenger who brings such tidings." As I spoke, I also listened to myself. I wasn't terribly impressed. I sensed that I sounded very much like a barnacle-encrusted, drydock sailor. Where was the daring, the decisiveness, and the joie de guerre of the submarine commander? Hollywood would never cast me in the role I occupied if I thought that way.

Still, I plowed on: "How can I tell the admiral that we picked a spot nine miles away from the one he designated—based on all the information he had but we didn't—because we thought the Japanese navigator would make a mistake. To me it sounds like a very weak excuse for not being in the correct position provided by Pearl. I have to stick with the admiral. We'll go to the 0600 posit designated in the message!"

So I protected my backside and went by the book. The result was that I lost an incredible opportunity to sink a Japanese carrier. We sighted her at 0555 through the morning haze. A great beauty! One of the large modern carriers, either the *Shokaku* or her sister, *Zuikaku*. Our *Japanese Ship Recognition Manual* listed them as displacing 30,000 tons. Since both had participated in the Pearl Harbor attack, either of them would have been a magnificent prize.

Unfortunately, she turned up nine miles distant from *Dace*

—right where my XO and navigator had figured she'd be if the Japanese navigator was ignorant of the reduced rate of speed of the Kuroshio. Right, too, where I had known in my gut she'd be. Right where everything I had learned at Annapolis and during active service in the decade since told me unequivocally she'd be at 0600 on that day. We never had a chance to attack the carrier. We were on her beam. The distance of nine miles might just as well have been 90 or 900. She was moving away at a speed of 22 knots. The best we could muster was 19 knots, and to achieve that we'd have to run on the surface. With daylight fast approaching, we'd be spotted quickly.

Grim-faced and angry at myself for not having the courage of my convictions—which had been strongly supported by the XO and navigator—I gave the order to dive. The crew made little effort to hide their disappointment, and the interior of the sub echoed with uncomplimentary asides. Obviously they wanted to continue the pursuit, at least until we were forced down by enemy fire. The men probably even considered the ramifications of firing me out of a torpedo tube.

What I couldn't explain to them was that *Dace* would be making a serious error if we now permitted the Japanese carrier group to see us at the exact position where it should have been —and would have been—if the current had been running at its normal rate. The enemy, once he discovered his navigational error and realized that it accounted for our nine-mile distance from them, could have deduced that the Americans were reading their code—a fact they never knew during the course of the war. Even my executive officer was not supposed to be privy to the fact that our intelligence had broken Japanese codes earlier.

I lived with that decision for a long time. I had based it on my experience that the greater the seniority and experience of the staff officer, the more convinced he was that his opinions were correct. Upon the completion of a patrol, with your type-written patrol report flat out in black and white on the desk of a reviewing officer, he could second-guess you to his heart's content. If the skipper had deviated from his order and been successful, well and good. However, if he had deviated from those orders and there had been a foul-up . . . grab your steel helmet and flak vest. Fault was certainly to be cited. It was a dilemma that I resolved to beat one day. . . .

Now, as skipper of *Archer-Fish*, I realized that pro forma thinking was not the way to get things done in the U.S. Submarine Force. The guerdons and plumes went to the audacious and the fearless, to the skippers of subs who demonstrated the derring-do and enterprise of cavalrymen like Jeb Stuart, Nathan Bedford Forrest, Turner Ashby, Wade Hampton, and "Fighting Joe" Wheeler. The submarine service had them in the likes of Fred Warder, Sam Dealey, John Cromwell, "Mush" Morton, Dick O'Kane, and many others. With skippers of their stripe, there was a constant awareness that they were, as Admiral Lockwood noted, "the man on the spot, strengthened with information personally observed and in a far better position to take appropriate action than a desk-bound officer hundreds of miles away." The authority for the final decision was in their hands, and they would exercise it to the fullest.

After I asked to be relieved as commanding officer of *Dace,* it took many months and long periods of examining my thought processes and the manner in which I went about my decision making before I came to the truth of Admiral Lockwood's axiom. Of course, in retrospect I came to the realization that I was too much the iron-bound traditionalist. I found it too easy to adhere to the rules of obedience imposed by my parents, the church, Annapolis, and the Navy. None of them ever intended that I shouldn't think for myself. It had no doubt been their intention to shape the twig with the ability to bend when necessary. But I had, perhaps, taken their emphasis on discipline a bit too literally.

In time, with the support of many of my contemporaries and the understanding of many empathetic senior officers, I came to realize that I was expected to think for myself on the basis of new information and observations, and to act accordingly. Nobody had all the answers. Of course, I would make mistakes; it's the fate of all of us. "The book" can only guide you, provide direction, delineate courses of conduct. Ultimately, I concluded that if I had used better judgment and sited *Dace* in ambush nine miles distant from the position designated by Naval Intelligence, Admiral Lockwood would have backed me 100 percent, as long as he believed I acted on the best information available.

Well, as the French say, "the more things change, the more they stay the same." And there I was a year later confronting another carrier and in almost the same location. This time the carrier was not homeward bound, but outward bound. This time I was determined it would not escape. The superstructure on the starboard side of the target had first alerted Seaman Stewart to the possibility that she was an aircraft carrier. As the target became more distinct on the late evening horizon, the doubts of everyone on the bridge dissipated. She was outfitted with a huge island! Then we sighted two more escorts for a total of three, and assumed that there was a fourth one either obscured by the hull or too far astern to be seen yet.

As *Archer-Fish* wallowed on the surface to the west of the oncoming carrier, I dropped below briefly to finger through the *Recognition Manual* for enemy warships in an effort to pinpoint the carrier's identity. The XO and I were reasonably well acquainted with the number of aircraft carriers still available to the Japanese and figured the manual could provide a fix on her. The way the war was going in our favor, there weren't too many big ones left.

To give credit where it is due, the intelligence data given to U.S. submarine crews during patrols was remarkably complete, accurate, current, and reliable. All of us held the two manuals (one for warships and the other for merchant ships, i.e., marus) in particularly high regard. If a target didn't appear in either of the manuals, our usual reaction was that it either didn't exist or wasn't Japanese.

The features we sought in identifying an enemy warship as a carrier were first the island itself—the huge superstructure on the starboard side of the ship with its many bridges, lookout stations, and various bridge batteries. In the manual the only carriers with the funnels enclosed within the island structure—which made it appear especially large—were the *Hayataka*[1] class (*Hitaka* belonged to this class) and the *Taiho* class. Then there was the flight deck. Did it extend from bow to stern? In the case of the *Hayataka*-class carriers, it was 690 feet in length and stopped short of both the bow and the stern. The deck of the *Taiho* class extended to the extreme bow but stopped short of the stern. It measured 844 feet.

We also looked for any open space underneath the flight deck. The *Hayataka* class of carriers had open spaces both forward and aft. The *Taiho* class had open space aft but none forward because the steel plates on the side extended up to the flight deck. We scrutinized the form of the bow. The ships in the two classes mentioned all had conventional or normal bows, with the *Taiho* class displaying a tendency toward a clipper bow. As for the form of the stern, these carriers all had sterns like those of a cruiser.

As we studied the huge shape on the horizon we knew we had a carrier but still weren't sure of the class. And we knew, too, that she was escorted by at least three destroyers. No. *Archer-Fish* was no longer contending with a tanker and a single escort. Now we faced an entirely different situation. An attack on a tanker that had one small warship for an escort was one thing. But it would be foolhardy for me to undertake a surface attack on a warship with multiple escorts on a bright moonlit night. Such an attack had never been implemented. To try it, I felt, with a cold stone of reality forming in my gut, would be practically suicidal.

"Mr. Andrews," I ordered, "we're going to have to get ahead. There's no way we can even consider a surface attack now. Their guns would blow us out of the water before we even got into good torpedo range."

"Yes, sir," he agreed. "Flank speed, sir. You've got it." He relayed the order to Chief Carnahan, who instantly repeated it to the maneuvering room. His enthusiasm, however, remained unflagged. "We can do it, skipper. *Archer-Fish* needs this one. They can't see us; I know it!"

It gave me a lot to think about. Going ahead of the carrier was our only chance of getting a shot at her. Even then we were too far off her track to dive and get into a favorable attack position. Our only chance was to maintain our best surface speed, keep running on a parallel track, and pray for the carrier to make a course change in our direction. I slapped at the rosary in the left-hand pocket of my khaki trousers to inspire the desired change.

It was now well over an hour since Lieutenant Bosza had made radar contact of a target at 2048. While *Archer-Fish* strained to turn around to course 210 degrees, I remained on the bridge with Lieutenant Andrews and four lookouts. The XO had gone below to supervise and coordinate the new activities by the crew. With the help of visual bearings and radar ranges our fire-control party had determined that the carrier's course was still 210 degrees at a speed of 20 knots. *Archer-Fish* was broad on the carrier's starboard bow, at a range of about nine miles. Yet we began to drop slowly behind. Our boat's four engines were all providing maximum power for a top speed of 19 knots. It didn't take an Einstein to deduce that the carrier would move imperceptibly ahead of us over a period of time. Victory seemed intent on outrunning us.

Oh, to get ahead of her. A few minutes ago we had been as high as sea gulls, keenly at our battle stations and hot to secure *Archer-Fish*'s first victory on her fifth war patrol. And me, to score my first victory as a submarine skipper. We just had to get ahead. Then we could submerge and approach the carrier off her starboard beam. The wind and sea state were ideal for a periscope approach. The wind intensity was force 4 on the Beaufort scale—11 to 16 knots, or nautical miles per hour— what we describe as a moderate breeze. The effect of this force on the sea, according to the Beaufort tables: "Small waves becoming longer; fairly frequent white horses." Waves this size were ideal for obscuring the periscope from enemy lookouts. With the light from the moon, we had the best possible conditions for an attack.

Below, *Archer-Fish*'s Fairbanks Morse engines revolved with amazing grace, but I wasn't in a very beatific mood. The Irish side of my nature wanted to take charge. Grasping the railing of the bridge, I bent my head to rest my forehead on the knuckles of my hands. I murmured a brief personal prayer. I would not give in to the black side. I had been that way before. This time I was determined to win for a lot of reasons, but especially for all the people who cared for me.

I raised my head to take in the beauty of the moonlit sea. The moonbeams flitted across the surface of the rolling sea to silhouette the enemy naval group. Even the Japanese warships appeared to be at peace as they moved over the ocean far to port. For a few moments it was difficult to believe that my country was really at war, that the ships in the distance were the enemy. And that I was so intent on my mission of putting them in harm's way. I took in the cool night air with several deep breaths, stretching and rotating my shoulders and arms to get the blood flowing and clear my mind of the despair and doubts trying to crowd my thoughts. It was time to get the old Celtic fighting spirit up. I remembered some lines from G. K. Chesterton that I had memorized many years before on a quiet Sunday afternoon by myself on the banks of the Severn River at Annapolis:

> For the great Gaels of Ireland are the men that God made mad;
> For all their wars are merry, and all their songs are sad.

Well, this was war, so let's get on with it. If it be merry, so much the better.

"Mr. Andrews," I ordered, "keep the lookouts sharp." Before he could even respond, I went below to the conning tower to check on the fire-control party. I told Chief Carnahan to have the engineering officer stick his head up the hatch. Lieutenant Cousins appeared at once and stood on the midrail of the ladder leading from the control room to the conning tower so we could converse easily.

"Rom, you and I both know how important it is that we sink that carrier. But she's making more speed and pulling away from us. I know you've had Chief Hoffman check the engine rooms and the maneuvering room for you. I know they're doing a great job, but I'd really appreciate it if you'd go back there yourself to encourage the men to do more."

As Rom nodded his understanding, I added, "Give them a fight talk. The old razzmatazz. Tell them to do whatever is needed to get more speed out of *Archer-Fish*. Nurse the engines. Cajole them. Coax, beg, kiss the engines if you have to. We need more speed. Even a few more turns will help."

Rom's succinct reply was, "Aye, aye, cap'n." Then he was gone.

There was no need for me to tell Rom to assign someone to stand by for him as diving officer during his absence. There were always people in the control room just waiting for things to happen. Rom only had to look at one fully capable petty officer and say, "Take over, will you?"

Our people were always gathering in the control room to wait for the next event. It was the best location on board for keeping in touch with the scuttlebutt. There old salts regaled the newer hands with exciting and overblown sea stories about the "old navy," earlier submarines, other war patrols, and all the colorful characters and skippers with whom they had served. The convivial atmosphere and ambience always reminded me of the way folks like to converge in the large kitchen of an old-fashioned home.

Whenever Lieutenant Cousins was on watch and not too busy he was assured of an attentive audience. He was by far the best storyteller on the boat, and none of us could claim to have had a more unusual and difficult life. Over a period of time I learned that Rom was an orphan. His first recollections were of an orphanage somewhere in San Francisco. He was told at some point that both of his parents had died in the Spanish influenza at the end of World War I. He lived for a while with a kind family named Cousins, and it was they who gave him his name. The Romolo came later, from the name of a friendly city square in San Francisco.

As a teenager he supported himself as a bootlegger in San Diego. His liquor supply in those Prohibition days was smuggled across the border from Mexico. Eventually he was arrested and taken into court, where an understanding judge asked him his age. "As best I know, I think about sixteen, your honor," Rom replied.

The judge said, "Rom, you look to be eighteen to me. I want you to join the Navy. It's a good life. You'll learn a trade, how to get on in the world."

"I've thought of that," Rom said, "but with the Depression, everybody wants to join up and each state is assigned a certain quota. If I'm not within a quota, I can't join up."

The magistrate was not to be put off. "Let me give you a suggestion in that regard. I would imagine that in your bootlegging here in San Diego you've undoubtedly had some Navy chiefs as customers. Go see them. A chief can do anything."

Rom wasted little time looking up a Navy chief, who talked to a doctor who gave physical examinations to potential recruits. When the doctor failed the physical of a young man in the Texas quota, he contacted the chief and told him there was an opening for Rom if he'd say he was from Texas. Rom became an instant Texan and enlisted in the Navy. Within a few years, he earned a commission.

I was still in the conning tower when Rom returned to the control room and called up to me: "Cap'n, everyone back there is doing everything that can be done to give us more speed. Charlie Wells is on watch in the forward engine room and he's as good as they come. No one could do more." Then after a pause: "While I was back there I visited the people in the after torpedo room. All their torpedoes are ready, and they're all hoping for a shot at the carrier. I also checked the main shaft bearings, and they're running cool." He smiled and added, "And, cap'n, all the guys back there asked me to tell you that they're ready to bust their asses if it will help sink that bastard."

I thanked him warmly and we gave each other the okay sign in unison, touching the middle finger to a thumb. Chief Carnahan, the telephone talker in the conning tower, was standing beside me and had heard my conversation. Turning to him I said, "Tell the guys in the back room they don't have to go that far, but thanks a lot."

In a matter of minutes, Rom's gang had performed the required witchcraft, magic, incense burning, oaths, or incantations sacred to the arcane members of engine rooms to raise the *Archer-Fish*'s speed. Damned if they didn't get her moving at slightly more than 19 knots! Yet it still wasn't going to do the trick for us.

Back on the bridge I could see immediately that the carrier group was pulling away. I cursed under my breath. Lieutenant Andrews remained a persistent optimist, assuring me: "*Archer-Fish* can do it, sir. We're going to get him." Yes, *Archer-Fish* needs this one. I had to look away, smiling, but nearly doing it through tears of frustration and anger.

The realization that our target was a naval ship rather than a commercial maru prompted me to reconsider the use of our radar. I knew from experience and intelligence information that Japanese naval ships were equipped with electronic countermeasure gear to detect our radar transmissions. According to the book, then, we should be using our radar only sparingly. The standard practice when in contact with an enemy warship was to train the unactivated radar dish to the bearing of the target, transmit a brief burst of energy, and watch carefully for an echo to obtain its range and bearing. In an effort to keep the operator of the Japanese electronic countermeasures unalerted, these pulses were sent infrequently and irregularly.

I had to conclude that this was another occasion when I shouldn't fall back on recommended procedures. If we were going to attack and hit an escorted, high-speed carrier, we needed all the help we could get. And right then I was ready and willing to take it from any source, including King Neptune if he were to rise from the ocean and proffer his services. *Archer-Fish* had to detect any change in the enemy's course and speed as promptly as possible. Only by using our radar continuously rather than intermittently would we be able to get the required information quickly enough to counter any new maneuvers by the enemy.

It was coming up on 2245. By then we had been using our active radar steadily for two hours. At no time was there any apparent reaction from the enemy. I figured that as long as he was willing to allow us this electronic advantage without retaliating or reversing course to return to Tokyo Bay, we should continue to use the radar. I wondered whether he even had electronic countermeasure equipment. I found it hard to believe that the carrier's captain wasn't aware of *Archer-Fish*'s presence. He had to know we were out there trying to position ourselves to destroy his great ship. What manner of man was he? Could it be arrogance? Were we so inconsequential to him, given the massive gunfire his carrier alone could train on us? Was he arming a flock of planes on deck? Certainly the destroyers could close on us quickly. Why hadn't he taken any notice of us? There we were dashing along a track parallel to him, nine miles distant. Lookouts on the nearest destroyer must be able to see us.

I asked Joe Bosza again to see whether the carrier group was using radar. Moments later he responded, "Negative, cap'n."

I held on to the bridge railing as *Archer-Fish* surged forward in an effort to remain within striking distance, and I gave a lot of thought to the captain of the carrier. Just who was he? Perhaps a Japanese naval hero who had been given command of the carrier as a reward for his intrepid and valorous service? One of the bastards who had struck our fleet at Pearl Harbor? Perhaps our paths had crossed before? Who could say?

Whoever the captain of the carrier was, he had me stymied. Talk about being checked. Whatever my options, they weren't going to be decisive enough to alter events now. If I tried any other course, he'd pull farther away. If I dived, he'd outrace us even faster. That one-knot superior speed he was maintaining was exhausting us. Moreover, if we remained on the surface in hot pursuit, we'd undoubtedly be sighted. There we were being offensive-minded to the limit. And he just seemed to be assuming a defensive stance—passive almost. Yet he was still winning. How come? That wasn't the way it was supposed to work in the real world. What we needed was a great hand from Lady Luck.

I was jolted from these musings by our sharp-eye lookout,

Seaman Stewart: "Skipper, the lead destroyer, I think she's coming our way."

No doubt about it! We could see the carrier and the escort like tiny toy ships in the moonlight. The lead destroyer had swung around and was racing toward us. So much for defensive tactics. The Japanese were on the offensive!

Without a wasted motion I ordered, "Lieutenant Andrews, alert the telephone talker to notify the crew. Secure for attack! Lookouts below! Hop to it, men!"

I glanced at my wristwatch. The time was about 2250. I stood by the ladder as the lookouts quickly descended. Each man was given a tap on the shoulder as he went below.

"Duty stations, men. On the double. Good work, Stewart." He gave me a big smile and disappeared into the conning tower below, where the officers and men had redoubled their attentiveness. Chief Carnahan was speaking quietly into his mouthpiece, relaying various messages to the compartments throughout the ship.

I had ordered the bridge cleared and the lookouts below, except for the OOD, in the event the onrushing destroyer opened fire. The fewer of us there were topside, the smaller the chance of casualties. I concentrated my binoculars directly on the destroyer, which was looming larger and larger as it closed on *Archer-Fish*. Boy, was she coming fast! It looked like a *Kagero*-class destroyer. They could hit up to 35 knots, or about 41 miles per hour. She'd be on us in no time.

"What's the range, John?" I asked the OOD.

Lieutenant Andrews twisted around and relayed the query below to Lieutenant Bosza, hunched over the radar screen. The reply came immediately: "Less than five miles and closing fast!"

"Got it, John," I said before he had a chance to relay the answer. With my binoculars still on the approaching ship, I knew I only had moments to do something. What were the alternatives?

Diving came instantly to mind. What better way to avoid the destroyer with its guns, torpedoes, and deadly depth charges? But if I ordered *Archer-Fish* to dive, the destroyer captain definitely would know what we were. Right now, he might still be in doubt. That's probably why he hadn't opened fire, although we were well within the range of his batteries. And if we dived, we'd almost certainly forfeit any chance of getting into a position to attack the carrier. Submerged, we'd lose a good deal of headway. The carrier could disappear over the horizon and right off our radar screen.

I decided to stay on the surface and bluff it out. We wouldn't "pull the plug" unless he opened fire on us. If I saw the "flashes and splashes," *Archer-Fish* would turn 90 degrees away and shoot a trio of stern torpedoes at the approaching destroyer. Then we'd dive. We'd hope for a hit on the narrow, foreshortened beam width of the enemy ship. Other U.S. submarines had scored with such shots. There wasn't much sense in turning away from him and making a run for it on the surface. The carrier would keep moving away, and the destroyer would catch us in short order. It would take only moments for its guns to blast *Archer-Fish* to pieces. So we just held fast to our course, with Lieutenant Andrews and me clinging to the bridge railing as *Archer-Fish* plunged through the ranks of running waves on a course still parallel to the carrier. And the destroyer rushed closer and closer as though she intended to ram our submarine.

Incredibly, my OOD continued to exude confidence and almost indifference to the onrushing warship. It was as though he was a cheerleader back in some stateside football coliseum and the destroyer was only an offside charging halfback, one he could sidestep at any time. There was no letup in his tautological chanting: "We can do it skipper! *Archer-Fish* needs this one. They can't see us. I know it!" He was making the impossible sound very possible.

God bless him for his spirit, but there was no doubt in my mind that we stood out like the Empire State Building in Iowa. You'd have to be blind not to see us. From the way the Japanese destroyer was hell-bent right on target, she already had. We watched her come, barreling full-speed ahead to run us over and send us to the bottom. I was conscious of faces staring up through the open hatch from the conning tower, particularly those of Lieutenant Bosza, Ensign Crosby, and Chief Carnahan. They were listening for my orders so they could act on them immediately. The order to dive would be executed by Lieutenant Rom Cousins in the control room. The OOD would then drop quickly into the conning tower. In one quick, helterskelter movement he'd be out of sight and then I'd follow, securing the hatch to the bridge while *Archer-Fish* was already beginning to plunge toward the asylum of deep water. We were coming close to that moment. The enemy destroyer was now about three miles away. She'd be on top of us within minutes. Why didn't she open fire? I couldn't understand it. At least challenge us by flashing signal light. Nothing.

"Stand by, John. Get ready to go below in another minute if he keeps coming. Fast!"

Actually it was profoundly exciting. I felt keenly exultant, like a kid in the first car of a roller coaster. It was a time to remember. A time to be burned as an indelible memory in my mind. John and I alone on the bridge, hanging on to the spray-slicked railing to keep our footing. *Archer-Fish* running at top speed across the inky, moon-streaked water. The enemy ship straining to put us within her grasp. Then, off in the distance, the carrier suddenly illuminated a bright red light high on her topmost mast. It flashed across the sea for ten seconds. What the hell, I wondered. I had never seen a warship show any type of navigation light at night. The light went dark for a few seconds. Again, it went on to hurl a bright red beacon into the night. For another ten seconds. Then off again.

"I think he's ordering the destroyer to fire!" I called to the OOD. I waited for the flashes and splashes. Nothing.

"She's *turning,* skipper. She's turning *away!*" Lieutenant Andrews cried. "Hell if she isn't!"

I couldn't believe it. What was going on? The carrier displays a light signal and almost instantly the destroyer starts to go about. Why? She obviously had us spotted. She was only about three miles away and would close on us in a few minutes. Instead the destroyer turned away without molesting us in any

"His course . . . on the chart. The one he's been following since we got our initial sighting. It's approximately 210 degrees, southwesterly. It's the course he's maintained for more than two hours. At least until he changed a few minutes ago to south. . . ."

"Right, we had it figured that on the 210-degree course he was headed for the Philippines," I noted. "Though why he'd want to head for an area dominated by our carrier task forces is beyond my understanding."

"Well, heading there is one thing. He could go off on another course farther along."

"Okay, so what are you saying, Bob? You think the 210-degree southwesterly heading is his base course. That this new course of 180 degrees is a zig leg. So he's going off to the left but sooner or later he'll zag to the right to return to base course 210 degrees."

"You got it, skipper," he beamed. "It's our only hope in any case. If he stays on his present course of 180 degrees, we can kiss him good-bye forever."

"You're right, Bob. So we don't go chasing after him on the new course. *Archer-Fish* remains fast on a course of 210 degrees and hopes that it's the carrier's overall base course, and that he'll come back to it. When he does, we could've gained on him and be in a favorable position to fire torpedoes."

"Exactly. I think it's the only way. Even if he goes out of sight, we can track him on the radar. It doesn't seem to bother him."

"Fine. And another thing—we shouldn't have to wait too long to learn whether or not this new course is just a zig leg. If he is making a reasonable distance good on his base course —such as 75 to 80 percent—he can't stay 30 degrees to the left of it for long. He will have to compensate by steering to the right also. I expect that when he thinks he has outrun us, he'll come back this way on a course as much as 50 or 60 degrees or more to the right of his present 180."

"I agree, skipper," Bob said.

I gave the information to Chief Carnahan to pass along on

the telephone. I also asked Rom Cousins to go back and discuss with the engine-room watch the possibility of obtaining more speed. Time for more magic. Elsewhere, *Archer-Fish*'s personnel were mostly relaxing and talking in low voices. There was only one topic of conversation: how much each man wanted our torpedoes to score on the carrier.

I checked the plot again to determine the position of the target. The clock showed that it was nearly 2330. I decided that I should notify Admiral Lockwood, Commander, Submarines, Pacific, Pearl Harbor, about our nocturnal activities. The admiral certainly would be interested in the news that a big enemy carrier was running loose. Perhaps another U.S. submarine was in a better position to intercept and sink her.

I went back to the bridge, thought about the contents of the message, and then called Ensign Crosby to the bridge. I didn't spell it out, just gave him the gist of it. As the communications officer, Gordon was very adroit at wording my messages.

"Encode it and get it on the air," I ordered. Off he went below.

It was now 2330, on the button. I had mixed emotions about sending the message. If nothing else had, this would certainly alert the enemy to our position. I'd begun to think of the carrier as *Archer-Fish*'s own special target, ordered up especially for us. But I knew that teamwork among all of our submarines was essential if the carrier was not to escape.

Gordon was gone longer than I had anticipated, and when he returned to the bridge I inquired, "How'd it go?"

"Tricky at first, skipper. The Pearl shore station was backed up and wanted us to wait. But I kept after them. Finally I impressed on them that I had a priority message. Then they let us go ahead. It was 4:00 A.M. Pearl time. Bet they're all buzzing back there. Admiral Lockwood must've been notified immediately."

I had to laugh. "I think you're right, Gordon. The admiral always wants to be informed immediately when one of his subs is after a big one. We'll have him up the rest of the night back at Pearl."

I looked off the port bow, across the intervening miles of open sea, to the target. By then the carrier was hardly visible even with binoculars. All too soon she was completely lost to view in the darkness. In my frustration I wondered whether I would ever see her again.

5. Flight

Against the rolling sea *Shinano* moved through the waves like a small city. Bounding along off her beams, *Hamakaze* and *Yukikaze* appeared more like two phosphorescent mackerel than like a brace of battle-ready destroyers. Far off to starboard, nearly five miles distant to the west, the flagship destroyer *Isokaze* bore down directly on the American submarine tracking along the huge carrier's course on the dark side of the moon. *Isokaze*'s intentions left little to anyone's imagination.

Captain Abe, his narrowed eyes on the runaway *Isokaze,* seethed as he stood with his officers on the lookout bridge of *Shinano.* His bare hands gripped the rail, the knuckles glistening like twin rows of fleshless agates. It was incomprehensible to the carrier's skipper that Captain Shintani, commander of the destroyer screening group, could be so derelict in his duty. Captain Abe had made his orders purposely specific. No one was to rise to a Yankee lure and go rushing off like some irresponsible knight-errant to seek single combat. How dare Captain Shintani disobey? How could he be so willful as to abandon his station and leave *Shinano* unprotected? And on the bow, where she was particularly vulnerable to attack by an ambushing American wolf pack. He wondered whether Captain Shintani could be suffering from battle fatigue . . . battle shock . . . some mental aberration . . . to so disobey his orders. And what about Captain Sunishi Toshima, the skipper of *Iso-*

kaze? Surely he was not a party to Captain Shintani's action.

"Should we signal him to return to his station, sir?" Navigator Nakamura asked with urgency in his voice.

"Wait a moment. See if he turns," Captain Abe replied. "I don't want to put on the truck light unless it's absolutely necessary. We still don't know whether it's an enemy ship."

The skipper, staff officers, and lookouts watched *Isokaze* through their binoculars. Not a word was spoken. The lookout officer had to admonish many of his men to return to watching other sectors of the silver-stippled ocean. This was no time to leave themselves open to attack from another quarter while all eyes were fixed on *Isokaze* and the mysterious ship.

"Range on *Isokaze?*" Captain Abe asked.

Ensign Yasuda, equipped with a telephone headset and in communication with the captain's bridge, repeated the request quietly into his mouthpiece.

"Almost five miles from *Shinano* by range finder, sir. Less than four miles from the unidentified ship," he reported.

"We'll give him just a few more moments, and then signal with the truck light if he hasn't turned," Captain Abe said unemotionally.

"Sir, Captain Mikami requests permission to open fire on the target," Ensign Yasuda said.

"No, not yet. Wait," Captain Abe answered.

"Do you think it's the same ship that's been emitting the radar signals, sir?" asked Navigator Nakamura.

"Must be, Nakamura. She didn't respond to our light signals. She's remained on the surface, although her captain must know she's visible to us. She's a decoy, I'm certain of it. She's been trying to entice one of our escorts to attack her so the other submarines can encounter less opposition in a submerged approach on *Shinano.*"

"She's succeeded in that, sir," Navigator Nakamura observed.

Captain Abe chose not to reply, keeping his binoculars focused alternately on *Isokaze* and on her target. He wondered why Captain Shintani, who had been so eager to go chasing off after the ship, hadn't opened fire himself. He certainly could have blasted her out of the water anytime he chose. He concluded that Shintani was intent on ramming her.

"Time to fire, sir? The range between *Isokaze* and the target is closing rapidly," Navigator Nakamura said.

"No, no, Nakamura. Our gunfire could be seen for many kilometers. It would attract every submarine in the vicinity to our location. Our orders are to deliver *Shinano* safely to Kure, not to attack enemy submarines. Order a zig to the left 30 degrees, from course 210 to 180."

Ensign Yasuda quickly relayed the captain's course change into his mouthpiece. Captain Abe nodded his approval for the quick response at the young officer.

"Time?" Captain Abe requested.

"Right on 2300, captain," Communications Officer Araki noted.

"Log it, Araki," Captain Abe ordered. He turned to the navigator. "Nakamura, signal with the red truck light for *Isokaze* to return at once to her proper station."

The navigator looked at Ensign Yasuda to note that he was already relaying the skipper's order. High above, the red masthead light flashed on for 10 seconds, off for 20 seconds, and then on again for another 10 seconds. Almost six miles away, *Isokaze*'s helmsman responded to Captain Toshima's order to turn "left full rudder," and the destroyer immediately heeled over sharply to starboard as she came left to the course that would reposition her on *Shinano*'s bow.

Captain Abe watched with grim approval as *Isokaze* resumed her designated screening station forward of *Shinano*'s bow and began her own zigzag maneuvers. He had already decided that Captain Shintani would be sharply reprimanded—if not court-martialed—for his unwarranted action in charging the unidentified target. Shintani might very well be one of Japan's foremost destroyer officers, but there was no excuse for his ill-timed and thoughtless decision to leave his station and deprive *Shinano* of badly needed protection forward. His day of reckoning would come, the captain promised himself, after *Shinano* reached the safety of Kure in the Inland Sea.

Without a word, Captain Abe left the lookout bridge and went below to his bridge followed by Navigator Nakamura, Communications Officer Araki, Ensign Yasuda, and Petty Officer Umeda. He was met by Captain Mikami, who also followed him to the bridge chart. There the officers gathered around as Captain Abe studied the large chart.

"Navigator Nakamura," he said, pointing to the chart, "*Shinano* will steer course south until further orders. If that is an enemy submarine nine miles to starboard, we'll leave it even farther behind with our superior speed. The best he can do is about 18, maybe 19 knots at most. With our 20 knots, we'll soon outdistance him. Even move out of visual range."

"He'll still track us on his radar, the way he's been actively maintaining it, sir," the navigator offered.

"True enough, but it's space I'm interested in putting between us. Of course, we still have to maintain a vigilant watch for other hostile submarines. I'm convinced that they are out there. Maybe even waiting on our current track."

"*Shoji itashimash'ta.* It will be done," the navigator replied.

The officers were silent for another minute or two as they watched Ensign Yasuda pencil *Shinano*'s new course on the chart.

Captain Abe walked away from his officers and went to the forward section of the bridge to take up his solitary vigil. He stood there silently, still eschewing the comfort of his command chair. Upon his departure, the staff officers resumed their various responsibilities and the captain's bridge took on an air of normalcy—although the atmosphere was riven with tension and anticipation in light of the captain's continued warnings about the proximity of a wolf pack of enemy submarines.

In his seclusion Captain Abe glowed a bit inwardly, almost smiling. The fact was, he personally was not concerned about any single hostile submarine that might be seeking to oppose *Shinano.* What he wanted to avoid was an onslaught by a host of them. He had not forgotten the reports of the numerous enemy submarines that had sailed earlier in the month from Guam and Saipan. They could be a problem. Meanwhile, it was best to occasionally raise the specter of the wolf pack deployment to keep his officers and men fully alert.

In seeking to bolster his own confidence in *Shinano*'s strength, Captain Abe recalled several conversations with Vice Admiral Fukuda, Japan's foremost designer of Imperial warships, when *Shinano* was still in drydock at Yokosuka. Admiral Fukuda had assured him that his ship was "not absolutely impossible to sink, but it would be very difficult to sink. Her designers have taken every eventuality into account to make her unsinkable." Comforting words, indeed.

Still, Captain Abe could not help thinking about *Shinano*'s onetime sister ships, *Musashi* and *Yamato*. They, too, had been designed and constructed to be unsinkable. Encased and wrapped in levels and myriad belts of steel, they had the power, protection, and weapons to outfight any warship in the world. *Musashi* had survived the torpedo attack of a lone enemy submarine. It was in March 1944.[1] The torpedo had scored on her bow. But *Musashi* had managed to return to port for repairs. She was not so fortunate the second time when, on October 24, she was attacked by hordes of enemy bombers. She went to the bottom after incurring a minimum of 10 torpedo hits and 16 aerial bomb strikes. Earlier, on Christmas Day, 1943, *Yamato* had been attacked by a single Yankee submarine, suffering one torpedo blow on her bow.[2] Despite the explosion, the dreadnought had remained upright and reasonably intact. At least 3,000 tons of water had poured into *Yamato*'s hull through the gaping hole inflicted by the enemy torpedo. Yet she had steamed to Kure for repairs and was back in active service by the end of February 1944.

In reviewing this information, Captain Abe reassured himself that his ship was nearly unsinkable. Certainly no lone submarine was capable of finishing off *Shinano*. He doubted whether even a wolf pack had the ability to accomplish such a feat. Let one of the detested foreigners attempt to thwart him in his quest to bring *Shinano* safely to Kii Suido, and he would run roughshod over the tiny boat.

As the hour approached 2322 Lieutenant Commander Miura, the division officer of the machinery division, which included four engine rooms, turbines, reduction gears, and the four main shafts with their bearings to the propellers, was enjoying a cigarette of cheap Sumatra tobacco in the main engineering control station. When his intership phone rang, he wondered, now what? and reached for it, snuffing out the butt.

It was the petty officer on watch in the shaft alleys. The news was not good. He reported an overheated main shaft bearing. In fact, the bearing had become so hot that he could not hold his hand on it.

Captain Bunji Kono, head of the engineering department, was immediately informed by Commander Miura. Captain Kono directed Commander Miura to meet him at once in the shaft alley with the hot bearing. As he hurried to the scene to give the bearing whatever emergency treatment was required, Commander Miura considered why the bearing had become overheated.[3] There were several malfunctions that could be responsible for the problem. The possibility that immediately came to mind was a lack of oil. The solution, then, was to check the oil supply and the filter. If, however, the problem was a clogged oil duct within the bearing, there would be no way to fix it before reaching port. Then there was the possibility of a few high spots on the bearing upon which the journal of the shaft rode. Or, a misalignment might have occurred between the shaft and the bearing pedestal that was mounted to the ship's structure. Either of these situations could also have led to the overheating.

Entering the shaft alley, Commander Miura noticed Captain Kono in the midst of a group of senior petty officers and warrant officers from the machinery division. He reported at once to Captain Kono, a tall, thin, aristocratic-looking officer with a broad brush moustache, hardly the type one would expect to find immersed in *Shinano*'s power operation. Commander

Miura was acutely aware that the carrier was already operating on only six of her dozen boilers, which had reduced her top speed of 27 knots to 20.

"Nasty business, sir," Commander Miura said as he studied the huge shaft from the starboard inboard engine to the No. 1 propeller.

"I've already checked for an interruption of the oil supply. No problem there," Captain Kono said calmly. "We've also tried to cool it down with a hose and seawater. No help."

"Actually, our problem is not an unusual occurrence for a new ship," Commander Miura said. "We've got to slow the ship to drop the temperature."

"Exactly," Captain Kono agreed. "But first I have to inform Captain Abe. He must be told. I know that he's not going to be happy about losing even more speed."

"We have no choice," the commander noted. "Remedial action must be taken. The propellers must be slowed before there is major damage to the shaft."

While Captain Kono went off to inform Captain Abe about the overheated bearing, Commander Miura considered the "worst case" scenario if the temperature of the bearing continued to increase. Ultimately, the babbitt metal, the soft white antifriction compound of copper, antimony, and tin from which the bearing was formed, would melt. If this happened it would no longer support the shaft. The shaft in turn would bind and halt. The deep scoring that could result would require that sections of the solid steel shaft, which measured 36 inches in diameter and was 150 feet long, be removed for rework or replacement.

Captain Kono returned to the shaft alley and took Commander Miura off to one side out of hearing of the working party. "Captain Abe was not very happy with my report. He talked as if I was personally responsible for the bearing overheating. Then, when I recommended that we slow the propellers by several revolutions per minute, I thought he would explode."

"But what is the alternative?" the commander asked.

"The captain is well aware of the alternative. The possibility of damaging the shaft is inconceivable to him. He finally admitted that we have to slow the ship until the bearing temperature begins to cool down."

"Good for you, Captain Kono. We must get on it immediately."

"Check with the OOD, *kanpan shikah,* on the bridge first. Tell him we are about to decrease the propeller turns. Keep him informed as we go along."

For the next half hour or so, Commander Miura was in almost constant telephone contact with the OOD about the efforts of the machinery division to lower the temperature of the bearing. Finally, when the bridge reluctantly allowed the propeller turns on the shaft to be decreased to 192 revolutions per minute, Commander Miura reported: "The bearing temperature is now dropping. I expect that we can hold this speed without damage to the bearing or shaft."

Captain Abe was informed that *Shinano*'s top speed had been established at 18 knots until yard repairs to the bearing could be completed. He shook his head in disgust. Of course a hot bearing was not unusual for a new ship on her maiden voyage. But *Shinano* was not some luxury cruise liner on a peacetime cruise. Japan was at war. The carrier was a prime target. Any of the many submarines lurking about could match her speed now, knot for knot.

Several decks above the engine rooms, Lieutenant Commander Kabuo Narute, the ship's chief supply officer, swept his eyes once more around the great breadth of *Shinano*'s main eating compartment. The sight was most pleasing to him. Under his direction the messmen had transformed the space into a cafeteria that would excite the envy of any shore-bound maitre d'hôtel and master chef.[4]

Commander Narute had come up with the idea for the *shiruko* several days before sailing from Yokosuka. It would be a special meal, to be served to all hands as midnight approached. The *shiruko* was prepared to both honor and celebrate the maiden voyage of Imperial Japan's newest and greatest pride. With some trepidation, he had broached the idea to Captain Abe and had been surprised and gladdened to receive the skipper's hearty approval.

"Splendid idea, Narute. Splendid," the skipper had agreed. "*Ryokai*. Do it up right. The best you can get. The men have been performing in excellent fashion and deserve the *sirouka*. Be sure to include the civilian and shipyard workers."

Commander Narute and his key staff had scoured the shops and markets throughout Yokosuka and its environs in their efforts to purchase the tastiest specialty foods for the occasion. When the men sat down to eat they would—at least for this meal—have no sense that Japan had been at war for years. It was a treat they would long remember. In fact, the meal was truly delicious. The cost had exceeded the supply officer's budget, but Captain Abe managed to transfer funds from another account. Unknown to Commander Narute, the skipper had also helped pay for the special meal with a personal contribution.

Mentally, Commander Narute went over the menu: the pièce de résistance was *adzuki,* a sweet black-bean soup with rice cakes. Just the thought of it made his mouth water. And there was more than enough for every man aboard. Great batches of sugar had been added to it—unbelievable, since sugar was on such short rations because of the war—and there were mountains of rice cakes for every table. There was fruit too, huge bowls of many kinds, an almost unheard-of luxury for a warship, and difficult at best to find anywhere in Japan. Commander Narute was confident that it was a meal the men of *Shinano* would boast about for years to come—one that would become a legend throughout the Imperial fleet, in every port of call.

Moments after 2332, Radioman Chisato Yamagishi, on duty in the radio room within the lower level of the ship's island, detected a radio transmission from a nearby ship.[5] He became instantly alert, quickly jotting down the myriad Morse code letters contained in the transmission. Of course they made no sense to him; they were encoded and impossible to read. However, he correctly identified the transmission by its strength and tone as one emitted by an enemy submarine, and definitely one within close proximity to *Shinano*.

The intercept was reported to his chief communications officer, Commander Araki, on the captain's bridge, who made it known to Captain Abe. As he studied the message and the notation that it was undoubtedly transmitted from a nearby hostile submarine, Captain Abe was strengthened in his conviction that *Shinano* was the target of an enemy submarine wolf pack. How could it be otherwise? *Shinano* would be an incomparable prize for any American submarine skipper. Who knew how many of them were out there, hoping to make his carrier their next personal trophy? They could be ringing the carrier right then, for all he knew.

Once again the captain was reminded that *Shinano* was not equipped to determine the location of the submarine that had transmitted the radio message. Neither was it equipped to ascertain the direction from which it had come. So where was the submarine? In what area of the sea could it remain hidden from view yet capable of keeping his ship in sight? Undoubtedly, it was the unidentified ship they had left far astern, no longer in sight. The one after which *Isokaze* had gone rampaging. What was the meaning of the enemy radio message? he wondered. It was in code, and his communications staff was unable to read it. To whom had it been sent? For what purpose? Were the enemy submarines gathering at that moment to strike *Shinano* en masse? Perhaps they had already loosed their torpedoes and they were now rushing underwater to explode against *Shinano*'s hull.

Captain Abe could not help peering with greater intensity into the sea around the carrier. His eyes searched for any telltale signs of approaching torpedoes. He knew them all. But there were none. Only his escort destroyers were visible as they darted about in their bewildering screening tactics. It was so much like a chess match, he thought. Except that I am a lone king, capable of only certain moves. Defended by only three knights, also limited in their moves. And confronted by six to a dozen queens who can move all over the board. Who ever heard of such a chess game? It is without rules and form. Well, they were not about to checkmate him. He'd play by his own rules. Bad enough that a bearing on one of the starboard engine shafts had to overheat and slow *Shinano*'s already depleted speed to 18 knots—now this radio report. His top priority was to deal with the message that had been transmitted by the enemy submarine.

Captain Abe went back to the bridge chart and spoke to Navigator Nakamura: "Change course to 270 degrees west. Now." He placed a finger to mark *Shinano*'s current course and then moved it sharply to the right.

Captain Nakamura nodded his understanding. "*Yosoro!* Helmsman, come right to 270 degrees, west. Immediately."

Petty Officer Daizo Masada, senior helmsman aboard the *Shinano*, complied at once as he repeated the order. Deftly, gracefully, he spun the big wheel to the right, and *Shinano* commenced a slow, wide turn to starboard and the course that would move her into the waters south of the entrance to the Kii Suido Strait. Course 180 degrees (south) became history. While bringing the carrier about, Petty Officer Daizo's mind flirted with thoughts of the celebration meal being served below in the mess decks. He hoped that he would be relieved at midnight to get his fair share of the delicacies. Because of the ship's grapevine, he could recite the menu's contents by heart.

Ensign Yasuda logged the course change at 2340—20 minutes before midnight, Tuesday, November 28, 1944. He immediately perceived the captain's intentions for the drastic course change. Obviously it was designed to thwart any enemy submarines lying in wait on *Shinano*'s 180-degrees (south) course and also to move her on a more direct line to the Inland Sea.

"Navigator Nakamura," the skipper ordered, "remain on this course until further orders. Have the deck watch and the lookouts maintain a particularly sharp lookout for the enemy submarine. We may sight him again on the surface. The bright moonlight will help. If the enemy sub followed us on the southerly course, and that is probable if he wanted to maintain visual contact, he should now be well astern. If, instead, he remained on the southwesterly course he was on when we lost sight of him, he can be ahead of us."

"*Shoji ihashimash'ta,*" the chief navigator replied. "Understood, sir."

Ensign Yasuda looked minutely at the bridge chart as the captain returned to his solitary position in the front center of the bridge. His eyes darted over and over it, retracing *Shinano*'s various course changes since leaving Tokyo Bay and tracing along the westerly projected course. The ensign recognized the need to turn west in order to reach the Inland Sea. He also realized that the turn took into account that the American submarine they had seen so recently was in that direction. But where?

6. Tenacity

Confidential
Subject: U.S.S. *Archer-Fish* (SS-311)--Report of
Fifth War Patrol

(B) Narrative

November 28, 1944

2300   Enemy group now determined to consist of a
large carrier and four escorts. One on either beam, one ahead and one astern.

2330   Sent contact message.

2340   Looks like a big zig in our direction.

2400   Probably a base-course change to the west.
We are now on his port flank farther off the
track than before. Changed our course to 270
and coaxed a few more turns from the already
overloaded motors.

November 29, 1944

From here on it was a mad race for a possible
firing position. His speed was about one
knot in excess of our best, but his zig plan
allowed us to pull ahead very slowly.

Although I realized it was useless, I kept sweeping my
binoculars across the horizon off the port bow of *Archer-Fish*
for even the slightest vestige of our big target ship. But it was
to no avail. It was fruitless to keep checking with the OOD and

the lookouts. They were as anxious as I was for any sighting, no matter how negligible or doubtful. The binoculars of the lookout assigned to the port forward quarter were fixed on the same far-distant area of the fidgety sea.

My mind relentlessly repeated a few phrases from William Blake's poem: "Tiger, tiger, burning bright . . . in the blackness of the night." Hell, I couldn't even put the familiar lines together. Something about "fearful symmetry . . ." How'd it go? "What fearful hand framed thy fearful symmetry?" No, that wasn't right. I just couldn't work it out. My mind was too much in a turmoil. How had I gotten on to that kick? I remembered. It was Mr. Andrews saying he wished he "had tiger eyes so he could see in the darkness." I wasn't even sure tigers saw that well in the dark. But I supposed they did, from the little I knew about them—laid up in the bush all day and then prowling around at night in search of their next meal.

Well, tiger eyes or whatever eyes, the best ones in the world couldn't see a target if it had slipped over the horizon. Then, of course, I had to remind myself about the message we had sent to Pearl and Admiral Lockwood. Were there other U.S. submarines south of Area No. 5? One would probably get lucky, and be right on the target's track, and score on my target. Damn, I wanted that carrier. It really bothered me that now one of our sister ships would get her.

From Blake my mind jumped to another English writer, John Milton, and something he had once written: "They also serve who stand and wait. . . ." Something like that anyway. Well, *Archer-Fish* and all of us were serving—standing, in effect—and waiting. By then, all of us had been on battle stations for about three hours. Geared up, waiting, standing by for a shot at the target. It just couldn't get away from us. Life couldn't be that unfair. But it just had.

It was coming up on 2400 and a new day, Wednesday, November 29, 1944. I had hoped that it would be a red-letter day in my life. I was overdue. I had turned thirty-four on September 18. Orders had been issued to me the next day to take command of *Archer-Fish*. I had a lovely wife. Virginia Robertson and I had been married in her hometown of Portsmouth, Virginia, on June 20, 1936. Our son, Joseph, Jr., was now seven years old. He had been born in Honolulu in those idyllic Hawaiian days before the outbreak of war. As commander of *Archer-Fish*, I was responsible for the lives of 81 officers and men, and an 8 million dollar submarine paid for by the American taxpayers. All in all, a lot of people were depending on me, looked up to me—I couldn't let them down.

I prayed again that the target's base course was 210 degrees. It just had to be. The enemy's new course of 180 degrees to the left was a zig leg, and shortly the carrier group would turn back to a course something to the right of 210. *Archer-Fish* was still maintaining flank speed on the 210 course. If the carrier made a course change big enough, ideally we could be ahead of him and be far more favorably situated to shoot our torpedoes. I kept my fingers crossed and occasionally patted the pocket containing my rosary beads.

Lieutenant Andrews made a quick move across *Archer-Fish*'s swaying deck to stand at my side on the bridge. "What do you think, skipper?"

"I couldn't begin to tell you, John. Praying mostly. Hoping that bastard will zig to course 210 degrees, or preferably more to the west. If he doesn't, I doubt we'll ever see him again."

The executive officer announced to the OOD that he was coming up to the bridge, and he joined me in searching the area where the target had disappeared.

He said, "Well, cap'n, what do you think? Will we see him again?"

I responded, "God only knows, Bob. This is a strange approach on a target. Different from any other I've seen or heard about. The target, from what we could see at a distance and in moonlight, has a silhouette quite similar to our *Essex* class. The big island identifies her as one of the only three Japanese carriers known to exist. The rest of their carriers all have small islands, or none. All of our big carriers have large islands. We have had no information from Naval Intelligence on the target's departure from Tokyo Bay, which is unusual."

Enemy destroyers were supposed to attack our subs, drive us down, and let the big ships escape. This destroyer hadn't attacked. When he turned away I had a fleeting thought: Are these even enemy ships? Or had the U.S. Third Fleet reinstated their previously scheduled attack on the Japanese mainland?

"You recall, Bob, that Captain Voge, SUBPAC operations officer, told me the day before we left Pearl on this patrol that Admiral Halsey was anxious to get that raid accomplished. His whole fleet was slated to be in this area about now. *Archer-Fish* was to be one of 12 subs in advance of the fleet to sweep the Japanese picket boats from a path so the main body would not be detected and the defense forces warned. On our fourth day this side of Pearl we received a message that Halsey's raid had been postponed."

The alternative operation, Burt's Brooms with seven of our subs, was then set in motion for training and to test the concept. They left the Marianas the day before we did. From the sketchy reports we got on daily summary of highlights on the evening submarine radio broadcast, the Brooms had a tough time of it. The Japanese resistance and firepower had been greater than was expected. Our subs had sunk four patrol boats, but eight others quickly replaced them, plus several aircraft. A few of our submarine people had been injured by gunfire. The rough seas and wildly pitching submarines caused *Ronquil* to fire two shells into her own pressure hull. The gun crews were fortunate not to have been washed overboard.

In any event, our surface ships could not be anywhere within hundreds of miles without our having been informed several times, and we would have had to acknowledge receipt of the message. I knew that all of Burt's Brooms had returned to port. There was no question that the ships we saw were Japanese.

"I think, Bob, we should be south of him when he comes back into view, if he does, because of the distance he has traveled compared to our travel in a straight line. Then we can try to be ahead of him when he returns to his base course. We've got to get between him and his destination, wherever that may be."

Just then my dream became a reality. Chief Carnahan stuck his head up through the hatch, a shadowy form in the eerie red light from the conning tower. "We've got lucky, skipper. Based on radar and the TDC, the target's made a sharp change of course. Almost straight west. Mr. Bunting says to tell you the range is 13,000 yards, bearing 060 true, and his angle on the bow is 40 port.

"Wonderful," I said. Turning to Bob I said, "I'm going to stay up here to look for him. You, please, go below to plot and have them project his track as soon as it's firm. Then project ours on this course and speed. Establish the minimum distance between the target and us, and the time it will occur. We must not be sighted. When the plotting is done, I'll come down."

Within a couple of minutes Bob was at the foot of the ladder below the hatch. "Cap'n, the tracks are now plotted. We are now at minimum distance, six and one-half miles. The range has commenced to open."

"Excellent, Bob. I'm coming down."

We met at the plotting table.

"Judd, now please pencil in a line nine miles south of his track and parallel to it. That will be our track. Bob, when we reach that line, change course to west."

Talk about everything happening at once. Chief Carnahan reported: "Cap'n, Lieutenant Andrews says the target's in sight again."

I whirled about and shot back up the ladder to the bridge, followed by the XO. I was exhilarated. I felt as if I had wings and could fly!

Mr. Andrews had a broad smile on his face and was pointing sternward. To port. "There, sir. Over there."

I trained my binoculars in the direction he was pointing. Damn it, there they were. The carrier and her escorts. I felt like shouting with joy. *Archer-Fish* might still have her moment of glory. The target was now astern! I figured our separation to be about eight or nine miles. While we had proceeded at top speed southwest on the course of 210 degrees, the enemy group had gone off to our left on course 180 degrees. When the group changed course to the west, it had begun to cut across our course—but astern of us. So now what? Was 210 degrees still her base course? It must be! This zag of his to the right would be logical. Next he will probably zig left again. Most likely some course near 210.

I went below again. Bob was still right behind me. Back and forth we went, like a pair of pent-up lions pacing a claustrophobic cage, between the radar people and the fire-control party. Shortly, with the visual bearings called down from the bridge by Lieutenant Andrews and the radar ranges provided by our radar operator, Earl Myers, we confirmed that the target was on course 270 degrees.

"Directly west," the XO noted, although he knew I had reached the same conclusion.

"Right, Bob. Damn it, though. What've we got? A zig 60 degrees off his base course? If in fact 210 degrees is his base course."

"I'm still of a mind that 210 degrees is his base course and that he'll come back to that because he was on it from the time we sighted him until 2300," the XO replied. "He must be going on that track."

I studied the chart, looking for a solution. Pointing with my finger, I said, "The course of 270 degrees would take him to the waters south of the Kii Suido. He could be headed for the Inland Sea. He could be, but I think you're right, Bob. He's going somewhere to the southwest."

"So what'll it be, captain?" Bob asked.

"All right," I said with all the confidence I could muster, "we'll remain on course 210 degrees until we reach a track nine miles south and parallel to his track. Then change course to 270. For him to make a reasonably good distance along his base course, he can't remain on a zig 60 degrees off that track for long, so he may come toward us at any time."

"You've got it, cap'n," Bob said. "In only a minute or two we'll be nine miles south of him and on the track you want to follow."

The minutes passed. Midnight was approaching. If the target

111

would only turn then to what we thought was his base course, we'd be in favorable position to get the big ship.

The clock turned its hands to 2400 hours. Midnight. The damn enemy group didn't turn! Now it was Wednesday, November 29, 1944. My lucky day? The enemy ship bore 008 degrees from us at a distance of nine miles.

"Come right to course 270 degrees," Bob ordered. "Parallel his course. Flank speed."

Archer-Fish swung quickly around in a tight turn to course 270 degrees. I looked at Bob and said, "Now we want to continue at maximum speed to get our bearing from him at 210 degrees."

"He could still turn to us," Bob offered.

"I sure hope he does soon," I said, but with little conviction. I was well aware that if he didn't turn toward us, we just didn't have the speed to get in front of him. He'd sail away from us just as *Shokaku* had done the year before.

Ensign Dygert looked toward me. "He's changing course, cap'n."

My heart leaped. Maybe we were going to be lucky. Maybe he was going to come right at us after all.

"Course now is 275 degrees," Judd said. "He's holding on it."

I checked the plot and the chart. Hell, five degrees' difference. What was that all about? I mean, why bother? To go from 270 to 275 degrees? It didn't help us at all.

I called down the hatch to Lieutenant Cousins in the control room. "Rom, go aft one more time and see if we can get some more speed. Even a few more turns will help." He went off, his diving duties quickly assigned to another man.

Our plan now was to keep the enemy carrier's true bearing from us at 030, if we could, so that we'd be ahead of him if he did make the anticipated course change. The distance between us was about nine miles, which was also about right. We could see the carrier and her escorts clearly in the moonlight, but they undoubtedly couldn't spot our low profile on the horizon to the south.

112

were late in returning from liberty. In those cases it was not unusual for the punishment assigned at Captain's Mast, if any, to be "restriction aboard ship" for one week, or two weeks in more flagrant cases—to begin on the day the submarine was leaving on a 60-day patrol.

Skippers themselves were not immune to being apprehended while relaxing and enjoying a bit of fun between patrols. In turn, we usually received similar consideration in the way of punishment from our superiors. Somehow it all worked, and I was thankful to be captain of *Archer-Fish*. While the daily routine was orderly and monotonous at times, the men for the most part found contentment in it because they had all been volunteers and carefully screened by physicians and psychiatrists for this type of underwater service.

Meanwhile, time was beginning to drag. There was nothing more we could do in *Archer-Fish* to get closer to the target without being sighted, resulting in the target again evading us or attacking and forcing us to dive. If we were to have a chance to attack, the commanding officer of the Japanese carrier either had to slow down appreciably or turn toward us. I willed him to do either, preferably to change course to 210 degrees. Other than that, we could only watch and wait.

While doing so, my thoughts turned to my family and friends who had made it possible for me to be where I was, close to enemy ships yet not close enough to hurt them. Those people close and dear to me all wanted to "do their bit" for the war effort, and I was their best chance. I was representing them and was obligated to them. The fulfillment of that responsibility was to sink the enemy ship nine miles away. Many thoughts raced through my mind quickly. My hand went into my pocket to begin fingering my rosary beads, although I didn't always say the necessary prayers. Weary of the impasse involving the Japanese carrier, I thought about how I had come to be where I was. I let my mind go back to other times and places.

I thought about my father, John L. Enright, who had been born in Northboro, Iowa, in 1883, and of his father, Michael Patrick Enright, who was born near Kilbourne, Wisconsin, in

1855. Young Michael in turn had been the son of Michael and Mary Lynch Enright, natives of Limerick and Tipperary, Ireland. They had fled the old country at the peak of the great famine in the 1840s, and perhaps had looked out over the ocean at night as I did now, sensing danger and opportunity together.

My father never finished high school. Instead he went to Chicago to live for several years with his aunt, Mrs. Anna McGovern, while attending La Salle Institute. At the age of twenty-one he claimed 160 acres of land under the Homestead Act near Ryder, North Dakota, and soon "proved up." That is, he made one quarter of a square mile productive.

Within a few years he had established a coal, feed, and grain store in Ryder, where he employed a young woman named Minnie Olson as his office manager. Minnie was the fourth child of Mr. and Mrs. Joseph Olson, my maternal grandparents, who had been born in Norway, married young, and come soon afterward to America. They had settled in Ferryville, Wisconsin, where my mother was born in 1885. The family relocated a few years later when Joseph Olson decided to homestead near Berthold, North Dakota. While still a young woman, my mother also "proved up" her 160 acres. Not long after my father went to work for a big coal company in 1907, he and Minnie were married and settled in Minot, North Dakota. It was there that I was born in 1910; later two sisters, Marian and Elizabeth, came along.

Warm memories of those early years flashed through my mind as *Archer-Fish* moved through the Pacific . . . school . . . old pals . . . all the delivery jobs . . . building my own radio set . . . getting to drive the truck for Jones & Webb Grocery in Bismarck, North Dakota. It was Uncle Frank, my father's brother, who had served as an officer in the Navy during the First World War and gotten me interested in Annapolis, mostly by sending me postcards from every port he visited. His message was always the same: "The Navy is great! Consider joining up when you're old enough."

And here I was. Father had prevailed upon U.S. Senator Gerald P. Nye to appoint me to the Naval Academy. After

116

much cramming, I had passed the entrance examination in April 1929 and entered Annapolis late in June of the same year. Four years later I graduated in the top 50 percent of my class of 1933 and received a commission as an ensign. I requested and got an assignment for the next three years to the battleship *Maryland*.

While I was remembering the many people and incidents in my life that meant so much to me, a spray of cold water in the face focused my attention on the target. It was still there, nine miles away. John Andrews was taking frequent bearings and passing them down to the fire-control party. I saw that we were gaining a few degrees of bearing. Obviously we had increased speed, or the target had slowed. There was no chance that our speed had increased appreciably, as we had been at maximum speed for three hours, and our engines couldn't do any more.

If the target had begun to zig, that could have accounted for some speed reduction; however, large zigs would have been needed to cause a noticeable reduction. That was not the case, because we saw no course change of more than a degree or so. A change of a few degrees left or right would have no effect on speed. I thought the Kuroshio might have variable speeds in horizontal gradients that affected the target and *Archer-Fish* differently. This would be possible in the Gulf Stream off Key West. There, within a distance of a few hundred yards, the current can change from three knots northerly set to zero, and then to a southerly set of a knot or two within a couple hundred yards. But there was no counting on a similar situation off Honshu without well-published reports, and we knew of none.

It certainly was not reasonable for a Japanese carrier, in an area infested with enemy submarines, to intentionally reduce speed. Our target was acting very strangely. It was spooky to think that it had slipped out of Tokyo Bay unannounced, then didn't shoot when the opportunity was ripe, disappeared into the darkness, then reappeared, and now had slowed for no apparent reason. Aircraft carriers could maneuver unpredictably to launch and recover their planes, but it was the middle of the night and there had been no signs of any flight operations whatever.

While I was trying to figure out what the carrier was up to, my mind went back to the decade earlier, the years of the Great Depression, when the American economy had been reeling from the stock market crash of 1929 and the loss of confidence in its traditional free enterprise system. Millions of Americans were out of work and on the dole. I was lucky to be a naval officer and permanently employed. At the height of the Depression, an ensign's monthly pay of $125, plus an $18 monthly subsistence, looked like a gold mine, especially since it was received on a regular and dependable basis. Of course there were all kinds of ways to spend money, and many of us were broke before the end of the month. But at least we knew there was a room with a berth, meals, free laundry, and movies available aboard our ship while we waited for the next pay day.

Completing my three years of duty aboard *Maryland*, I had opted for submarine training at the school in New London, Connecticut. There Virginia Robertson of Portsmouth, Virginia, and I spent seven idyllic months after being married in the summer of 1936. Then we went on to Pearl Harbor, where I was assigned to the U.S.S. *S-35* and our only child, Joe Jr., was born in 1937. Late in October 1938 I sailed aboard another sub, *S-22*, for New London. Virginia and our son sailed on a cruise ship to San Francisco, then traveled to Bismarck, North Dakota, to visit with my parents.

As the years passed, I built up my experience on submarines out of New London, Annapolis, and Key West. They were halcyon at times but also hectic with preparations for the conflict we felt was coming, particularly when the Nazi juggernaut rolled into Poland on September 1, 1939. I recalled being at Argentia, Newfoundland, when the Japanese attack on Pearl Harbor occurred. We were stunned, angered, and then eager for revenge. We sailed quickly aboard *S-22* for New London and then on to the sub base at Coco Solo, Panama. We made five patrols with a trio of other submarines some 600 miles out into the Pacific, but saw no action.

118

Platforms for three lookouts, attached to the periscope shears. The forward periscope (right) is the smaller day attack scope. Its field of view is from horizontal to directly overhead. (National Archives)

Cutaway view of a fleet submarine. During the war, 339 boats were ordered and 221 completed. *Archer-Fish*'s hull number was 311, indicating she was the 311th submarine commissioned in the U.S. Navy. (Courtesy of Fred Freeman)

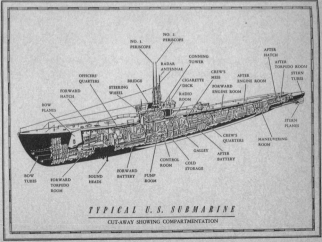

NO. 1. PERISCOPE
NO. 2. PERISCOPE
CONNING TOWER
RADAR ANTENNAE
AFTER HATCH
AFTER TORPEDO ROOM
STERN TUBES
OFFICERS' QUARTERS
BRIDGE
CREW'S MESS
AFTER ENGINE ROOM
STEERING WHEEL
CIGARETTE DECK
FORWARD ENGINE ROOM
FORWARD HATCH
RADIO ROOM
BOW PLANES
STERN PLANES
CREW'S QUARTERS
MANEUVERING ROOM
BOW TUBES
FORWARD TORPEDO ROOM
SOUND HEADS
FORWARD BATTERY
PUMP ROOM
CONTROL ROOM
COLD STORAGE
GALLEY
AFTER BATTERY

TYPICAL U. S. SUBMARINE

CUT-AWAY SHOWING COMPARTMENTATION

U.S.S. *Archer-Fish* after the war, engaged in oceanographic work. Her guns had been removed. (U.S. Naval Institute)

A 21-inch Mark 18 electric torpedo powered by a lead-acid storage battery being loaded into the forward torpedo room of *Archer-Fish*. Its advantage over steam-driven torpedoes is that it left no air-bubble wake on the surface. (U.S. Naval Institute)

A Mark 14 steam torpedo, with an exercise head, being loaded aboard a postwar submarine. Four of this type of torpedo, with high-explosive warheads, sank *Shinano*. (U.S. Navy)

Outboard Profile

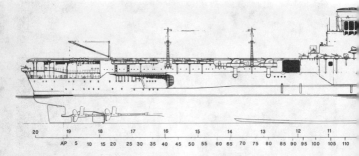

20	19	18	17	16	15	14	13	12	11
AP 5	10 15 20	25 30 35	40 45	50 55	60 65	70 75	80 85	90 95 100	105 110

Topside View (October 1944) *Shinano*

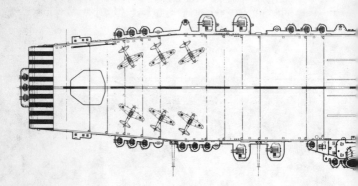

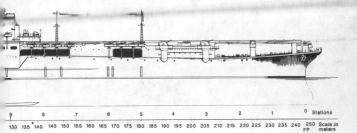

	8	7	6	5	4	3	2	1	0	Stations
130	135 140	145 150 155 160 165	170 175 180 185 190 195 200 205 210 215 220 225 230 235 240							250 FP	Scale in meters

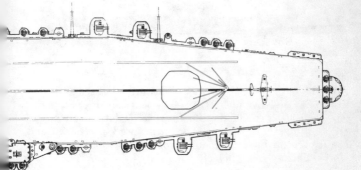

No detailed photographs exist of the *Shinano*. This is an American drafter's conception of the side and top view. (U.S. Naval Institute)

An artist's rendering of the *Shinano* underway, showing its unusual canted funnel. In the background is one of *Shinano's* destroyer escorts. (Courtesy of Richard Allison)

This photograph of *Shinano* was taken during her sea trials in Tokyo Bay on November 11, 1944, by a civilian aboard a tug. The carrier was conducting steering trials, which accounts for the slight heel. Only one print of the picture was retained, and it was presented to Lieutenant Commander (Construction Corps) Shizuo Fukui, IJN, after the war.
(Courtesy of Fukui Collection)

A rare photo of *Shinano* taken high above Yokosuka by a B-29, piloted by Captain Ralph Streakley, on November 1, 1944. Neither the existence nor the location of the aircraft carrier was provided to *Archer-Fish*.
(Courtesy of W. G. Somerville)

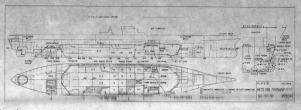

The four small arrows along *Shinano*'s starboard side indicate the locations of hits and the flooded compartments that resulted.

The central armored citadel and the essential spaces it enclosed can be seen in the side and top views.

The two hydraulic machinery rooms, just forward of the outboard engine rooms, are labeled. It was in the starboard one that Lieutenant Inada and eight enlisted men gave their lives in an effort to right the listing ship.

The half-section in the cutaway drawing at right labels the "H" beam that *Archer-Fish*'s third torpedo drove through the bulkhead between No. 3 and No. 1 boiler rooms. (Office of Naval Intelligence Review)

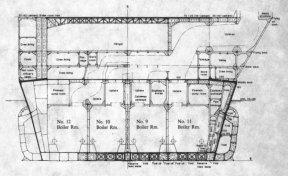

The midship sectional view of *Shinano* indicates dimensions pertinent to her sinking. The distance from the water line to the bottom of the hull is 33 feet. The 10-foot depth setting on the torpedoes was optimum for striking the ship near the joint between the upper and lower armor plates and also the transverse beam. One torpedo hit the "H" beam in No. 3 boiler room, two compartments forward of No. 11, and the beam acted as a battering ram to punch a hole between No. 3 and No. 1 boiler rooms.

The width of the flying off deck, 129¼ feet, provides an indication of the size of the boiler rooms. (U.S. Naval Institute)

AT LEFT: The insignia produced for *Archer-Fish* by Walt Disney. (Author's collection)

BELOW: An *Archer-Fish* party at the Royal Hawaiian Hotel at Waikiki Beach in October 1944. The ladies are with Lieutenant (jg) Bosza and Chief Hoffman. (Author's collection)

Archer-Fish people being entertained by USO celebrity Ginger Rogers at the Royal. Boatswain Dan Ellzey has a girl and Judd Dygert has a drink. (Author's collection)

Standing on the bridge, kneading the rosary, it was coming back to me in bits and pieces, some reminiscences sharp and clear, others blurred by time. When I focused across the sea on the enemy group, so near yet so far from *Archer-Fish*, I felt like a boy with his face pressed against the plate-glass store window, seeing but unable to reach inside.

I was very impatient for the carrier to make a zig our way. Our plan of attack was based on the enemy's having a base course of 210 degrees. After seeing him zig to the left of that to 180, and then at 2340 zig right to 270, I expected him to come back to 210. When he did, we would be in a good position to get him. At 0030 we had increased the carrier's bearing from us to 013 true. We were on our way to reaching a bearing of 030 so he would be heading directly at us when his change to base course did occur.

We still had to wait for him to change course, and it gave me time to think back to my first command, *O-10*, when I was known to my friends as "Oh Boat Joe of the Oh-One-Oh." After a training stint with *O-10*, I was given command of U.S.S. *Dace* and became one of the first in my Annapolis class to receive command of a new submarine right from the building yard. *Dace* was supposed to have brought me fame and renown, but it didn't work out that way. On my first war patrol aboard her in the Pacific, we had several excellent target opportunities, but nothing seemed to go right. I had missed ambushing *Shokaku* by nine miles. Blaming myself for the poor showing on *Dace*'s first war patrol, I asked to be relieved of her command.

New orders came through at the end of 1943. I was to report for duty with the submarine relief crews at Midway. It was important work, but still a place where time dragged and became a tedious burden while great events unfolded elsewhere. I was thoroughly convinced that I was going to miss taking part in the one great adventure of my life. My only war, and I wasn't taking an active role . . .

Lieutenant Andrews was at my side, talking about what a great opportunity the target presented for *Archer-Fish*.

119

"I remember," he was saying, "one of my profs telling us that crisis is opportunity riding on dangerous wings."

Fixing my eyes on our target, I nodded silently. Opportunity was present, all right, at about eight miles distance. We knew we had the carrier within range of our five-inch gun. But that would be like tossing marshmallows at an elephant. We had to bring *Archer Fish* in to a range close enough to fire her torpedoes. They alone would make the opportunity a reality.

7. Optimism

At 0215 on Wednesday, November 29, 1944, the Imperial Japanese aircraft carrier *Shinano* steamed along the course of 275 degrees—almost directly west—eight hours plus into her maiden voyage. Off *Shinano*'s bow, the wayward destroyer *Isokaze* raced about erratically on her screening station. The destroyers *Yukikaze* and *Hamakaze* duplicated *Isokaze*'s unpredictable movements off both beams of the carrier. Overhead the moon was beginning to drop in a western sky daubed with wispy clouds. Visibility remained excellent. Optimism was mounting that *Shinano* would pass safely through the Pacific waters believed to be swarming with Yankee submarines.

Captain Abe stood above, as if transfixed, at the front of *Shinano*'s bridge. Behind him staff officers and crewmen went about their tasks quietly and efficiently. More than an hour earlier, Captain Mikami, the XO, had gone below to convey the captain's compliments to the ship's officers and men partaking of the celebratory *shiruko* meal.

Ensign Yasuda, the assistant navigator, advanced his plot of the carrier, recording the position and time on the bridge chart every 15 minutes, his activities observed by Navigator Nakamura, who had yet to find any reason to comment on them. In the navigator's mind the young officer was born to the sea and required little direct supervision. Though mindful of the captain's interest in the young ensign's performance, the

121

navigator would not hesitate to criticize him if he found it necessary.

Periodically, Captain Abe came back to look at the bridge chart. Most of the time he studied the chart, and *Shinano*'s plot, without comment. He was mainly concerned about the enemy submarine that had been detected by the Direction Finding Network 18 hours earlier. He thought about that particular submarine almost obsessively. Nasty business. She had to be the same submarine that had been defiantly operating her radar in the presence of *Shinano* since the initial radar emissions had been detected at about 1915. Submarines seldom remained stationary, and in those two days it could have moved in any direction, and for a considerable distance. She could be anywhere. At 0230 *Shinano* would be passing only 25 miles south of the site of the reported detection, well within the range of a patrolling sub. If he could constantly detect the radar signals, it could only mean that the American boat was remaining surfaced. And as long as the submarine rode on the surface, she posed no real threat to *Shinano*. His lookouts would spot her long before she could come within torpedo range. He would be seriously concerned, however, if the signals could no longer be detected. That would mean she had dived, with the assumed intention of attacking the carrier.

Abe was convinced that just before the submarine submerged, she would send out a radio signal giving *Shinano*'s location to the other submarines with her in the wolf pack. Accordingly, his people had been alerted to listen for any further radio transmissions. He was to be informed immediately. *Shinano* would then quickly come about to a new course, as she had done earlier. The Yankees were going to learn that they were dealing with a superior mariner.

If they attacked en masse, he believed *Shinano* could withstand the damage caused by any torpedoes lucky enough to hit. The enemy's torpedoes, as he well knew, were substantially inferior to the Empire's on several counts. And the man hours and millions of yen spent on *Shinano*'s construction made it nearly inconceivable that a few torpedo hits would put her out of action. Yet he knew what would come to mind next, even before the thought was fully formed. He fought it, but there again was the image of *Hiryu* silhouetted by a pallid false dawn. The proud carrier was listing badly. Once again he saw Admiral Yamaguchi and Captain Kaku lashed to *Hiryu*'s bridge as the final instructions were carried out. The powerful surface-ship torpedoes from the destroyers *Kazagumo* and *Yugumo* raced each other through the calm sea and exploded with deafening concussion against the carrier's hull.

As he stared with widened eyes through the dark expanse of the window on the bridge, Captain Abe relived *Hiryu*'s death plunge. He had not been close enough to witness the actual sinking, yet he could envision it readily. He saw the carrier list farther, farther, until she rolled over and slipped under the surface. Gone.

How had Admiral Yamaguchi and Captain Kaku died? Did they hold their breath at the last moment as the seas broke over the bridge? Did their opened eyes apprehend anything in the dark waters that boomed over them and marked their end? Their lungs would have burst, and death would have enveloped them before *Hiryu* smashed against the ocean mount, sliding finally to a halt on the floor of the Pacific. Were their . . . were they still tied to the bridge?

He shuddered, a chill passing through him. Enough, he told himself. You cannot do anything about Midway. *Hiryu* is gone. The admiral and the captain chose their deaths; you dishonor them with such morbid reminiscences. Still, what manner of men were they that they could die so willingly when life was still held out to them? Life was precious; how could any man give it up so easily? There were so many things to live for and so little time to indulge them. The Emperor and the Empire. To live to serve them. His career and his pending promotion. How proud he would be when he assumed his new rank. There were too many other captains on the ship. To be captain of *Shinano* and a rear admiral at such a young age—what deeds she would achieve under his command! His name would enter the annals of his country's naval history.

The war currently was not going well for Dai Nippon. That could not be denied. The Yankees held a strong edge in the Pacific war, for the time being. But he was convinced that the situation would change. The Empire was marshaling a huge fleet in the Inland Sea.[1] *Shinano* was the prime carrier. This battle force would steam out of Kii or Bungo straits and turn back the enemy flotillas. Japan would prevail and be established as the paramount power in the Pacific Basin.

Captain Abe did not want to think about his own death. There was too much to accomplish. Each of us was allotted only so many years. How could he possibly get it all done? Yet he was too much the pragmatist not to be aware of his own mortality. Why else had he put a certain degree of ritual into his last visit with his family? He had taken a brief leave during the three weeks *Shinano* was redocked to repair the damage caused by the caisson mishap on October 5. It was only for a few days. He had gone to his home in Kamahura, a suburb of Tokyo, for what could be the last pleasant interlude of the war with his wife, Fumi, and their thirteen-year-old son, Toshikiko.

Mrs. Abe maintained an orderly and serene household in a modest dwelling adequate to the rank and salary of her husband. Once home, Captain Abe had put aside his uniform and worn only the traditional Japanese kimono and padded clogs. No visitors were invited. Captain Abe chose instead to pass the few days only with Fumi and Toshikiko, reminding them in subtle words from time to time of the family's duty to the cause in which he was engaged.

More than once Captain Abe retreated to the privacy of his study to sort out old papers and documents covering the many years of his family's history and the events of his own life. Now and again he would go into the small garden to shred and burn records and scrolls he felt should not be left for the eyes of others. At other times he chose to be alone either with Fumi or Toshikiko. There was so much he had to say to each of them before he returned to his duty.

In quiet moments he skimmed volumes of favorite authors, especially poets, and contemplated the meaning of their words, whether expressed in taka, haiku, or free verse. His attention returned repeatedly to a free-verse funeral piece by the young poet Minoru Yoshioka, who he knew was then serving with the Imperial Army in Manchuria. For him Yoshioka's poem about a man who has drowned articulated in a masterful way much of what was on his own mind. How many times had he wondered whether he would drown at sea. Whether he also would know the "quiet wholeness" of Yoshioka's drowning victim. There was a certain aura of piquancy about the poem, yet he knew in his heart that it had also been crafted to evoke a sense of horror. It did, at least for him.

Captain Abe had returned to the Yokosuka Naval Shipyard before the end of the month. Fumi and Toshikiko had requested permission to see him off at the train station, but at his insistence farewells had been made in the privacy of the family home. The day before *Shinano* sailed, her skipper dispatched a meticulously bound package to Kamakura. Fumi was informed that it contained clothing and some personal effects he would no longer need. She rewrapped them and stored them away to await the day of his return.

Ensign Yasuda, standing at his battle station, could see by now that *Shinano* was in serious jeopardy. They all did. Even the skipper. He knew it most of all. The staff was constantly reminded to relay the word to all to be alert—an exhortation that meant danger was omnipresent. How unfortunate, Ensign Yasuda thought, that Captain Kono, head of the engineering department, had been forced to the embarrassing expedient of slowing the ship because of a hot bearing. *Shinano* was now making only 18 knots—less than the top speed of the Yankee submarines they had outrun only hours before.

8. Fulfillment

Confidential

Subject: U.S.S. *Archer-Fish* (SS-311)--Report of
Fifth War Patrol

(B) Narrative

November 29, 1944

0231 Sent second contact message when it appeared he planned to stay on 275 and not much chance of us reaching a firing position.

0300 Looks like another change of base course or big zig southward. Range closing rapidly and we are ahead.

It was more than two hours into the new day as *Archer-Fish* pounded across the Pacific in hot pursuit of the enemy carrier group. Realistically, of course, it could not be called "hot pursuit," because the target wasn't running ahead of us and we weren't directly behind. Rather, we were still paralleling the carrier's westerly course from about eight miles to the south, hoping we wouldn't be sighted again. We were also attempting to keep the target's bearing from us to about 030 degrees, the reciprocal of the southwesterly course—210 degrees—that we were hoping the Japanese ships would come back to. It had taken us from midnight until 0200 to increase the target bearing from 008 to 030. I was becoming increasingly concerned about the time, especially as 0200 had come and gone, and the hands on the ship's clocks had advanced in clicks toward 0230. The moon was beginning to set. As dawn approached, visibility would increase and the enemy would soon spot us slamming along on the surface to port of them.

As time passed I began to doubt that the enemy group would turn south toward us on a course for the Philippines. I went below to the conning tower once more, to compare our manual plot with the Torpedo Data Computer. They confirmed again that the carrier's speed was about 18 knots, or the same as *Archer-Fish* was now logging after slowing a few turns. I didn't know how to explain this. Perhaps his engines had faltered a bit. Perhaps our engines had outdone themselves to produce a few more revolutions per minute. Whatever, I was grateful to Lieutenant Cousins and the engine-room watch for their performance. Who knows what magic they had managed to work back there?

Although we were slightly ahead, there was still no way we could make an "end-around" on him—that is, pass him while keeping out of sight, then pull in front to launch an attack. If we headed for him on the surface, we'd soon be sighted and taken out by their gun batteries. If we submerged to approach, the carrier and her escort would quickly leave us far behind. We could only wait and attempt to will the Japanese ships to turn toward us.

I was back on the bridge when Chief Pharmacist Mate Bill Hughes called up through the hatch for permission to come to the bridge. The OOD looked at me, and I nodded. Hughes came up to the bridge, his eyes fixed on the horizon to the north rather than on me. In a hushed voice, he asked whether I wanted a No-Doz pill to help me stay awake. He said that it would keep me alert.

"I think we've got enough excitement going on around here to keep me awake, doc," I told him. "I'd consider taking one, though, if you think it will keep me more alert and there aren't any side effects."

"Well, there is one side effect, cap'n. When it wears off in

127

a couple of hours, you'd have to get to your cabin and rest."

I chewed that over for only a moment. "No, I better not, doc. By then we could be under depth-charge attack . . . and I don't want to be sacked out in my bunk."

"I understand, cap'n," he replied. He looked at the northern horizon for a moment, then went below. I chuckled to myself. Doc didn't really think I needed a pill to stay awake. He just wanted to see the carrier we had been chasing for more than five hours. Who could blame him? Most of the men who serve on submarines never get even a glimpse of an enemy ship. They know when the torpedoes are launched, when a target is hit and sinks, or when an enemy ship is stalking or depth charging them because they can hear the telltale noises—but the majority of the crew do their jobs blind.

Lieutenant Andrews kept prodding the lookouts, trying to make sure they were maintaining an alert watch not only on the target but in every other sector. It was important that we not become mesmerized by the carrier group and fail to spot an ambush developing from another direction. The OOD also had to keep track of the precise number of people on the bridge at all times so that everybody could be accounted for if we had to dive in a hurry. Any man wanting to come topside had to ask the officer of the deck's permission. Conversely, they had to report to him before leaving the bridge. Rank having its privileges, Commander Bobczynski and I were exempted from this important procedure. We would simply say, "I'm comin' up" or "Going down."

Below, the only real activity on *Archer-Fish* was concentrated in the engine rooms. The men in the other compartments were playing acey-deucey or card games, relaxing, and chatting in low voices. The main subject of conversation continued to be how each man aboard couldn't wait to put a series of torpedoes into the big carrier. I'd settle for that. Give me this carrier, this chance to do my bit, and I'd never ask for another target—not that I would ignore one if opportunity put it in my path. But my cup would overflow with gratitude if I could just have the chance to get a torpedo into that immense hull.

With my head once more between my fists, I stared glumly across the waves at the enemy ships. Life sure was a mystery, the twists and turns it takes. The heady rewards it bestows on some, early and undeserved death on others. The broken dreams for many. As in a card game, you could only play if you sat down at the table. No one knew better than I. Then my mind skimmed over all the card games I had played in so many places, on so many ships, at so many stations. Card games have always been a popular pastime for men at war—wherever. For money, of course; and what better time or place to gamble some away. Tomorrow you could die, and, especially at sea, cash was only paper. Always, though, one particular poker game will remain forever fixed in my memory . . .

I had been in the submarine relief crews at Midway, and eventually I had written to Admiral Lockwood to request reassignment as skipper of a fighting submarine. My letter had been routed through Captain Pace, the admiral's subordinate commander on Midway. Captain H. L. "Howie" Clark, my commanding officer, who had recommended approval of my request for combat duty, knew my spirits were a bit low and suggested that I join him and some of the other senior officers in a poker game at the Brass Hat Club, a preserve for senior officers. I hesitated because I wasn't sure I was up to mingling with a group of top brass, and with only $100 in my pocket I wasn't sure I had the cash to go the distance. In the end, we went off to the club together.

The game was just about ready to begin when we arrived. All the players were personal friends, with one exception. The exception was Captain Pace. I had never played cards with him before, though I did remember him from my first year at Annapolis, when he had been a duty officer at the Naval Academy. He greeted me cordially. Howie and I took the last two vacant chairs. Seated to my left was Captain Pace. I expected to break out in a big sweat any minute. I was overreacting, thinking of my request, then being routed through him, for combat service.

I managed to stay composed as the game began, with the cards dealt quickly to the players around the table. The conversation was convivial and the betting pleasant, occasionally evoking wry comments. There was a sense of fellowship and camaraderie—we were all enjoying ourselves.

I'm not one of the world's best poker players, and I knew my limitations. Surprisingly, though, as the evening progressed I won a fair share of pots. In time, I had about $200 stacked in front of me. I knew I had made the right decision in accepting Captain Clark's invitation. The world was a kind of fun place after all. You just had to get on your own two feet and confront it.

When it got to be about 10:30 P.M., a half hour before the game usually ends, Howie Clark was dealing. He announced that the game would be five-card stud. "Let's boost the ante to ten dollars."

The game ultimately came down to just two players—me and Captain Pace. After three rounds, Captain Pace had two jacks showing and a third card facedown. I had two fives showing, but my hole card was another five. The other players began to fold after viewing the captain's high pair. Then the fourth round was dealt, and Captain Pace drew a six; I received a two. Apparently no help to either of us.

Captain Pace held the boss cards with the pair of jacks showing. He bet $20 to show that it was still a friendly game. In my gut I knew then that he had a third jack in the hole. With a trio of jacks he was in the driver's seat. He also had more money on the table than I did, and he could have made a larger bet. If he had, I would have had to either fold or cover his bet as far as my cash would go.

It was all intellectualizing. I knew I was going to call his $20 bet. What I had to decide was whether I should bump his bet up. I had to improve my hand or get him to fold. Realistically, he didn't look as if he was in any mood to fold. I badly needed a five or a two. Neither of those cards had shown anywhere else on the table during the game. I had to gamble that most of them were still in the remaining deck. I figured I had a reasonable chance of getting one or the other. If I did, I'd have either four fives or a full house with a trio of fives and a pair of deuces.

I threw down the gauntlet, matched his $20, and raised him $40. I took a deep breath and held it momentarily. Captain Pace studied first his cards and then mine. Not a sound was heard in the room. Finally he called me, pushing his $40 over to the pot. I let out my breath. Thank God he hadn't raised me. I didn't have much to bet with then.

Howie dealt the final cards. His hand slipped my card off the top of the deck. He reached across the table and flipped it over. It could have been the Holy Grail the way it held everyone's attention.

It was a two! Now I had two pairs showing. But with my hole card, I had a full house. I was ecstatic but tried not to show it.

The attention shifted to Captain Pace. Howie stretched across the table to drop his last card. What luck! He got an eight. No help, obviously, for his jacks and six.

With the two pairs showing, I got to bet. I pushed my stack of cash toward the pot. Did I still wear a poker face?

Captain Pace fluttered his hand. "No need, Joe." He flipped over his hole card. It was a third jack. He had capitulated. Ever the gentleman, he said softly, "I was sure you had three fives, but filling a full house on the last card is too good. Nice going, Joe."

"Thank you, sir," I replied, beaming all the while. "I was lucky."

The game broke up and we all mingled around talking about our various hands and enjoying a nightcap. The final game was the topic of most of the conversation. I received warm congratulations from all the players. After a bit Captain Pace took me off to a quiet corner. I worried that I had overplayed my hand after all.

Captain Pace looked me right in the eyes and asked, "Joe, would you run a submarine the way you play poker?"

"Yes, *sir.*"

"Okay, Joe, I like your spirit. You can have the next available submarine."

I was incredulous momentarily. His announcement was too good to be true. Yet I knew he could make it happen, and he was going to. As the commander of Submarine Division 201 with administrative responsibility for six submarines, he had a direct line to Admiral Lockwood. I was exultant. I was about to get back into the war.

As Howie and I were driving back to the quarters we shared, I said, "Cap'n, I was glad to win that pot from Captain Pace, but I hope his promise to give me a command was based on my capabilities as a skipper and not on my luck at cards."

Howie replied, "Not to worry, Joe. His question about running a sub the way you play poker was just a friendly quip. You and I both know that no one in this Navy has ever been given a command unless he's fully qualified."

Captain Pace, of course, was a man of his word. The very next day, September 8, 1944, he endorsed my letter requesting a command with glowing comments and recommended to Admiral Lockwood that I be assigned command of *Archer-Fish*, one of the six submarines in his division. Within ten days, the Bureau of Naval Personnel issued orders for my assignment as skipper of *Archer-Fish* in accordance with his recommendations. What a birthday present! My own boat again.

Captain Clark detached me as the executive officer of the U.S. Submarine Base, Midway Island, Territory of Hawaii, on September 24. On the same day I reported aboard *Archer-Fish*, which had just returned from her fourth war patrol. She was on her way to Pearl Harbor for a routine outfitting and to give her crew some rest and recuperation. Lieutenant Commander William H. Wright was the skipper of *Archer-Fish*, and I was to ride as a passenger with him to Pearl. We agreed to make use of the transit time for change-of-command routines, with me relieving him on our arrival there. Then, without delay, Commander Wright could leave for the States to assume his "new-construction" command. This process would give him a month's leave, then another two or three months at a submarine building yard while final construction and tests were implemented on his new ship. Selection for a new-construction assignment was usually the reward for excellent performance of duty and the completion of a series of war patrols.

Archer-Fish got under way from the pier at Midway on the afternoon of September 24, with a host of friends dockside to wish me bon voyage. We sailed to the music of Ray Anthony and his band—sailors all—who had been assigned to SUBPAC and were on Midway for a few weeks.

For the next four days during the passage to Pearl, I inspected my new submarine with affectionate thoroughness. The crew was exercised at battle stations, fire quarters, collision quarters, and was mustered at abandon-ship stations. I also counted and checked all registered, secret, and confidential publications aboard. There were 70 of them. I was given the combination to the safe in the captain's cabin and the keys to the magazine and the small-arms locker. I inspected the Fleet Regulations and the Force and Unit Instructions to determine that they were correct to date. I also scrutinized the inventory of food supplies in the commissary department and the latest report to the Bureau of Supplies and Accounts. Even then, fighting ships involved a great deal of paperwork.

I was halfway through these bureaucratic but necessary details, when it occurred to me to ask why the name of the submarine was given as *"Archer-Fish"*—two words joined by a hyphen—on all the logs, reports, inventories, and other documentaries. The names of other submarines in the fleet were written as a single word. None was hyphenated. I was informed by Chief Yeoman Carnahan that at the time she was commissioned, the crew considered *Archer-Fish* to be a very special submarine—worthy of a distinctive name. They had simply begun forwarding documentation showing her name spelled with a hyphen. Over a period of time, incoming mail was similarly addressed—although a few establishment diehards continued to write it as one word. Another mystery solved.[1]

The inspections of the ship and the exercises by the crew are requirements for all relieving commanding officers. Every function and department must be certified as "satisfactory"—with exceptions noted in a turnover letter—before the new skipper assumes responsibility. The system is designed to protect the new skipper from preexisting problems for which he is not responsible, or of which he might otherwise not be aware. *Archer-Fish* looked good, and I was so happy to get command again that I would have been tempted to say the operative words— "I relieve you, sir"—even if there had been major discrepancies. In fact, there were none.

I had had ample time during that four-day trip to Pearl Harbor to meet the men of *Archer-Fish*. Her complement comprised 8 officers and 72 enlisted men. They were the finest band of brothers I ever had the privilege of serving with in the Navy.

"Cap'n, how about a hot cuppa coffee?"

I was shaken from my reverie by a voice that seemed a long way off for a moment. I looked around. It was Lieutenant Andrews.

"Thanks, John. But no thanks, I'll skip it." I glanced at my watch. We were coming up on 0235. Fully alert now, I looked across at the target. Nothing had changed. We were just holding our own. Maybe a bit ahead. Damn it. If he wasn't going to turn southwest for a run for the Philippines, then he must be headed for Kii Suido, one of the two main straits leading into the Inland Sea. If that was his destination, he'd probably change course 15 to 20 degrees to his right shortly—taking him even farther from us.

I knew that the moon was due to set at 0430. When it did, the light I needed to attack by periscope would be gone. Soon thereafter, the eastern sky would begin to light up, signaling the approach of dawn. When that happened, we'd have to submerge in order to avoid being sighted by lookouts. Prospects for an attack were diminishing steadily. I considered sending a second contact message, and I thought about the difference a year's time had made in this respect. Back in 1943, Allied submarines in Empire waters had sent radio messages only when there was a pressing need to do so. The Japanese would detect the transmissions, get radio bearings, and probably send out an aircraft or two to try to catch the sub on the surface and attack. Their response time was generally slow, but their positions were accurate. Over time, however, we had come to be less conservative about breaking radio silence.

On this patrol we had sent several messages. The first evening we'd been in Area No. 5, COMSUBPAC asked us if we had made any contact with the U.S. submarine *Scamp*. She had been assigned to an area adjacent to us. On the submarine radio schedules for a few days, we had noticed messages obviously intended to elicit some word from commanding officer John Hollingsworth, a friend and submarine school classmate of mine. It was the normal routine in the event Admiral Lockwood and his operations officer were becoming concerned about the sub's safety. I was sorry to have to send: "Regret we have had neither sight nor radio contact with *Scamp.*"

The other messages we had sent were meteorological data for the B-29 weather forecasters, transmitted from positions 20 to 30 miles north of where we were now. Pursuing our target on his southerly courses took us out of Area No. 5. I knew that when we did transmit, our signal would be heard by the target. But so what? We couldn't catch him under present conditions. No matter what we did, our chance of attacking him could not be diminished. Furthermore, he had turned *toward* us within minutes of hearing our radio a little before midnight. We couldn't fathom the reason for that turn, and it would remain a mystery to us for many years. I decided we had nothing to lose, and even a slim chance of improving our lot if we did open up again.

I called down the hatch to have Ensign Crosby report to the bridge. We had to send another radio message to COMSUB-PAC at Pearl. Without a doubt, Admiral Lockwood and his staff were awake and anxiously awaiting a status report from us. They should also be informed that the Japanese carrier's base course obviously was now 270 degrees, and not the 210 we had previously reported. Once again I gave Gordon the sense of the message and asked him to stay with the radioman in the radio shack until the coded text was transmitted to Pearl on the ship-to-shore frequency. The radioman was then to shift to ship-to-ship frequency and repeat the message for the benefit of submarines who might be on their way to assist us.

Within a few minutes, Gordon returned topside to report

that Pearl had provided "perfect cooperation" for our message. This time the communicators in Hawaii had recognized the high priority of the message being sent by Radioman First Class Dick Scanlan as soon as he began transmitting. ~~on before they had decoded it. Even as it~~ was being received, Pearl began to relay it on the submarine broadcast frequency for all U.S. submarines in the western Pacific. We were undoubtedly the chief topic of conversation at Admiral Lockwood's headquarters and throughout the fleet.

I was delighted with Gordon's report. "What time did Pearl receipt for the message?"

"At 0241, cap'n," he responded with a big smile of his own. "Couldn't have been any faster than that, now that Pearl knows we're chasing a big target."

I turned to keep an eye on the enemy carrier group. "Let's see if those people react to our message to Pearl. No way they couldn't have detected it."

"Good luck, cap'n," Ensign Crosby said as he went below.

I nodded my thanks and trained my binoculars back on the Japanese carrier. Would she turn in our direction on a course of 210 degrees or somewhere in that vicinty? Or would she turn away to the northwest or north and disappear? Would she do anything at all?

The minutes passed. It was 0250. No change in her course. Nothing. I prayed silently. I willed her to turn. Come on. Turn toward us, you bastard . . . I looked at my watch. Just coming up on 0256. Then the fates who had been guiding the enemy must have fixed their attention elsewhere. She was turning. Toward us. All the way toward us. To course 210 degrees, southwesterly! Speed 18 knots! The big carrier and her escorts were headed directly for *Archer-Fish*.

9. Zigzag

Navigator Nakamura retained his favorite post, standing to one side of the bridge chart and staring at the back of the captain's head. He was hardly conscious of Ensign Yasuda, who was busy maintaining the plot a few feet away. The navigator was beginning to feel fatigued and thought about how restorative it would be to stretch out in his berth—even for a few minutes. But he stood ramrod straight, not even appearing to blink his heavy eyelashes as he looked past the captain's ear into the milky sky far off *Shinano*'s bow. Tired as he was, he would have no difficulty in working around the clock another 24 hours if necessary. His energy and strength were legendary.

With his very junior officer tending most efficiently to the navigating chores, Navigator Nakamura worried about the many defects still to be corrected aboard the ship. He had heard a litany of them at the time *Shinano* was delivered. And just an hour ago, when he had gone below for a quick bowl of sweet black-bean soup, Lieutenant Inada had confided to him about his fears for the ship's pumps. The navigator had been in no mood to listen to more negative reports about the ship, particularly when the problems were not his responsibility. Besides, they would be at Kure shortly, and *Shinano*'s deficiencies would be corrected. But Lieutenant Inada was one of the most dedicated and diligent young officers aboard, and the senior officer had allowed him to express his concern while he sipped his soup.

Lieutenant Inada said that there had been no time allocated to operate the pumps, to test what amount of water in the bilges could be shifted to correct listing. Neither had there been any testing of the ship's electrical system to rehearse the shock of a torpedo hit, and the lieutenant predicted that if torpedoes did strike *Shinano,* an electrical failure could cause a malfunction of the pump valves.

Navigator Nakamura had complimented Lieutenant Inada for his concern, but suggested that he was not to worry too much. All would be made shipshape once they arrived at the naval yard. And even as they spoke, several hundred civilian workers aboard were pressing to correct many of the ship's deficiencies. The navigator had to smile to himself. There he was telling Lieutenant Inada not to worry about the ship, and that was all he himself did. He could think of little else—and of the irony of it all. She was the world's largest aircraft carrier, yet not one of her assigned aircraft was aboard. Where was her complement of fighters, of bombers—of scouts? Where was Lieutenant Commander Shiga, who was to lead *Shinano*'s planes into battle against the Americans. *Shinano* just wasn't ready for them.

Navigator Nakamura thought back to the builders' trials on November 11, when Commander Shiga and a group of his baby-faced pilots had conducted a series of tests on *Shinano*'s flight deck. The landing equipment, consisting of 15 sets of arresting wires, had caught the tail hooks of the planes in fine fashion. But without any catapults—*Shinano* had none—takeoffs were tricky. The ship had to steam into the wind at good speed, while the planes raced at full throttle down the 840-foot flight deck to gain sufficient speed to launch themselves.

The navigator shook his head as he thought about their current situation. First they had to make the run for Kure at night because there were no Japanese aircraft available to provide air cover. And then *Shinano* had to put to sea without her own planes because of other commitments.

138

Would there ever be an end to inspections and the correction of design and construction deficiencies? A time when *Shinano* could at last go to sea fully equipped and ready to engage the enemy in battle as her designers had envisioned? If this were to be, the remaining problems would have to be resolved within a two-week period after arriving at Kure. Headquarters had allotted only that brief time span for work to be completed on the ship's four remaining boilers, for pumps to be installed to complete the fire main and drainage systems, and for the correction of deficiencies in the watertight integrity system. Once this work was finished Commander Shiga, his pilots, and their aircraft would come aboard. The day couldn't come fast enough for the navigator.

Captain Mikami, *Shinano*'s executive officer, returned to the bridge for a few moments after attending the *shiruko*. He went forward to converse quietly with the skipper. Ensign Yasuda thought the XO looked tired. Shortly afterward the XO had taken his leave, telling the communications officer, Commander Araki, to have him called at 0400. He was going to his cabin for a nap.

As Ensign Yasuda's eyes darted back and forth on the chart between *Shinano*'s present position and the entrance to Kii Suido, he wondered about his classmates from the Naval Academy at Etajima. They were all good, solid men, eager and ambitious. Now they were at duty stations aboard ships throughout the fleet. How many had already seen action? Perhaps even been wounded or killed? Some, probably, had won high decorations and wonderful glory. He rejoiced for them. Soon, he was confident, he too would have an opportunity to show his mettle in battle.

The clock turned to 0242. Commander Araki left his post beside his radioman and hurried over to Captain Abe. "Sir, we've just detected another enemy radio transmission. From the strength of the signal, it's close by."

Captain Abe asked simply, "How close?"

"Very close, sir," the communications officer replied. "Ten

miles . . . 20. The transmission was very loud and clear. Encoded, of course."

Captain Abe nodded and rubbed his strong jaw with his right hand. "Damn Americans! It must be an operational message from the commander of the wolf pack to his other boats. But what did he tell them?" he said rhetorically.

Captain Abe turned and walked back to the bridge chart. "Navigator Nakamura, the communications officer has just reported the detection of a strong enemy transmission. Very close by. Prepare for another course change."[1]

The skipper realized all too well that the coded radio message from the submarine undoubtedly provided the wolf pack with his position, course, and speed. The enemy ships would soon station themselves en masse along his current track. To avoid their trap, he must change course immediately.

The chief navigator nodded his understanding and ordered his helmsman to stand by to make the change in course. Captain Abe leaned over the chart to decide on his new course. At his side were the senior navigator, Ensign Yasuda, and Commander Araki.

"All right, gentlemen, we have to believe that the transmission was sent from the lead submarine of the enemy wolf pack. Undoubtedly reporting our position and speed. He could also have ordered them to prepare to attack. We have no idea of his location. Which way do we turn?"

The staff officers were well aware that Captain Abe's question had already been answered in his own mind. He was thinking aloud, not seeking their advice. Ensign Yasuda, knowing that he was the last one who should offer an opinion, remained silent with the others.

"Let's see," said Captain Abe. "*Shinano* is now here. Our speed, unfortunately, is below 19 knots. A submarine could just about match that. But only if it remained on the surface."

He became silent again, tracing a finger along *Shinano*'s course on the chart. Which way?

"Commander Araki, are we still detecting the enemy's radar signals?"

"*Yosoro*. They haven't stopped since we first picked them up."

There was a pause as Captain Abe considered. "Good," he said. "At least the wolf pack commander's boat is still on the surface. But I'm worried about what he has just ordered his other boats to do."

Captain Abe looked at his watch. As if thinking aloud some more, he said, "Submarines have been in this area almost constantly since the war began. When one leaves, another takes its place. They patrol the coastal route without letup. Any routes the merchant ships favor between Tokyo Bay and the Inland Sea are a magnet for them. They concentrate, too, off peninsulas where ships tend to bunch up—points of land like Shiono Misaki. Such dangerous areas are to be avoided."

Again he was silent for a few moments, all too aware that eight minutes had elapsed since Commander Araki reported the detection. Could it be 0250 already? Hmm, north was out. The westerly course wouldn't do either. In those directions, a host of enemy submarines could be in place and submerged, anticipating their approach. What to do? The commander of the wolf pack had one thing in mind: to sink the carrier. The thing to do was not to offer him a fight. There would be opportunities later for *Shinano* to display her prowess, once the work was completed on her at Kure. The great battles of the war were still to be fought, with the approach of the Yankees to the Empire's home islands. They could very well herald Armageddon itself, at which *Shinano* would be the key ship because of her planes, weapons, men, and resources.

"Navigator, *Shinano* will come left from 270 to course 210. Log it."

Navigator Nakamura immediately repeated the order to the helmsman: "Come left 60 degrees to course 210."

Ensign Yasuda leaned over the chart and marked *Shinano*'s new course to the southwest. The time was also noted. It was 0256, November 29, 1944. As he did, he could already feel *Shinano*'s huge hull turning to port, hardly heeling as she did so.

"Commander Araki, I want the keenest watch possible. Every lookout must be attentive to the greatest degree. This is no time for slackers."

The communications officer spoke to his chief who relayed the captain's orders to all the watch stations. A few more moments passed as the carrier came left to the new heading.

The helmsman called out: "Steady on course 210 degrees, sir." Navigator Nakamura acknowledged the report of the completion of the turn to the new course and checked the time. It was now 0258. He told Ensign Yasuda to log the information.

Captain Nakamura and Ensign Yasuda stood side by side, staring at the bridge chart. Neither spoke. The younger officer knew that every minute now *Shinano* was making another 600 yards. Every minute she was putting a greater distance between her and the gatherings of "Xs" on the chart. There was a group of them to the north of her, the sites where enemy radio transmissions had been detected or friendly ships sunk.

Captain Abe, standing by himself at the brow of the bridge, was confident that he had chosen the correct course for his ships. In fact, he knew it was the only possible one. Before long it would be dawn, and his lookouts would have the advantage. By then *Shinano* would be close to the shoreline and to the security of the guns protecting Kii Suido. He hoped they could even count on some air cover.

Commander Araki appeared at his side with an ominous report. "Sir, the enemy's radar transmissions ceased at 0305. Abruptly."

Captain Abe sighed. So the submarine has finally dived.

"Commander Araki, have a signal sent at once to the screen commander. Order him to approach for an important message."

"*Hai!*" the communications officer replied and hurried away to the outside bridge with his signalman. There the signal was flashed from the lights on the tips of the yardarm for Captain Shintani to maneuver close to the starboard beam of *Shinano*. *Isokaze* promptly acknowledged the signal by dropping back to a position some 200 yards off the beam.

142

Captain Abe came out on the platform and clung to the railing.

"Message, sir?" asked Commander Aroki

"Inform Captain Shintani that *Shinano* is in great danger. An enemy submarine submerged in close proximity at 0305. It could attack at any time. *Shinano* will zig shortly."

The signalman, using the signal lights on the tips of the yardarm, sent the captain's message. Captain Abe's message was acknowledged, and *Isokaze* turned right and sped up to resume her patrol station. Captain Shintani ordered his lookouts to keep a sharp watch for periscopes.

Captain Abe, back inside the bridge, was considering his next move—a zig to starboard or to port? *Shinano* had now been on the new course of 210 degrees for about 14 minutes. He had moved about five miles. Enough time and distance for a submarine to set up an attack. So where were the Yankees?

At 0310 Captain Abe ordered a zig to the left, to course 180 degrees. *"Hidari kyusoku senkai, hyaku hachiju do!"*

Shinano would head south for a few minutes. Her escorts swung about. The skipper went back to talk to Navigator Nakamura. Ensign Yasuda was not privy to their conversation. Within a few moments they came around together to discuss something in front of the bridge chart.

At 0315, November 29, 1944, Ensign Yasuda informed Captain Abe and the navigator that *Shinano*'s position was "longitude 137 degrees 41 minutes east, latitude 33 degrees 1 minute north . . . 108 miles bearing 198 degrees from Omae Zaki Peninsula."

Navigator Nakamura was attempting to stave off the feeling that something terrible was about to happen. Never before had he felt such a premonition of disaster. It mounted like a column of cool mercury up his spinal cord. Despite his bulky woolen uniform, he shivered perceptibly. The enemy was going to attack. He was convinced of it. Very soon now. He knew it as he knew the clock was coming up to 0316 in a few seconds.

But he also thought the attack could be blunted if the captain would just order the escorts to go after the submarine with their guns and depth charges in the event an enemy sub was sighted again. The sonar on a couple of the destroyers—or was it just one of them?—was still working. Yet he sensed it was too late. The escorts should have attacked the submarine on the surface at 2245 the previous evening. Now she could be anywhere.

Navigator Nakamura shook his head. He wished he had the courage to suggest that course of action to the captain. But Captain Abe was obsessed with the idea that *Shinano* was surrounded by a wolf pack, and all his actions were based on that belief. The navigator no longer accepted that premise. In fact, he didn't think there was more than one hostile submarine in their vicinity. In such situations, his instincts rarely failed him.

10. Onslaught

Confidential
Subject: U.S.S. *Archer-Fish* (SS-311)--Report of
Fifth War Patrol

(B) Narrative

November 29, 1944

0305 Changed course to 100 and submerged. Range
to carrier 11,700 yards. Sighted carrier in
periscope at 7,000 yards. Changed course 10
degrees to left to keep from closing track
too much. A small starboard angle on the bow
and range 3,500. Escort closed carrier to
receive blinker message. This caused him to
pass nicely ahead of us at 400 yards.

0316 Carrier zigged away about 30 degrees. Picture improves. Good position, 70 starboard
track, 1,400 yards. Gyro shots a necessity
due to late favorable zig.

0317 Started firing all bow tubes, Mk 14
torpedoes, set depth 10 feet--first gyro 28
degrees right, track 100, spread from
cards, aft to forward.

Damned if the big carrier hadn't turned and headed right for
us. I could have jumped for joy, right there on the bridge.
Lieutenant Andrews was practically beside himself. He went on
nonstop about how *Archer-Fish* was going to get the target. I

had to slap him on the back and urge him to calm down. All of us on the bridge just kept pointing toward the target.

Finally I went to the hatch and called down to Commander Bobczynski. Bob was below in the conning tower, and he came over to the hatch where I could see him.

"The target's turned, Bob. Coming right at us. Get a report from radar right away."

"Aye, aye, sir," Bob replied. "Myers just noted a change, and he'll give us the information in a minute."

Shortly before 0300 Bob came back to the hatch and called up: "Cap'n, both plot and the TDC give his course as 210 and speed at 18 knots."

"Hey, that's terrific, Bob. Can you believe those Japanese ships are coming right at us? Headed directly for us."

I took another hard look at the carrier that was moving toward us from the north.

"Bob," I called down, "I don't want to dive until it's necessary. If this is a short leg of a zig, we may have a chance to gain valuable distance to get ahead of him. Keep me informed of the range. It's imperative that we get out of sight before the enemy ships see us. I think we're safe outside of 12,000 yards."

Archer-Fish raced westward for some five minutes. It was crucial that we obtain a position a short distance to one side of the target's expected track. Firing torpedoes from directly ahead of a target is not the best tactic because you are presented only with the narrowest view of the ship. I wanted to attack from the beam, to have the largest target possible for our six bow torpedoes. I also wanted to get within a range of 1,000 to 2,000 yards. When I estimated that *Archer-Fish* was far enough off the track, I turned right to head on a track parallel to and toward the carrier for a couple of minutes. Then *Archer-Fish* turned right again—east—to reach an ideal firing position.

Based on advice from the fire-control party below, I ordered the helmsman: "Come to course zero nine zero." The course gave us an approach angle of 60 degrees starboard on the target. *Archer-Fish* had six torpedoes ready forward, and four in the after tubes. Heading in toward the target would therefore be preferable to heading out and firing the stern torpedoes.

It was a few seconds after 0304 when Bob called to me: "Cap'n, the range is now 12,000 yards, and the target is still on course 210, speed 18 knots."

I whirled around to Lieutenant Andrews. "Okay, John, let's take her down!"

Instantly, the OOD bellowed, "Lookouts below! Dive! Dive!" He sounded the diving alarm simultaneously. It resounded throughout *Archer-Fish:* Ah-oooooh-gah! Ah-oooooh-gah!

In the control room below the conning tower, the chief on watch was already opening the vents to the ballast tanks. The seawater could be heard rushing into the tanks in a noisy surge. The air it forced out whined through the topside vents like so many fearsome tornadoes. *Archer-Fish*'s down angle increased to ten degrees as we started to slide beneath the moon-dappled Pacific.

I shot down the ladder right behind the lookouts. I remained in the conning tower, while they continued below to the control room and their various battle stations. I positioned myself between the pair of periscopes.

The last officer to come down from the bridge was Lieutenant Andrews. It was his duty as he came below on the ladder to use a toggle he held in his hand to pull the hatch closed. Then he stepped back to permit the quartermaster to reach up and spin the wheel to secure the hatch.

The OOD's voice reverberated in the conning tower: "Hatch secured, sir."

I called below to the diving officer, Lieutenant Cousins: "Level off, Rom, at 60 feet."

It all went like clockwork. From the time the alarm was sounded until we leveled off at 60 feet, about one minute had elapsed. Sixty seconds was in fact about the average time it took to make such a dive, and that was just the way I wanted it. It was not my intention to be hurried about this attack. I knew that we needed—all of us—to work as a team in a smooth but deliberate fashion. Almost as if it were a training exercise rather than the real thing. The point was to be accurate and deadly, not just "fast on the draw."

Our battle stations diving team was outstanding. It was led by Lieutenant Cousins, who had been waiting for hours for the diving alarm to sound. So had the forward-plane operator, Torpedoman First Class "Gunner" Ford. Charlie Wells, the motor mate second class from Detroit, had hurried forward from his engine-room station the moment he'd heard the diving alarm and had taken control of the stern planes. These men were a top-notch team that could hold *Archer-Fish* within inches of any depth I designated.

Standing by to assist me with the periscopes was Bill Sykes, who called out the range and bearings when I announced: "Mark range," or "Mark bearing." He also raised or lowered the scope, using a lever that controlled the hydraulic pressure. Two of Bill's most important pieces of equipment were a lead pencil and a stopwatch. It was his responsibility to start the watch when I said "fire" and to mark the watchcase with the pencil when he heard each torpedo explosion. In effect, he was the official timer who would let us know how many hits we had scored on a target and how much time the torpedo had taken to reach it. If we got a hit, the information he compiled with his pencil and stopwatch would provide an exact range between *Archer-Fish* and the target, confirming or refuting the information I received from the periscope. These data were very helpful in reconstructing the firing procedures and in accounting for any misses.

About a minute after *Archer-Fish* had leveled off at 60 feet, I asked Bill to raise the number two periscope. *Archer-Fish* was equipped with two periscopes: an attack scope and a night scope. The attack scope was finely tapered to the 1.4-inch exit lens. A skilled attacking officer could raise it, observe the target, and lower it before any lookouts on the enemy ship—even with excellent visibility—could see and identify it. However, the small glass aperture and the 40-foot length of the periscope tube tended to limit the amount of light transmitted. The night scope

148

had a much larger exit lens to compensate for the lower visibility after sunset and therefore transmitted far more light. But its upper column was much larger and could be spotted more easily by enemy lookouts.

I considered using the attack scope because the larger one might be sighted in the bright moonlight. But I still didn't know the identity of the target and decided that the night scope offered a better opportunity to obtain a good view of her. I went with the big night scope and cautioned myself to use it sparingly. As the periscope rose from the deep well in the center of the conning tower deck, Lieutenant Bunting called out the target bearing generated by his TDC. Quickly, efficiently, Bill Sykes turned the tube that housed the periscope and folded down the handles for my grasp. This procedure made it unnecessary for the skipper to search for the target when he peered into the scope.

I pressed my head against the rubber cushion around the glass before the scope was fully raised and glared into the eyepiece. The cross wires were fixed right on our target. Just keep coming, sweetheart, I murmured to myself. Don't turn away.

"Stand by for a setup," I ordered. "Range, mark!"

Quartermaster Sykes called out, "Seven thousand yards."

"Bearing, mark!"

"Bearing three three zero."

By way of confirmation, Lieutenant Bunting said, "TDC checks."

We were now in the final stages of the attack. The huge Japanese carrier was approaching at about 600 yards every minute. *Archer-Fish* was lined up. Unless the target zigged, the next move was ours. *Archer-Fish* was engaged in a typical approach, one that many of us had rehearsed hundreds of times on training runs in various submarines over many years—nine in my case. The principle for firing torpedoes is almost the same as the way I was instructed to fire a rifle at the Naval Academy: "Settle down; steady; squeeze the trigger gently!" Do otherwise and the bull's-eye is missed. I was determined that my fire-control party and I would be steady, accurate, and successful.

There were about ten of us crowded into the conning tower, each concentrating on his particular task. Talk was kept to an absolute minimum. We looked like so many black cut-outs in the red glow of the lights.

As the range closed rapidly we prepared our Mark 14 torpedoes for firing.

"Make ready all tubes," I ordered. "Flood the tubes. Set depth on the torpedoes at ten feet."

Commander Bobczynski, who was right at my elbow, observed: "Cap'n, that seems a pretty shallow setting for a target that probably draws 25 to 30 feet."

"Right, Bob, but I'm going to capsize the bastard. You'll see. I'll explain it to you later."

There wasn't time to tell Bob about a conversation I'd had with Rear Admiral Freeland A. Daubin, Commander, Submarines, Atlantic, during his informal visit the year before aboard *Dace* in New London. During a chat in the wardroom, Admiral Daubin had told me that if he ever had an opportunity to torpedo an aircraft carrier, he would set his torpedoes to run shallow. He figured that given the great weight of the flight deck well above the waterline, any additional weight high in the carrier—namely in the form of flooding—would tend to capsize her, perhaps even more effectively than a greater amount of flooding lower in the hull. It made a lot of sense to me.

I was also concerned about the performance of the torpedoes we had. Earlier in the war they had been known to run deeper than set. Many sub skippers blamed this for their frequent misses. I was among them. While on *Dace* I had missed three great targets because—at least this is what I suspected—the torpedoes ran lower than the depth for which they were set. Corrective measures reportedly had been taken to upgrade their performance, but I was still leery. If I set them shallow, they might still score even if they ran deep. Nothing in the book recommended it. I had never received any instructions regarding it. The pro forma setting for torpedoes in attacking a carrier was to select a depth of between 25 and 30 feet. It was a procedure I now confidently ignored.

Within a few seconds, Chief Carnahan, our telephone talker, reported: "Forward room reports all torpedo-tube doors opened. Tubes are flooded. Torpedoes are set for ten feet."

He reported the same status from the after room.

To all the crew in the conning tower I announced: "We are sharp on the bow of the target. It's not a desirable position, but we'll shoot when the target's within range. Despite the fore-shortened ship, we should get some hits."

I had Bill Sykes raising the scope for me for only quick peeks at the target. Up and down it went, silently within its smooth casing. Even though it was still dark on the surface, I didn't want the periscope breaking the surface any more than was necessary. It was during the course of this process that I noticed something strange about the enemy carrier, something I couldn't figure out. During a quick scope observation, when we were almost dead ahead of the carrier, I saw that its huge island appeared to lean to starboard. Strange, I thought. How could that be? I had never heard of a carrier island being sloped like that. I knew that when you're on the beam of a carrier there is a sense of a forward slope to the island because the lower section of the structure is larger than the upper sections. The tapering effect from the flight deck to the top bridge gives this appearance. But that wasn't the case with the carrier I now had under observation. The hull of my target looked as if we were sharp on the starboard bow. I was sure that's where *Archer-Fish* was in relation to her. Yet such an apparent slope to the island should have been visible only if we were farther aft, closer to the beam.

It made me wonder whether, unknown to us, the carrier had changed course. Frankly, I was confused. My curiosity aroused, I sidled up to Lieutenant Bunting and asked in a whisper, so that my confusion would not be noted by others, "Does the TDC show a zig to the left?"

"No, sir. He's still on the same course."

Still puzzled at the carrier's appearance, I had the scope raised to obtain another bearing.

"He's on the same course, cap'n," Dave replied.

During this observation I saw another strange sight occurring on the surface. The carrier was using the white lights on the tips of the yardarm to send a signal that could be seen for many miles around the darkness. As I watched, a destroyer ahead slowed until the carrier came abeam at a distance of some 200 yards. At this juncture there was further signaling by the target. What the hell was that all about? Incredible! Warships never used open light signals at night and certainly not those visible in all directions, as the yardarm lights were.

Now the range had closed to 3,500 yards. We still had a small angle on the target's bow. Almost in unison, Bob and Dave said, "We have to fire quickly."

"I know," I said. "We will. We'll shoot in the normal order. Number one tube first. Eight seconds between fish. Tell the forward room to stand by. My next look will be a firing observation."

I ordered Sykes to raise the periscope. "Up scope!" I was still using the wider night scope. As I looked into the eyepiece, I noted immediately: "He's zigged away!"

We were prepared for that possibility. We had established a procedure on *Archer-Fish*—one we had rehearsed on numerous practice approaches—to handle such a situation. The important thing was not to waste valuable time obtaining the new range and angle on the bow. With a bit of historical research, our fire-control party had examined all the prescribed zigzag plans used by our warships and concluded that the average zig was approximately 30 degrees. So when I informed the party that the target had zigged away, Lieutenant Bunting used this average and within seconds had inserted the change of 30 degrees into the TDC.

"Change made. Ready light," he said to acknowledge that the computer had caught up with the insertion. The TDC was automatically sending new, corrected gyro angles for the torpedoes in the forward room.

Lady Luck must have been there with us in the conning tower. The target's course change provided us with a perfect setup—one submariners dream about: The carrier's full starboard side was our target. She was now on a course due south, and we were pointed east, on a track perpendicular to hers. The distance our torpedoes had to run had increased to approximately three-quarters of a mile. In this new situation we had another two minutes to wait before firing.

I was anxious to obtain the identity of the carrier. Hell, how many of the big ones did the Japanese have left in their fleet? Aloud, I described the carrier again to the men around me. The shape of the island. The exaggerated clipper bow. Cruiser stern. The proximity of the forward end of the flight deck to the ship's bow and the after end of the flight deck to the stern. Ensign Crosby was beside me, holding the *Recognition Manual* so I could study the carriers with large islands.

"None of those, Gordon. Give me a piece of paper."

He handed me a clipboard and a pencil and paper. I drew a quick sketch of the key features of the enemy carrier. It was weird-looking. Gordon looked at my crude drawing. Then at the manual.

"The Japanese don't have anything like that."

"The hell they don't. I'm looking at it."

I peered through the scope and saw an unexpected maneuver by the screening destroyer on the carrier's starboard beam. Damn it, he was changing course and heading straight for our piece of the ocean. There was no doubt that he had a bone in his teeth, as they say, and was making knots in our direction. Time for another decision, and quickly.

I announced to the conning tower complement: "We've got an enemy destroyer coming our way. He'll pass about 200 yards ahead."

In truth, I knew his course would bring him much closer. But why alarm everyone else when there was nothing any of them could do about it? What I needed to know was whether the destroyer was making an attack on us or just returning to

153

station. If he was attacking, he would be using his echo ranging sonar to locate us and obtain a range.

I turned to our sonarman, Radioman 1/c Scanlan, and asked, "Is the destroyer pinging?"

"No, sir."

I wanted to be absolutely certain. "Scanlan, look me in the eye and tell me whether that destroyer is pinging."

Scanlan turned the frequency knob on the sonar set through the entire band on which the receiver could detect sonar transmissions. Then he looked me right in the eye. "No, sir. The destroyer is not pinging."

If he had picked up pinging, I would have had two choices: go deep to try to escape the almost certain depth charges, or remain at periscope depth and hope for the best while firing our torpedoes. Since we did not appear to have been detected by the destroyer, I ordered Sykes to lower the scope and called down to the diving officer. "Make our depth 62 feet."

All of us could now hear the sharp sounds of the destroyer's propellers as she headed our way. They got louder. When we dropped to a keel depth of 62 feet, we would have about 10 feet between *Archer-Fish*'s upper periscope support and the destroyer's keel. The Japanese warship churned closer. The noise of its propellers increased in volume as she was whipped through the water. Inside the conning tower not a word was spoken. We just looked at each other, with an occasional raised eyebrow, and listened. Men held fast to anything available. Some probably said a prayer. I did.

Then the destroyer was roiling the water right above us. The beat of the big propellers so close was breathtaking. She thundered overhead like a locomotive. The whole submarine vibrated and rolled from the shock waves. We waited. Would she drop the ash-cans? We squinted and listened. No depth charges! Then the destroyer was past us, the sound of her propellers diminishing rapidly.

I quickly motioned "up" with a jerk of my thumb, and Sykes raised the scope. I rushed to peer into it. The target was there, clearly visible. I put the cross wires on the carrier's island and hastily called: "Mark, bearing."

Speed was of the essence because the target had already passed from our port bow to our starboard and beyond optimum firing position. We would have had torpedoes already on their way toward her if that damned destroyer hadn't forced me to lower the scope for about 60 seconds.

"Stand by," I ordered. "Fire one."

Chief Carnahan, off to my left, pushed the firing button. *Archer-Fish* jerked as if she had been smacked by a whale, as the huge compressed air blast ejected the first torpedo from its tube. It swooshed away in a cloud of bubbles at a depth of ten feet, with a 28-degree right gyro angle steering it on the course for the Japanese carrier. Now I had time to stare at the target and take in all the details. God, she was big! An immense ship. She filled the scope. I said to myself again, *Archer-Fish* needs this target and we're going to get it. Thank heaven for this chance.

Chief Carnahan, almost like an automaton, turned the selective switch to the No. 2 tube and waited for the eight-second interval, then fired the second torpedo. *Archer-Fish* lurched again. Then the third and fourth torpedoes were fired. I kept watching the nearby carrier through the scope. Things were getting a bit tense. Where were the hits? They should be registering now. But I was a bit premature, trying to hurry up the running time on the fish.

After the fourth torpedo was on its way, Commander Bobczynski called out: "Check fire! Get a new setup!"

The chief passed the word over the phone. I began to get a range, bearing, and angle on the bow of the target.

When I assigned Bob the responsibility of coordinator, I also gave him the authority to step in at any time to correct or initiate any action he considered necessary. That included any of my actions. Like anyone else, I could become so engrossed in one facet of the approach that I might neglect others. It was Bob's job to keep us from concentrating on one tree while ignoring the forest.

Bob later mentioned that under other skippers it had been the practice, when a full salvo of six torpedoes was being launched and no hit had been registered after the initial three were fired, to check fire at once and get a new computer setup. It was the best and the quickest way to prevent the remaining torpedoes from being fired with incorrect data. In our approach on this carrier, he had waited for four torpedoes to be fired before calling for the new setup. It was an excellent idea but it caught me flat footed; we hadn't rehearsed that method before.

All I knew was that Bob had ordered the new setup at a critical stage of the attack. I had complete confidence in him. This was not the time to begin questioning his order. My instinct was to give him whatever he thought was required to sink the damn carrier. Incredibly, however, while setting up, we all felt the unmistakable jolt of our fifth torpedo swooshing away. Talk about a surprise. But however it had happened, I had no intention of asking why then. It had been fired. That was all I needed to know. Later I'd find out how it happened.

Lieutenant Bunting soon had the new data in the TDC. The ready light flashed. Chief Carnahan, without any sign of emotion, fired off the sixth torpedo. As *Archer-Fish* jumped anew we awaited the results. We used a spread of 150 percent—with the first torpedo fired to pass behind the target, four fired to strike along the carrier's hull, and the last to pass ahead on the bow. Doctrine rationalized that in this way we should score multiple hits, despite any likely errors in estimating either the course or speed of the target.

They say one's heart leaps into one's mouth, and that is exactly what I felt. In the glass I saw a huge fireball erupt near the stern of the target. Then we heard the noise of the first hit, carried to us through the water. Then *Archer-Fish* felt the shock waves created by the 680 pounds of torpex explosive.

"Got 'em!" I yelled. "Got the son-of-a-bitch!" Still, it was too early to celebrate. There were hits to count. And there would be depth charges to avoid, all too soon.

As I continued to peer into the periscope, I saw the second

explosion rip the target's hull eight seconds later. It erupted about 50 yards forward of the first blast. Yahoooo! I cried to myself. The spread appeared to be exactly right, with the torpedoes evidently moving forward on the target.

I swung the periscope to watch the reaction of the destroyers. One was already headed for us from the carrier's starboard quarter. The one that had gone pounding by overhead only a minute before was completing a tight turn to head back toward us. I got one more fast look at the carrier as we felt and heard further torpedoes rip into her hull. Incredibly, she was listing already. The ocean must be pouring into her guts. She looked as though she would capsize any minute. Without counting them, I heard more torpedoes strike the target.[1]

I wanted badly to remain at periscope depth and watch her go under, but it wasn't possible. We had done everything we could to sink the target. The destroyers were rampaging about in their search for us. *Archer-Fish* was now a target.

"Take her down to 400 feet," I ordered. "Rig for depth-charge attack."

As *Archer-Fish* began her descent, we had the opportunity to express our excitement and congratulations. It was tough, though, to make out what anyone was saying, as we were all talking at once. But no one cared.

"I counted six hits!"

"So did I," chimed in another voice. "That carrier's going to sink."

"Down goes another big one."

"It's about time, men! Thank God for this one."

No one among us in the conning tower was more excited and jubilant than Bill Sykes, who had raised and lowered the scope for me throughout the approach. "We hit the bastard. We hit him lotsa times. He'll sink. Damn, if he won't!" Like the teenager that he was, Sykes kept jumping up and down, shouting.

I looked at the clock above the chart desk. It was 0322. We had submerged at 0305. An eventful 17 minutes. Ones we wouldn't forget in a hurry. I patted my rosary. *Archer-Fish* had done it, triumphantly. I was a winner at least. We were all

157

winners. We had achieved our moment of glory in the big war.

Operating his sonar gear, Radioman Scanlan kept tabs on the destroyers by picking up the sound of their accelerating propellers. He also picked up a lot of noise that he translated as various death throes of our target. She was breaking up. The ocean was drowning her, tearing and twisting her bulkheads. It was music to our ears.

Then the Japanese destroyers were on top of us, and their depth charges rolled into the water above *Archer-Fish*.

11. Gutted

The time was 0317, November 29, 1944. *Shinano* had completed her turn from course 210 degrees left to 180 degrees. Captain Abe was determined to outsmart the Yankee submarines, especially the persistent commander of the wolf pack. He'd zigzag all night and into the morning hours if necessary to keep the American submarines at bay.

Navigator Nakamura and Ensign Yasuda were recording the new data and making updated notations on the bridge chart. The chief navigator was growing concerned at the lateness of the hour. Soon the moon would set and the sun would rise. Daylight would expose *Shinano* to any B-29 bombers passing overhead on their way to Tokyo. Had they really gained that much by the nighttime passage?

At that moment the first torpedo smashed into *Shinano*'s hull some ten feet below the surface. There was a tremendous roar, and a huge ball of red and orange flame rolled up the starboard side of the ship and shot into the dark sky. The torpedo had struck the carrier at frame 194, 115 feet forward of the rudder. This first hit, the one farthest aft, ripped into large refrigerated areas and one of the empty aviation gasoline-storage tanks. The blast ruptured and caused prompt flooding of other refrigerated spaces on the deck below. The explosion also burst through the deck above, killing engineering personnel who were asleep in their compartments.[1]

Within the next 30 seconds three more torpedoes slammed into *Shinano* at frames 162, 118 and 104, advancing toward the bow. There was an eight-second interval between each hit. The number two torpedo thudded into the stuffing box compartment for the starboard outboard propeller shaft. The sea rushed into the hull at this point and flooded the outboard engine room. The engine-room personnel managed to escape.[2] The third torpedo punched through *Shinano*'s hull with a mighty explosion, causing the No. 3 fireroom to be engulfed with seawater within minutes. It was one of the steaming firerooms, and every man on watch was killed. Soon there were leaks and ruptures in the bulkhead between the No. 3 fireroom; and the No. 1 fireroom, which was inboard of No. 3, resulted in flooding to No. 1. Just as quickly, the No. 7 fireroom became inundated.[3] The last of *Archer-Fish*'s Mark 14s detonated against the side at the starboard air compressor room, flooding it. Seawater rushed into the neighboring magazines that held antiaircraft ammunition, and the explosion also ruptured the starboard-ready oil tank. Shortly after, the adjacent No. 2 damage-control station—one of the ship's nerve centers for the coordination of firefighting, antiflooding measures, and emergency repairs—was awash with inrushing water and had to be abandoned.[4]

The No. 1 damage-control station, located on the carrier's island, took over responsibility for saving the ship. The primary concern was the flooding. Captain Kono, the chief engineer, had been in the No. 2 control station when the Yankee torpedoes ripped into his ship. The stricken station was just below the armored deck,[5] four decks above and directly over the site of the last torpedo hit.

Captain Kono, already alerted to the attack on *Shinano* by the hollow thudding noises from the first three torpedoes, had rung up Commander Araki on the bridge. The communications officer acknowledged the skipper's awareness of the submarine attack and requested a damage-status report as quickly as possible. Then the fourth torpedo burst below. But the great mass of the carrier muffled it. Captain Kono expected a severe jolt, even to be knocked off his feet or sent crashing into a bulkhead.

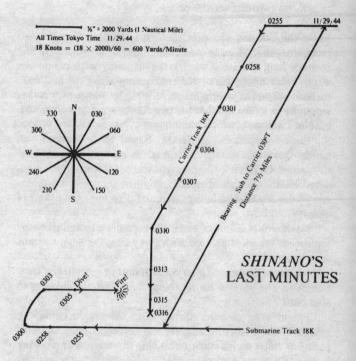

½" = 2000 Yards (1 Nautical Mile)
All Times Tokyo Time 11/29/44
18 Knots = (18 × 2000)/60 = 600 Yards/Minute

0255   11/29/44

0258

Carrier Track 18K
0301

0304

Bearing Sub to Carrier 030°T
0307   Distance 7½ Miles

0310

0313

0315

0316

N
330   030
300   060
W   E
240   120
210   150
S

0303   Dive!
0305   Fire!
0300   0258   0255

Submarine Track 18K

SHINANO'S
LAST MINUTES

Archer-Fish
0256—Sights Target Turning
0255—0300—Gets Off Track
0305—Dives—SJ Antenna Goes Under
0313—Lowers Scope—Destroyer Passes Over
0315—Fires Initial Torpedo

Shinano
0255—Turns to Port
0305—Radar Indication Vanishes
0307—Sends DD Light Signal
0313—DD Returns to Station
0316—First of Four Hits

Instead, his sensation was a great gale of air whipping through the passageways of the ship.

"I'll get back to you, commander. We've got a fourth hit. Just below us somewhere. We're already taking water," Captain Kono rattled over the phone.

From the dreaded sound of the first explosion, Captain Abe recognized that *Shinano* was under submarine attack. He had been too long at sea and was too familiar with battle conditions not to know immediately that concussions along the hull were torpedo warheads holing his ship. Well, let the enemy do his worst; he was firm in his belief that *Shinano* could sustain this kind of damage.

"Enemy torpedoes, gentlemen. Sound battle stations—all hands. Quickly. Damage-control status reports. Immediately. Casualties. Get to it." Captain Abe seethed inwardly. He wondered whether he should break radio silence to notify headquarters of the attack. No, best to wait and determine the extent of damage.

"Navigator Nakamura, order the helmsman to maintain our top speed. We must proceed with every knot the engine rooms can provide."

Lieutenant Sawamoto interjected almost immediately: "Captain Abe, the ship is listing. Nine . . . now ten degrees to starboard."

Captain Abe glanced through the window fronting the bridge. *Shinano* was heeling, far too quickly. Could four torpedo hits cause such a situation? A ship this huge, with so many inches of armor—something was wrong. Weren't the antitorpedo blisters along the hull effective?

After relaying the captain's order to the helmsman, Navigator Nakamura told Ensign Yasuda to be sure to write down *Shinano*'s exact position when the torpedoes struck. The young officer promptly did so, also noting the time. *Shinano*'s ordeal had begun at 0317 hours on November 29, 1944.

Commander Araki called out: "Sir, Captain Kono reports he has had to abandon the No. 2 damage-control station. The damage there requires it. He's making his way to the No. 1 station."[6]

Captain Abe responded: "I want those full reports on our damage and from damage-control station. Tell them to get on it." He went to the bridge chart, where Navigator Nakamura and Ensign Yasuda had unrolled a set of *Shinano*'s blueprints and were studying them to determine the specific location of the torpedo hits. An initial report from the No. 1 station came back almost at once. The first torpedo had struck the condenser room toward the stern on the starboard side.

Captain Abe turned to Lieutenant (j.g.) Michio Sawamoto, the OOD, or *kanpan shikan*, who was also the son of the Imperial Navy's vice minister, and gave him an immediate order. "Deck officer, check the damage to the condenser room. Obtain a report from the steering room on damage and flooding there."[7]

Lieutenant Sawamoto, who only a short time ago had been enjoying the late portion of the *shiruko* celebration meal in his cabin, snapped off a cursory salute and hurried below.[8] He passed through numerous watertight compartments while making his way through the interior of the ship to reach the condenser room, which was located near the after steering room.

Captain Abe's mind was in some turmoil as he thought about the fate of the carrier *Akagi*, which had been deprived of its electric steering by the Yankee bombs at Midway, resulting in a jammed rudder. *Akagi* had turned in huge circles to port until Japanese ships were forced to scuttle the carrier with torpedoes.

While Lieutenant Sawamoto proceeded toward the stern, Captain Mikami, *Shinano*'s executive officer, rushed toward the damaged areas to get a firsthand estimate. Only moments earlier the XO had been knocked out of his bunk in the middle of a nap by the effects of one of the torpedo explosions. The whistling sounds of escaping air were everywhere as he passed closed watertight doors indicating leaking gaskets. The same ominous high-pitched noise came from several sources, such as pipes, ventilation ducts, and electric cables passing through

163

bulkheads. To the experienced captain, these were serious danger signals.[9] He recognized that the air being vented was caused by the pressure of seawater entering the ship. The huge amount of water was staggering and indicated real danger.[10]

As he advanced through the confusion, Captain Mikami surveyed the mutilated decks above and below him. Spanking-new storerooms, refrigerated spaces, and sleeping quarters had been blown apart. Reports of many dead and wounded were being called out to teams of medical corpsmen who were making their way to the crew's sleeping compartments. Captain Mikami reached the No. 1 damage-control station and instructed all personnel to proceed to their stations and secure all watertight doors. As he gave the orders, he was filled with resentment toward headquarters and the builders of *Shinano*. If we had been permitted time to air test the compartments, we would be able to control this flooding now, he thought. Within minutes he received reports of four large gaping holes in the hull. When one of the reports told him that the flooding was close to the starboard pumping station deep in the ship, he again felt a chill for the safety of everyone aboard. If we lose the pumps, he thought, it will be impossible to keep the ship righted.

Captain Mikami telephoned Lieutenant Inada, who was at his general quarters station in the hydraulic pump room, forward of and below the outboard starboard engine room.[11]

"Inada, what are you doing to correct this list?"

"We are pumping from the bilges in the No. 3 engine room to the bilges in a port engine room, sir."

"You are not getting the list off, Lieutenant," the XO said.

"I know it is disappointing, but there is a lot of water flooding the ship. We will do all we can, Captain Mikami."

"I'm sure you will, Inada. Keep pumping. Do you have any flooding in the pump room?"

"Not yet, sir."

Even as they spoke over the telephone *Shinano*'s list to starboard had increased to 13 degrees, making it difficult to walk along the decks. Ringing off, Captain Mikami made his way to the first generating room next to a flooded compartment. Seawater, reeking of bunker crude oil, swirled above his knees. The generator was out of commission. When the auxiliary generator kicked on, the dim light revealed that the water in the generator rooms was rising to waist height.

Captain Mikami returned to the No. 1 damage-control station, where he received a new order from Captain Abe: "We're going to try to make Shiono Point. Do everything possible to right the ship."[12]

Acknowledging the order, Captain Mikami then called Lieutenant Inada. "Lieutenant, we must do more to correct the list. It has now increased to 13 degrees. Can't you do more?"

"We are pumping from starboard to port as fast as we can. Some of the valves are not working properly now. We have already shifted 3,000 tons of water into the port bilges. That hasn't helped."

The executive officer now realized that *Shinano* probably would not make port.

When Lieutenant Commander Yasuma, chief medical officer, heard and felt the impact of the torpedoes, he rushed from his cabin and headed for the medical department.[13] He had to make his way through a crush of officers and men who were overloading the passageways and ladders on their way to scores of different battle stations. He shook his head in disgust and shouted at groups of civilian barbers and laundrymen, and Korean forced-labor-yard workmen who were milling around unproductively and clearly were about to panic. Unmilitary and untrained for combat conditions—how could the authorities have permitted so many of them aboard a capital ship in such unsafe waters?

When he finally shoved his way through to the medical bays, Doctor Yasuma was relieved to see that many of the patients were up on their feet, helping his personnel to close and securely dog the watertight doors. One exceptionally calm patient, ignoring a severe arm wound, informed him that he had been aboard two other ships that had been torpedoed. In this man's unbidden opinion, *Shinano* was in no danger of sinking.[14]

The department was rapidly filling up with incoming wounded and dying men, and Dr. Yasuma moved through the crowded sick bay, trying to ascertain their number. His complement of doctors and corpsmen had begun the task of triage—separating those who would live if treated first from those who were less seriously hurt or beyond help. Some of the seriously injured were already under the surgeons' knives.[15]

As the physician toured this semiorderly chaos, he was also able to assure himself that his department had escaped the immediate consequences of the torpedo explosions. The bulkheads appeared to be in good shape. There was no sign of flooding, and, thankfully, no sign of fire. This section of the ship appeared, for the moment, to be out of harm's way. Shortly after, however, the ship listed farther to starboard. Dr. Yasuma would have to order his people to evacuate their medical facilities. Supplies and instruments cascaded from storage cabinets; sinks spilled over. The angle of the deck was making it impossible to provide treatment to the growing number of wounded men. He directed his medical personnel to begin moving the injured and the disabled up to the relatively safe hangar and flight decks.[16]

Ensign Shoda, the carrier's chief quartermaster, had been enjoying a peaceful nap when a torpedo exploded close enough to knock him out of his bunk.[17] He dashed out of his tight quarters and headed for his battle station at the emergency steering station, choking on the heavy brown smoke and the odor of cordite explosive. He staggered through the dimly visible, suddenly unfamiliar passageways. As he covered the length of one corridor, he noticed that a section of the bulkhead had been peeled back. Ensign Shoda could peer into what had been one of the seamen's quarters. The bodies of many of the sailors, killed in their sleep by a torpedo blast, floated eerily on the surface of the ocean rushing in from a gaping hole in the hull.[18] The ensign climbed to the flight deck, which was covered with

crew members and panic-stricken
the flight deck there was a large
blast of a torpedo, where antiaircr

Despite the sharp list, Ensign S
tion in the after steering room to
standing by at this post, ready in t
the bridge failed. The officer confirm
from the bridge was still operatio
sponding.[19]

This was welcome news for the
vinced that *Shinano* could make i
maintain electrical power. The ens
Nakamura on the bridge through a
steering is fine, sir. What's happeni

The chief navigator replied: "We
starboard side. If we can check the
Keep an eye on steering and let us k
power failure so we can switch to n

Lieutenant Commander Miura,[21]
watch officer, was on duty in port int
when the torpedoes pierced the hull
a shoji screen. He knew immediatel
attacked and wished again—too late
been ordered to sail from Yokosuka
Actually, he had been depressed at
since she had been damaged by the
drydock.

The phones in his watch station
hooks. Battle-damage assessments ca
them began with reports of massive
bulkheads the length of the ship. T
caused finite initial damage, but now th
the seawater cascading through the ope
smashing through one compartment a
hull was resulting in greater destructio

tially co
pressure
expected

Meanwh
denser r
shikan,

The
keep up

Seaman
being e
bowled
when th
head to
force th
room.
whined
his sens
to find
partme

Sea
ately a
Kuroka
and ma
electric
ing. W
wet rag
hot fu
climbe

Captai
No. 1
No. 3
damag
a port

through the bulkhead between the two firerooms the "H" beam had pierced.

"What's your situation, Mr. Inada?" Captain Mikami snapped.

"The flooding isn't too bad here, sir," Lieutenant Inada replied. "But we have to get this pump going. We're also counter-flooding the port outboard voids to correct for the starboard list."

"Good, but we don't seem to be making much headway against the list."

"Yes, sir, I know. The water keeps pouring into *Shinano.* The holes are so big and the water is coming in so fast. We'll keep trying."[26]

The carrier's starboard list had now increased to over 13 degrees, making it even more difficult for the survivors of the submarine's onslaught to carry out their duties. Captain Mikami left the engine room to continue his rounds of gathering firsthand information about *Shinano*'s survivability. He had to walk at an angle and brace himself against the bulkheads in order to stay on his feet.

After the war, Seaman Kanenari informed Japanese author Jo Toyoda of his experience. Toyoda wrote:

At the time *Shinano* shuddered from the impact of *Archer-Fish*'s torpedoes Seaman Kanenari was ordered, along with four other sailors, by Petty Officer Kato to assist in the boiler rooms. The direct passageway to boiler room No. 1, their specific assignment, was filled with water, so Seaman Kanenari and his comrades made their way by first going topside and then going below into the No. 1 boiler room. The new hands were warmly welcomed by the boiler-room chief. The relief men could see why immediately. The bulkhead that separated them from the No. 3 boiler room was bulging from the enormous water pressure behind it.

Already, small streams of water were passing through any tiny cracks or openings. We began helping the boiler men by shoring up the bulkhead with beams and blankets. As we worked we could hear squeaks and shudders from the tortured metal under at least 100 tons of pressure. The rivets were shaking and appeared almost ready to burst free from their holes.[27]

As he worked, Seaman Kanenari thought, "My life will be over in a minute." Fortunately, the officer in the boiler room realized that a bulkhead collapse was imminent and ordered all personnel to evacuate. "As we hurriedly climbed the ladder," he said "I heard the shouted order, '*Sooin,*' that 'all hands' were to assemble on the flight deck. At that moment I knew *Shinano* was going to sink soon."

Seaman Kanenari and hundreds of other officers and seamen responded to the order to go up to the flight deck. Ironically, however, the intended announcement, "*Kooin,*" was directed only to the civilian workers from Yokosuka. Captain Abe wanted the civilians out of the way of the fighting men. However, because of the error in pronunciation, hundreds of men who might have been trapped below now had a chance for survival.[28]

Seaman Kobari, who later made his diary available to Jo Toyoda, had been in the Japanese Navy for only six months when *Shinano* sailed for Kure. Kobari had run to his station in the No. 12 boiler room when the torpedoes struck. Incredibly, the room was already ablaze when he arrived. The asbestos flooring, supposedly unable to burn, was in flames.[29]

"Superior Engineer Sato," he recalled, "ordered us to get sand to smother the flames, but even that wouldn't muffle them. We then saw that crude oil was leaking from a fuel injection nozzle and closed off the pipe to douse the fire."

Seaman Kobari heard Captain Abe announce over the loudspeaker system, when it was still functioning, that *Shinano* would not sink. "But I was so anxious I couldn't even taste the biscuit the messmen distributed to us. We brought in timbers to strengthen the closed hatch of the lower compartment, which was flooding. Although Mr. Sato had also guaranteed that the ship was impregnable, I shivered when I saw the main steam pipe under water. I knew then the ship was doomed."

Seaman Kobori was convinced that the flooding "had to stop our engines. When we were finally ordered topside, the list was 40 degrees. Before we began to climb, Mr. Sato kindly told us to put our socks on over our canvas shoes so we wouldn't slip on the greasy decks."

Seaman Ishii also kept a diary and permitted Jo Toyoda to use it. The youngest sailor aboard at sixteen years of age, he was at his battle station with antiaircraft battery No. 125, 6th Group, when *Shinano* staggered from the enemy torpedoes. "I was napping and crashed onto the deck," he reported. "Chief Petty Officer Matsumoto ordered all gun crews to search for the periscope and to open fire on sight."[30] Seaman Ishii felt that no enemy submarine would show itself to his ship at this point. He wrote:

> Our weapons were useless against an underwater enemy. After a while, when we had our first power failure, our battery group was sent below to the steering room to help manually steer *Shinano*. Even when we pushed with all our strength, we could only turn the rudder five degrees.
>
> Under the dim light from the emergency generator, we looked like half-naked red devils as we toiled at the steering pump normally turned by an electric motor. In the dark, polluted air, the whole place was like Hades itself. When the second generator failed, I almost gave up hope of surviving. Fortunately, we received orders to gather on the flight deck. [Author's note: These orders were delivered personally by Ensign Shoda.] On the way up, someone almost sealed a hatch above me. I believe I was the last one of our group to escape.

In the pumping station far below many decks, Lieutenant Inada and eight enlisted personnel had struggled in vain to pump water from the ship.[31] Now they were trapped in the rising water. Their only escape door had been jammed shut by water pressure. Several of the men began to thrash about in the water and to scream out in terror. The officer's efforts to calm them were useless. For himself, he had no concern, only thoughts to perform his duty in an honorable manner.

Captain Mikami informed him over the voice tube that a rescue team was on its way. The members would try to burn their way into the enclosed compartment with the aid of acetylene torches.

As the water rose higher, forcing the trapped men to tread water or clutch for a hold overhead, Captain Abe spoke to Lieutenant Inada through the speaker tube: "Keep up your spirits, men. Our people are cutting their way into your area from above."

Lieutenant Inada replied, "Thank you very much, sir, but I'm already prepared to die. We're in total darkness down here, and the water is rising all the time. But we'll keep trying to fix the valve as long as we can."

Captain Abe expressed his hopes for a happy ending to their situation and signed off. As the rescue team worked feverishly to cut through the steel plate to Lieutenant Inada's party, *Shinano* listed farther. When the engines stopped and the edge of the flight deck was already awash, the rescue team had to withdraw.[32]

Some five hours after *Shinano* was attacked by the American submarine, Lieutenant Inada called the bridge. Ensign Yasuda was standing by.

"This is Lieutenant Inada in the pumping station. The water is now almost at the top of our compartment. We'll soon be unable to communicate with you. I will not be able to report again."

The doomed officer then asked for the time. Ensign Yasuda replied, "It's 0830 hours, lieutenant."

Lieutenant Inada then shouted his last words into the speaker tube: "I'm going before you, and I will pray for *Shinano* and her company."[33]

Ensign Yasuda relayed the gallant officer's final words and sentiments to Captain Abe, who shook his head sadly. "Lieutenant Inada's courage and that of his men are in the finest

172

tradition of the Imperial Navy. They will all be remembered for generations."

Aboard the destroyer *Yukikaze,* which was steaming off the carrier's port side, Captain Terauchi and Lieutenant Shibata were on the bridge discussing their concern about the radio transmissions detected from the enemy submarine when the torpedoes slammed into *Shinano*'s hull.[34]

In a postwar interview with Jo Toyoda, Lieutenant Shibata would later recall vividly the moment the first torpedo struck *Shinano* on the starboard side. "In fact," wrote Toyoda, "Shibata was staring right at the huge ship when the initial explosion lit up the entire area. The blast illuminated the surrounding expanse of ocean to such a degree that Shibata wondered whether the torpedo actually had hit the port side instead."

A lookout immediately reported to the bridge: "A torpedo has struck *Shinano!*"

Captain Terauchi ordered action stations and prepared for a depth-charge run. Aware that *Shinano* had been hit by at least three more torpedoes, Lieutenant Shibata was surprised that the carrier still maintained speed. Shrugging his shoulders, he figured Captain Abe knew his ship. In any case, *Shinano* was not supposed to sink. Still, he wished Captain Abe would change course and head for shallow water.

Shinano's starboard list worsened to 15 degrees. Over the parts of the public address system that were still functioning came Captain Abe's voice: "I have given orders for *Shinano* to head for Shiono Misaki. Remain at your duty stations. We must correct the list!"

Shinano was still making almost 18 knots. Yet the sea poured into her broken hull. The cries of the wounded and terrified civilian and Korean workers echoed throughout the ship. Now the muffled screams of men trapped by rising water could also be heard at many points within the hull.

The reports of damage-control parties continued to be received and recorded in the log of the damage-control central station, located on the flight deck level of *Shinano*'s island. Each report was relayed immediately to Captain Abe, who had withdrawn with key members of his staff to the steel-enclosed command station on the bridge.

Captain Mikami had rejoined the captain. His examination of the reports confirmed Captain Abe's worst suspicions. The enemy torpedoes had unaccountably torn deep into the interior spaces. *Shinano*'s protective bulges, or "blisters," around the ship's hull had failed to absorb the impact of the torpedoes. They had ripped through those concrete-filled barriers like a sword through butter.

"Bad as it can be, captain," Captain Mikami reported. "Four hits, and three of them struck in the citadel. I just don't understand this damage."

Ensign Yasuda, listening to their conversation, was stricken with a momentary sense of doom. *Komatta na!* The citadel! It was the most heavily protected area of the carrier—her very heart—containing the most essential equipment. Located between frame 70 and frame 186, and extending the width of the ship, the citadel housed the boilers, engines, steering equipment, electronic and communication gear, and the ammunition magazines. The ship's most important functions were implemented from within it.

Soon after the torpedoes hit, Captain Abe called for his chief communications officer, Commander Araki. Together they drafted an SOS message to be sent in the clear, rather than in code, to Yokosuka Naval Station. Taking valuable minutes to encrypt at that point made no sense; the enemy already knew the location of *Shinano*.

"Get it off at once, commander," the captain ordered.

The communications officer gave the message to Chief Radioman Yamagishi, who transmitted it quickly: "SHINANO TORPEDOED AT 0317 X POSITION 108 MILES BEARING 198 DEGREES FROM OMAE ZAKI LIGHT." It was the same position that Ensign Yasuda had reported to the skipper earlier.[35] It was signed off at 0330. The radio communication also served to

174

warn other Japanese ships in the area of the presence of submarines.

By 0420, despite the efforts of the damage-control and repair parties, *Shinano*'s headway had been slowed by the damage inflicted by the torpedoes. As the list to starboard increased, Captain Abe approved the flooding of the port outboard void tanks. For a brief interlude, this counterflooding reduced the list to some 12 degrees.

Toward 0500 a perturbed Captain Mikami reported to the ship's skipper that the civilian workers and the Korean complement had become more of a liability than a help to the crew's efforts to save the ship.

"Our men are mistaking them for ship's officers because of their uniform-type clothes and caps. The shipyard people are panicking and shouting orders, confusing the crew members, who are trying to keep the ship afloat. The men don't know who to obey."[36]

"The panic could become contagious?"

"Yes, sir. We've got reports of men fighting and punching each other to get up ladders. Others are just huddling on the hangar deck, refusing to obey all orders."

Captain Abe shook his head in understanding. "All right, let's get them off the ship. I want them transferred to a destroyer. How many are we talking about?"

"I'd say all 300 of them, sir."

"Fine. Let's get rid of them."

The orders were given for the transfer of the civilian workers, and Captain Abe went down to the flight deck to talk to them before their departure:

"Workmen of the Navy Yard, you have had a most unusual experience. I realize you are not members of the fighting fleet. Still, you should profit by this. You are the ones who built this ship. Now you are seeing her destroyed. You have good reason to understand why you must struggle more diligently at your building tasks. You must work ever harder and do the best you can to build stronger ships to protect Japan and the Emperor. Good-bye to all of you."

The skipper turned hurriedly away to return to his command station high in the ship's island. The moon had set, and a slim hand of pink lay along the eastern horizon. A momentary thought of the doomed carrier *Hiryu*, as ephemeral as the dawn, hovered at the edge of his mind. Surely history was not going to repeat itself?

12. Reflection

Confidential
Subject: U.S.S. *Archer-Fish* (SS-311)--Report of
Fifth War Patrol

November 29, 1944

0312-57   The six hits with a spread can be explained by considering the data as correct; the overall spread from the card for a 600-foot target is 10 degrees and our target, 750-feet long (estimated), is 10.5 degrees at 1,400 yards. The six hits are certain [*sic*].
Breaking-up noises started immediately. With the bright moonlight the identification is quite accurate. The carrier appeared to be similar to the *Hayataka* class except it is believed to have had a raked stern. Perhaps our recco plane over Yokohama has a picture to further identify this one.

0345   Last depth charge. The hissing, sputtering, and breaking noises continued. At one time they covered 90 degrees around the scale on the sound receiver.

Archer-Fish, rigged for depth charges and silent running, hunkered down at a depth of 400 feet in the Pacific and awaited the Japanese onslaught. None of us relished the thought of the enemy's depth charges plummeting into the sea and wafting down on our boat. Most of us had suffered the torments of the damned in other such attacks. We were so inconsequential, and our boat so vulnerable, when confronted by this terror.

God help us now, I whispered. We've done what we had to do; now just let us go home. Victory was sweet, but sweeter still when you were around to enjoy it.

There was a pair of destroyers above us. The churning noises of their screws were clearly audible to us in the conning tower over the sonar gear manned by Radioman Scanlan.

"There's the first one, cap'n," he reported without emotion.

We braced ourselves. There was a muffled blast in the distance. The shock waves hardly moved the ship. I began counting. Within a period of 15 minutes I counted 14 depth charges. Incredibly, none of them even came close to *Archer-Fish*.

"They don't know where we are," I said to no one in particular. "Damned if they don't know where we are."

There was a murmured "Praise the Lord." I didn't recognize the voice, but I echoed the sentiments anyway.

"They're moving away, cap'n," the sonarman reported.

"Probably back to the carrier to pick up survivors," Lieutenant Bunting guessed. "They must be abandoning ship."

"Back to business, men," I said. I looked around the conning tower at every one of them. "Okay, tell me, how many hits did we get?"

One after the other they responded, "Six hits, sir." Chief Carnahan called the forward and after torpedo rooms for their response. Everyone agreed that *Archer-Fish* had scored six hits. Rom Cousins chimed in from below in the control room with the same number.

Six out of six, I thought. Very unusual. Yet all the men confirmed the figure. I knew that when the air or alcohol used to make steam was expended in a torpedo and the propulsive steam fizzles away, the weapon sinks. At a deep depth, the exploder is activated and the igniter normally fires the main charge. The resulting self-destruct, or end of run, blast could unintentionally be counted as a hit on a target.

I turned to one last source, the extremely elated Quartermaster Sykes, our teenage quartermaster, and inquired: "How many hits?"

At first all I could get out of him was: "We hit the bastard! We got enough hits! He'll sink! I know it, he'll sink!"

In his exhilaration, Sykes had forgotten to use his pencil to mark the case of the stopwatch. If he had, we would have been able to determine the range to the target at the time of firing, and the correct number of hits. In essence, I would have been able to determine the identity of the explosions—on or off the target—by the time they had occurred. As soon as I had time, I planned to look at our data more carefully and see what we could establish.

Nearly 20 minutes had passed since Radioman Scanlan had heard the first of what we took to be the carrier's breaking-up noises and the depth-charge attack of the destroyers. Our happiness increased with each of those passing minutes as the sounds of the carrier breaking up were carried to us through the ocean. I was convinced that she must be sinking. How many bulkheads could she have before there were no more to implode? Gradually the sounds grew weaker and more distant. Was she gone?

Whatever, it was time to announce: "Secure from depth-charge attack and silent running."

Archer-Fish vibrated with renewed life. Power was turned back on to heighten our spirits even more. The ventilation fans whirred again, circulating cool drafts. Doors and hatches between compartments were swung open, and the officers and crew shared a heartwarming camaraderie born of the thrills and hazards they had recently experienced in the attack on the big carrier. It was like New Year's Eve in Times Square. The boat echoed with Indian war hoops and rebel cries as the crew exchanged congratulatory backslaps and handshakes. Everyone wore mouth-cracking smiles and flashed "V" for victory signs.

179

Commander Bobczynski made his way toward the bow through the jubilant crew to have the men in the forward torpedo room reload our six empty tubes. We were a most happy ship, although I was beginning to drag a bit by then. Still, I had Bob go through the boat to relay my compliments to the crew for a job well done, and to tell them that if the carrier hadn't already gone down, she would shortly as a result of our torpedoes. Men who had been standing watch all night were now finally to be relieved. We were going to remain deep until daylight in case a destroyer or two were standing by to attack us as we neared the surface.

I began to realize just how tired I was. I hadn't sat down since sunset the previous evening. I also hadn't had anything to eat since the previous noon. But this was no fault of our wardroom steward mates, Bill Brown and Levi Scott. I recalled that they had come to the conning tower several times during the night to ask whether they could fix something for me. At the time, I just didn't have any appetite.

Actually, there wasn't a seat in the conning tower except for the one used by the sonarman. Nothing for me but to sit down on the deck with my feet dangling down the hatch. Boy, I didn't realize how tired I was.

Quartermaster Ed Mantzey looked as though he'd like to join me. "C'mon," I said. "Rest your weary bones." So he duplicated my seating arrangements with his legs swinging in space. We chatted in low tones about the attack.

For a while everyone seemed satisfied with the job accomplished by *Archer-Fish* and had little to say. Mostly, we just kept to our own thoughts. It took too much effort to talk at any length. I wanted very much to take my boat up to periscope depth and look around as soon as it got light enough for good visibility.

"Mantzey," I asked, "will you please work out the time of sunrise. I'd like to be at periscope depth at first light, find out what the hell's going on."

"Yes, sir, cap'n." Off he went. He was back in ten minutes with the time of local sunrise.

"Our dead reckoning position, cap'n, is not very accurate. We didn't take time during the night to maintain a navigation log as accurately as usual. I used 32 degrees north and 137 degrees east as our present position to enter the Nautical Almanac."

"That's fine, Ed." It was accurate enough for our purpose. With all that had happened during the night, it was understandable that the best we had was an approximate dead reckoning position. We had spent all our efforts maintaining position relative to a moving target rather than keeping track of our precise geographical location. With the water thereabouts as deep as it was, and with the distant coast clearly visible, there had never been any danger of going aground.

Mantzey said, "As soon as it's light, cap'n, we'll obtain our position from landmarks."

At about 0610 *Archer-Fish* came up to periscope depth, and I took a careful look around. The sun was rising bright and yellow. The sea, deep blue, was still choppy, with sporadic whitecaps. Visibility was excellent. Not a ship or aircraft could be seen. In no direction could I find any trace of our target. There was not a piece of debris.

"Secure from general quarters," I ordered, and then went below and forward to my cabin. I was exhausted and slipped into my pajamas in about a minute. I fell into my bunk, threw a blanket over myself, and was soon fast asleep. I still had no thought for food.

It was a fatigued but still spirited crew when most of us were able to get some sack time. Just before I fell off to sleep, I had to chuckle again over the story about Carl Wilken, our damage-control repairman, who had gone immediately to sleep the previous evening while waiting to be called if needed during the attack. Carl's slumber was not interrupted until *Archer-Fish*'s initial torpedo was fired and the jolt of it registered throughout the ship. Up he bounded, instantly awake with his tool bag in hand and a curt query: "What happened?"

From way down in the well of my sleep, I felt someone

181

calling me awake. I snapped to immediately. It was a messenger from the control room.

"Cap'n sonar heard—in fact we all heard—a deep rumbling explosion pretty far off. The OOD says to tell you that he thinks it was our target going to the bottom."

"Fine, thanks," I said. I glanced at the clock. 1055. I rolled over and went right back to sleep.

I was up by noon. The ship was at periscope depth, conducting a routine daylight patrol in Area No. 5 of the "Hit Parade" section in Empire waters off the coast of Honshu. Reawakening to such normality, it was difficult to believe that only hours before we had sunk a big enemy carrier.

Chief Yeoman Carnahan had begun to gather data on the attack for submission with our patrol report. We were slightly uncertain about one key detail—the precise geographic position of the target when we torpedoed it. We decided to go with the dead-reckoning position Mantzey had provided earlier in the day.

After lunch Commander Bobczynski, Lieutenant Bunting, Ensign Crosby, and I met in the wardroom to draft our message for Pearl about the attack. We realized that Admiral Lockwood and others would be anxious to hear our news. I wanted it completed, encoded, and prepared to send as soon as we surfaced after sunset.

Our foremost task was to determine how all six of our torpedoes could have scored with a 150 percent spread. We resolved it by drawing a scale sketch of *Archer-Fish* and the target at the time we fired. We concluded that it was possible. If the actual range to the target had been less than 1,400 yards, separation between torpedoes would have been less, making the spread under 150 percent. Since the carrier was not identifiable from our *Recognition Manual,* we had no means of knowing the height of her mast. So the range we had estimated could easily have been too much. I tried not to think about the fact that if young Sykes had used his pencil and stopwatch we would have known how much time it took our torpedoes, running at 46 knots, to reach the carrier. Knowing that, we'd have had an exact fix on the range at the time of firing.

In our report we emphasized that our carrier was not shown in the *Recognition Manual.* All we could report was that it resembled the *Hayataka* class more than any other Japanese carrier listed in the manual. In my patrol report I claimed that *Archer-Fish* had sunk the big carrier, for the following reasons:

· Six certain hits (2 observed).
· Heavy screws stopped and did not restart.
· Loud breaking noises (heard) for 47 minutes.
· Escorts gave us slight attention and closed carrier, probably picking up survivors.

From everything I had heard, I was convinced that U.S. Naval Intelligence would quickly learn the fate of our target. They were exceptionally skilled at intercepting and decoding Japanese radio traffic. While we had not seen the carrier sink, there wasn't the slightest doubt in our minds that she had gone to the bottom. That's what we'd do: claim we sank an enemy ship rather than only damaging her. I knew that should Naval Intelligence learn of the carrier's sinking through their own sources, they could easily support my claim. If they learned that the ship, somehow or other, had not been sunk, they would say there was insufficient evidence to support my claim of a sinking but would still support my claim of damaging an enemy warship.

If my initial claim was only for damaging the ship, on the other hand, and Intelligence later learned through their own sources that she in fact had been sunk, they would not be able then to openly, officially upgrade my claim. Why? Because the loss of big enemy ships was reported in our press. If the newspapers reported that the carrier had been damaged, then later reported that it, indeed, had been sunk instead, the Japanese might begin to wonder how they had come by that information. Logically, they would have to consider whether the Americans could read their coded radio messages.

At 1830 on Wednesday evening, we began sending Pearl the

report of our attack. It was a great feeling to know that I was back on the first team. My attack report was sure to brighten Admiral Lockwood's day. Maybe he'd put my picture on his piano.

When the lengthy message cleared, along with the required weather report for the B-29 bombers, I took a break. I wanted to get my mind off the target for a while. In 1944, Thanksgiving Day—the last Thursday of the month—fell on November 30. The traditional meal of turkey and all the fixings would be served the next day aboard *Archer-Fish*. I looked forward to it. I now had a lot to be thankful for.

Still, I couldn't help wondering exactly what had happened to the huge, unidentifiable carrier I had last seen in my night scope, and whose looming silhouette still plunged toward me in my mind's eye.

13. Extinction

Depending on the size of the holes in her hull, water poured, streamed, or jetted into *Shinano*'s myriad passageways and compartments. As the internal bulkheads gave way, the carrier's topside weight increased inexorably. She groaned like a whale being torn to pieces by sharks.

Within an hour after the torpedoes struck Captain Abe realized that his huge seagoing castle had been significantly breached. The overlapping reports from damage-control and repair parties attested to this. There was little in them to bring him optimism. What was especially depressing were the reports telling of hundreds of crew members trapped by jammed doors, smashed bulkheads and rising water throughout the ship. Most attempts to rescue them had failed, as they had with Lieutenant Inada's party.

The skipper turned to find Ensign Yasuda looking at him. There was a pained cast to the young officer's face, as though he were trying to communicate, in a personal way, his sympathy and loyalty to his skipper. Captain Abe uncharacteristically nodded his head at the ensign, then looked away.

At 0530 another radio message was transmitted[1] to Yokosuka, giving *Shinano*'s position as 72 miles, bearing 113 degrees, from Shiono Misaki. By then *Shinano* had made 36 miles on course 270 degrees from the point where she had been torpedoed by *Archer-Fish*. She was soon limping along at only about ten knots.

No one's concern for *Shinano*'s condition was greater than that of Commander Miura, the engineering officer of the watch, who had been receiving nothing but negative reports by the minute at his watch station in the No. 2 engine room. The flooding was almost uncontrollable. The ship's list was back to 13 degrees. Elements of her huge power plant were still operating, but engineering and machinery officers were expressing doubts about how much longer any of the engine and firerooms could continue to function.

Even after the counterflooding had reduced the list to seven degrees, there was little time to be optimistic. Soon it was reported that the starboard inboard engine room had been hopelessly flooded. *Shinano*'s list increased again, to *20 degrees*. Then came the report that the trimming tanks on the port side could no longer be used to correct the list because their flood valves were now above the waterline. On receiving this information at 0600, Captain Abe ordered his ship's course to be changed from 270 degrees to 300 degrees—northwesterly—in an effort to reach the vicinity of Kii Suido and shallow water. With luck they might be able to beach the carrier at Cape Ushio.

The sun was low on the eastern horizon, rising like a golden disk and pulling the light-blue cloak of the new day into the sky. *Shinano* was exposed, her speed dropping below ten knots.

Commander Miura lit up another one of his ragged Sumatra cigarettes. *Komatta na!* It tasted awful! Just like the others. But what was one to do? This many years into the war, you took your tobacco from wherever you could get it. Too bad Turkey hadn't come in on the side of the Axis Powers. It was then that he learned for the first time that a damage-control party was trapped in the No. 1 fireroom.[2] Their escape seemed impossible. He gave their rescue a key priority for one of his subordinate officers.

Many compartments had flooded due to leaks in the bulkheads and around doors. Because of the urgent order for *Shinano* to depart Yokosuka Naval Shipyard, there had been no time to detect and repair them. Hundreds of gallant officers and seamen fought to halt the water, even though the majority of them lacked the experience or the equipment to make much headway. Bucket brigades were formed to control the flooding, but the water swirled around the men and continued to rise. It was like bailing out a small boat under a waterfall. The buckets were left to sink in the flood waters, and the men began to clamber topside on ladders throughout the ship.

Captain Abe made necessity official at 0800 when he ordered the men on watch in the firerooms and engine rooms to leave their posts and proceed to higher decks. Captain Kono was then ordered to flood the three outboard port boiler rooms[3] in a desperate effort to reduce the ship's list. Captain Abe realized that this action was his last resort if *Shinano* was to be kept from capsizing. His ship was doomed if the list could not be corrected.

The crew sprang to their duty. They turned the series of valves on seawater lines through the bottom of the hull, which allowed the sea to enter the port boiler rooms on the higher side of the ship. As the tons of water filled the spaces, the carrier began to right herself. All too soon, however, she again started to heel to starboard under the weight of the water and that of her steel island.

Radioman Yamagishi was given leave from the radio room to help many of the men who had set up additional bucket brigades to fight the flooding. The brigades became necessary because the ship's pumps were failing at almost every point. "The flooding from the breaches in the hull poured in far more water than could be removed in this way," he later wrote.[4] "Suddenly I had to urinate. But as I made my way to a lavatory, I saw water streaming through the riveted seams in the officers' quarters. I gave up all thought of my errand."

His thoughts actually became fixed on the belief that "there must be some structural fault allowing water to pass through the seams. How else could the rivets become loose? "My resentment was not directed toward our attackers," he wrote, "but toward our headquarters, which had put us in such a predicament."

He hurried as best he could back to the radio room and

reported the flooding through the seams to his superior. The officer suggested "that everyone in the radio room be prepared to abandon our posts at a moment's notice. He directed us to put on our freshest underwear. He said this was the day we might die. When you swim, he said, tuck up the bottom of your shirt into your trousers and tie up your sleeves and cuffs. Since this officer had survived several sinkings, all of us listened to his advice quite closely."

Engineering Petty Officer Ueno,[5] at about 0500, suddenly decided that he also had to urinate. Climbing a ladder to reach a lavatory, he later reported:

> I saw that a watertight bulkhead was swollen as tight as a drum. I realized that we could have massive flooding immediately if she let go. I rushed back to the engine room only to learn that all engineers had been ordered to a lower [sic] deck. Suddenly a new order came, sending us midship. Just as fast, a third order arrived telling us to move topside. When I reached the port antiaircraft gun deck, I was upset to see how far the listing of the ship had progressed. The officer in charge, however, Petty Officer Kurokawa, remained calm, and after calling the roll to be sure none of us was trapped below, he had us dog each hatch securely. I was lucky to survive. I later learned that four of my fellow engineers had been blown to bits when the torpedo struck outside their quarters.

Engineer Petty Officer Itoh was not convinced that *Archer-Fish*'s torpedoes had caused severe damage to his ship. But later, as *Shinano* lost speed, he discovered that the No. 3 outer shaft alley on the starboard side had taken a hit. Two men on duty were killed. Not only was this alley totally wrecked, but the starboard inner shaft alley had quickly filled with live steam and could not be entered. At this point the ship was being driven only by the propellers on the port side.

When the list reached 18 degrees, the ship's freshwater evaporator shut down. If *Shinano* needed boiler water, it could only be distilled from seawater. As the reserve feed water had been exhausted, there was a heated discussion among the officers whether *Shinano*'s boilers would suffer from the use of salt water. At this time, no one believed the carrier was going to sink.

Engineer Itoh said the officers finally decided to use a small tank of fresh water that was located near the bow. Unfortunately, torpedo damage had cut the transfer pipe to the forward section of the ship. So they decided to begin shutting down the boilers rather than use seawater.

When the engines shut down for lack of steam at about 0700, Engineer Itoh was ordered to go topside with his crew at once. He called the roll and then led the men to the upper deck. It was then that he remembered that he was responsible for many valuable possessions his men kept in the ship's safe. On his own and without orders to do so, he made his way through a lengthy section of the ship to the site of the safe, where he removed his men's bankbooks and other key holdings to be returned to them.

By 0900 *Shinano* had lost all power. Headway fell off. Her speed slowed. The huge bow hardly rippled the sea. Serried ranks of waves slapped at her hull. The ocean poured into the openings created by the torpedoes. Soon she was dead in the water, without electricity or steam pressure—little more than a hulk. The escorting destroyers circled around her. *Shinano* now had a list of more than 20 degrees.

With no headway on the ship, movement of the rudder had no effect. Ensign Shoda recognized that the men sent to the steering station to provide emergency hand power were no longer needed there.[6] The station was located in the most remote part of the ship, directly above the rudder. The people there would have no chance to escape when the carrier capsized. Ensign Shoda also recognized that the loyal enlisted men would not leave their assigned duty stations unless directed to do so by an officer in their division.

Telephones were no longer operative because of electrical failure, and the voice tubes on the lower levels had been flooded out. That left only one way to order the men out. He went after them.

He requested the navigator's permission to leave his useless helm and go down to the steering station. Captain Nakamura immediately agreed.

The list of the ship made walking very difficult. The chief quartermaster, Ensign Shoda, descended from the bridge to the hangar deck, crossed to the port side, and walked well aft to the trunk leading to the lower decks. The hatches were all closed tightly for damage-control purposes. He therefore undogged the manhole in each hatch, lowered himself through the opening, and then closed and dogged it again. Because the ladders were no longer vertical, the operation was more difficult than usual. There were five decks in this area.

The men were near exhaustion because since the power failure the motors had stopped, and they had turned the pumps manually, forcing the hydraulic oil to move the rudder. Seaman Ishii, aged sixteen and the youngest man aboard, was in this group.

Their rescuer told them: "Since the telephones [and voice tubes] are out, I have come below personally to tell you that Senior Navigator Nakamura has ordered everyone to go topside to the flight deck. Hurry!"

Ensign Shoda then proceeded through the listing ship to the central gyroscope room, where the men there were also anxiously awaiting the order to go topside. He went in turn from compartment to compartment, passing the word to as many members of the crew as possible. By the time he returned to the flight deck, he saw that the water already covered a large section of the lower deck of the island. At this point the balance of the crew, misunderstanding the captain's orders intended only for the civilian workers, began leaving the lower decks and crowding onto the flight deck. There almost 1,000 or more men milled around, most of them clutching any object that would help them to maintain their balance on the sloping deck. It was then that panic took hold of some members of *Shinano*'s crew.[7] The less experienced men began to jump over the sides. Some drowned, but most of them were able to stay afloat until rescued.

Senior Medical Officer Yasuma watched the fainthearted in

disgust. His sick and wounded had been brought all the way topside to the flight deck, but their position remained precarious due to the ship's list. In the postwar article that appeared in the magazine *Maru* Dr. Yasuma had written:

> There was no other alternative but to jump into the rough sea hoping to be rescued by escorting destroyers. Since there were no means available to rescue those wounded men lying on the flight deck, I went around to look at their faces with a deep feeling of apology. Probably deeply determined in their minds, all of them merely looked back at me with a bow in silence. Overwhelmed by deep sorrows, I could not say a word to them. The skipper stood beside me and looked around his men gathering on the flight deck with a pale face. Then he calmly walked toward the ship's bow. . . . After giving instructions to my men to patiently wait for a chance to be rescued, I climbed down a rope into the sea.

Seaman Sua was attempting to steady himself on the flight deck when Commander Araki ordered him to go below several decks to one of the radio rooms to retrieve several important files.[8] Seaman Sua recorded in the diary he later made available to Jo Toyoda:

> I went below, struggling along because of the terrible list. After I had obtained the stupid files, I noticed graffiti written on the bulkhead. Some of the sayings were patriotic and wished long life to the Emperor and the Imperial Navy. But right next to them were several drawings of our officers with such descriptions scrawled alongside as: "You stupid bastard!" "Officers are no better than drug cans or hatboxes." "Officers have far lower rank than drug cans." [These expletives were puns on the Japanese word *kan*, which means "officer" but is also a homonym for *cans* or *containers*.]
>
> I supposed one of the officers must have harassed the artist unmercifully, but even so, it seemed rather humorous that some sailor had taken the time while *Shinano* was sinking and listing to vent his feelings before hurrying topside. What a tough sort he must have been to linger down there to express humor no one would ever see.

191

Sometime after 0800 Captain Abe sent a semaphore message to *Hamakaze* and *Isokaze* requesting that they approach to take on tow lines.[9] Ensign Shoda shook his head in disbelief as he watched the two battered destroyers approach and assume stations off the bow of *Shinano*. With a combined displacement of some 5,000 tons how could they hope to tow a 72,000-ton carrier flooded with thousands of tons of water?

A pair of two-inch-thick steel cables were relayed to both escorts. Then the destroyers attempted to put on headway. *Shinano* failed to move. Her weight was too much for the small ships. Shortly after, the cables parted. Again they were taken aboard the destroyers, but this time they were secured around heavy gun mounts in an effort to make them hold fast. When the tow was ready for a second try, it was obvious to all that the cables would undoubtedly snap again, injuring many sailors aboard the ships. In addition, *Shinano*'s list was becoming so severe that it appeared she could plunge below any moment. Captain Abe ordered the cables released, and the two destroyers dashed away.

The skipper had allowed himself to pin his hopes on the towing effort. If they had just been able to get her to move through the sea at a few knots, it might have been enough to bring *Shinano* to Cape Ushio. The ship just couldn't sit there, an inviting target for Yankee bombers on their way to Tokyo. He turned to his executive officer, Captain Mikami. "Our situation appears to be hopeless. What else is there that I can do to save *Shinano*?"

Captain Mikami had no answer. From his tours below right after the torpedoing, he was vividly aware of *Shinano*'s torn entrails and the tons of water she took on each minute. He had surmised even then that the ship was mortally wounded. The only question in his mind was how soon she would list to the point where she would capsize.

At about 1000, Lieutenant Sawamoto[10] requested permission from Captain Mikami to take the portrait of the Emperor to safety. The XO spoke to Captain Abe, who granted permission for its removal. Approaching the portrait, the young officer bowed his head in respect and reached up to lift it from

192

the after bulkhead of the bridge. Captain Abe watched him openly; his staff officers did so in a more clandestine manner.

Lieutenant Sawamoto took the portrait to a table covered with scattered blueprints of *Shinano*, where he wrapped it in waterproof paper and canvas and tied the package to his waist. He also attached a life preserver so the portrait would stay afloat no matter what happened to him. Then, because Lieutenant Sawamoto, as a damage-control officer, still had key responsibilities to handle aboard *Shinano*, the esteemed package was handed over to Radioman Yamagishi for safekeeping.

Meanwhile, the destroyers had been positioned alongside *Shinano* for some time in an effort to take aboard her sick and wounded, and to pick up the men who had jumped overboard. The ship's list had increased to 30 degrees. The carrier was fatally stricken. It was time for Captain Abe to give the able-bodied men permission to leave the ship.

"Captain Mikami," he said, "it truly saddens me, but it's time now for the officers and men to leave the ship. To save themselves. Have the order passed to the men as quickly as possible. I want them to have the best possible chance to save themselves."

At no time could Captain Abe bring himself to give the order: "Abandon ship!" How could he abandon *Shinano?*

The order to leave was passed beginning at 1018. With the loss long since of the public address system, scores of men were ordered to pass among the throng, jamming the tilted deck, and relay the captain's command: "You are all released from duty. Save yourselves." Almost immediately, great numbers of the crew began to jump into the sea to join hundreds of others who had done so earlier. Any object that would float was tossed into the sea by the veterans to aid the men in the water or those who fell into it while attempting to board one of the destroyers. There were no lifeboats or rafts for this rescue work.

Aboard *Yukikaze*, [11] Lieutenant Shibata kept up a running account of the ship's rescue efforts to Captain Terauchi, who was then at the helm. Captain Terauchi, viewing the hordes of men trying to clamber across several gangplanks between the ships and the hundreds of others jumping into the sea, said, "Lieutenant, don't pick up any sailors who cry or call for help. Such faint hearts can do our Navy no good. Pick up only the strong ones who remain calm and courageous.

Lieutenant Shibata cringed and said to himself: "What a price to pay for the lack of spirit. How cruel he is."

All the time, *Yukikaze* was dropping lines to the sailors in the sea. Some held on until the men aboard the destroyers could haul them up. Others, too exhausted to help themselves, were abandoned to drown. Far more men fell from the lines and drowned than were rescued.

Within his command post, Captain Abe had ordered all the seamen and petty officers assigned to the bridge and command post to save themselves. "You have performed nobly and gallantly in the service of the Emperor and the Empire," he told them. "Go quickly now with a clear conscience and the realization that you have done your duty to my great satisfaction."

Then he was alone with his staff officers. It was time to make their farewells, and quickly. They hung on to secured tables, chairs, and pipes to maintain their footing.

"Gentlemen, you now have my permission to leave *Shinano*. As I told the men, you too have performed gallantly and with great dedication ever since I first met you. I am very proud of everyone of you. You go with my gratitude for your dedicated service to *Shinano* and myself, but most of all to the Emperor and the Empire. Never cease to believe in Japan's cause and eventual victory. Now go."

Captain Mikami, grasping the back of a chair, was the first to speak for the staff. "Sir, your gratitude and compliments are most welcome. We shall never fail Dai Nippon. But what about you, sir? Surely you will leave the ship with us."

Captain Abe was silent for a moment. "Captain Mikami, staff officers, I shall remain aboard. I take this action alone. I was at Midway and witnessed the decision of Admiral Yamaguchi and Captain Kono not to abandon the *Hiryu*. I have concluded in the years since that their way was correct for a commanding officer. Farewell, gentlemen."

The Japanese officers were too imbued with the samurai tradition and with respect for their superiors to consider arguing against the course decided upon by their captain. One by one they came by on the slanting deck to salute and bid him farewell. Then they lurched and crawled across the command station to the doorway.

To Captain Mikami, *Shinano*'s faithful XO, Captain Abe commended his final words for his family: "Express my shame at the loss of my ship. I alone was responsible. Give them my blessings. They were in my thoughts to the very end. My wife is to remain faithful and diligent in her endeavors on behalf of the Emperor and Dai Nippon. My son is to be raised in the old traditions. Ask them to respect my memory and to pray for me annually in the temple at Yasukuni."

"Sir—"

"You may go now."

After the XO had managed to gain the outside platform and begin his precarious descent to the waterline and an awaiting destroyer, Captain Abe noticed that Ensign Yasuda was still in the command station.

"Ensign Yasuda, you must make your farewell and leave quickly. Our ship will soon be gone now."

Ensign Yasuda attempted to come to attention on the tilted deck but had to grab hold of a pipe with both hands to remain standing.

"Sir, I'd like to maintain the log to the end. With your permission."

Captain Abe sighed. "Ensign Yasuda, once the ship begins to go down, the suction will take everyone still aboard with her."

"I'd like to believe, sir, that there are many compartments that aren't flooded and that *Shinano* will live for hours yet. I'll take my chances, sir. I feel it's important to make all notations properly in the log and that it be preserved for history."

"Yes, of course. You could be right, Ensign Yasuda. Who ever knows the exact moment of his death. *Shinano* could live for hours yet. But I, frankly, am not of that mind."

Captain Abe turned away and made his way outside. Ensign

Yasuda followed close behind. The skipper was staring at the ship's new naval ensign, with its red sun radiating across a field of white. "She's hardly had time to get sprayed with salt. I'd appreciate it if you'd strike *Shinano*'s colors, Mr. Yasuda."

Ensign Yasuda[12] had to crawl up the side of the carrier's island to reach the drooping flag. He lowered it quickly and without ceremony, tying it around his waist. He returned along the side of the island to Captain Abe. Together, the skipper and the ensign clambered awkwardly along the steep incline of the deck toward the bow.

Radioman Petty Officer Yamagishi, the Emperor's portrait tied about his waist, was tossed into the sea when *Shinano* suddenly increased her list. He went deep, but a few sweeps of his strong arms brought him to the surface. He felt the water tugging at him with what seemed a hundred hands. What was happening?

His eyes widened in horror! The carrier's huge elevator, used to raise and lower the aircraft, was wide open, causing an enormous suction that was pulling mobs of sailors into it.[13] Despite their screams and thrashings, a tremendous waterfall pulled them into the huge opening, where they disappeared from view into the maw of the ship. He was certain that he, too, would be sucked into the maelstrom with the other victims. Luckily, he caught on to some loose trash snagged to the flight deck. Holding it fast, he was able to secure his position until he spotted a rope dangling from the flight deck and managed to grasp it. He then climbed across the width of the deck, swung himself over the port railing, and slipped and slid along the port side into the sea.

An expert swimmer, Radioman Yamagishi swam away from *Shinano* as fast and as straight as he could. He didn't want to be anywhere in her vicinity when she sank. Out a good distance, he turned about and threw the dying ship a formal salute. Sighting a two-meter wooden ladder floating nearby, he grabbed hold of it and then pushed it toward a group of enlisted men struggling to remain afloat in the oil-covered water. Each grabbed a portion. Then he spotted Seaman Koguri, whom he had known since coming aboard *Shinano*. He called for him to join them for a share of the ladder.

The young seaman was most grateful. He had seen scores of his teenage shipmates go under screaming for their mothers at the end. He himself had been waiting without a cry for one of the destroyers.

Radioman Yamagishi saw a large piece of lumber bobbing on the waves and grasped it. He invited another group of enlisted men, their faces coated black with crude oil, to grab the board. One of the youngest couldn't swim a stroke. Knowing how to swim was required at Etajima, but not for everyone in the Japanese Navy.

Radioman Yamagishi called to him: "Don't panic. Relax. You'll make it—if you do as I tell you. Don't push the board under. Just cling to it enough to keep yourself afloat. Face leeward."

His small party was finally approached by *Yukikaze,* which moved slowly by, trailing a series of lines to be grasped by the men in the sea. Each line had a loop at the end. The men had only to slip it over their heads and under their arms, then they were hauled aboard.

When Radioman Yamagishi clambered onto the deck of the destroyer, he suddenly realized that he had suffered a severe laceration on his chin. At what point, he couldn't remember. A medical officer quickly stitched the wound without using anesthesia.

Yamagishi yelled, "*Komatta na!* It hurts!"

"Be grateful you're alive to feel the pain," the doctor said.

The injured survivor had to agree. This pain is the only proof I have right now that I'm alive, he thought. It was then that he realized the Emperor's portrait was missing.[14] It had slipped from around his waist when he was in the water. He hurried to report the loss to Captain Terauchi. *Yukikaze*'s skipper flashed a message to her sister ships to be on the lookout for the package containing the portrait. Soon afterward, sailors aboard *Hamakaze* sighted it floating on the oily sea and brought it aboard, still untouched by the seawater.

When Radioman Yamagishi learned that the portrait had

been found and was in good shape, he collapsed in a bunk and fell into a deep sleep.

Seaman Sua was informed by Lieutenant Yokote, the officer in charge of a section of antiaircraft weapons, that he and his mates could abandon ship. He later wrote:

When we were released I went over the port side into the water and immediately got sucked into a huge exhaust vent about three meters below the deck along with many of my comrades. Most of them screamed in vain for help as they disappeared in the swirling water into the bowels of the ship. Just as I was about to give up hope, I managed to seize hold of a wire cable and pulled myself out of the vent and crawled back onto the deck again. This time I jumped into the sea from the bow bulge.

As I floated away from *Shinano*, I seized hold of a big section of lumber. Some of my shipmates were singing to encourage others until we were picked up. When I looked back, *Shinano* was heeled way over to starboard. What an incredible sight! Such a huge ship, and to suffer such a fate. I could see two men still clinging to the bow rail. One was heavy, undoubtedly Captain Abe, and the other was tall and lean. I guessed he was Ensign Yasuda. I prayed that they would get off the ship safely.

Nearby a trio of veteran sailors clung to a long section of shoring timber. A young seaman, who couldn't swim very well, came by spluttering and swallowing water. He begged the old-timers to let him join them. He said his throat was extremely sore from swallowing oil. One of them said, "No! Get away. There's no room for you." When the youngster continued to plead for assistance, one of the veterans punched him and pushed his head under the water. I looked on in shock but could do nothing. The boy suddenly popped up to the surface, spluttering worse than ever. A stream of water gushed from his open mouth. He cried loudly in desperation. I shouted for him to join me on my board. I pushed the board to him. But it was too late. He sank silently and gently beneath the waves. How sad, I thought, but without any real feeling. Death was all around me. Men were dying by the hundreds on *Shinano*. Others were drowning in the oil-coated sea. What was one more death?

Finally the destroyer *Yukikaze* approached our group. The

men on deck shouted to us to put our legs through the loop at the end of a host of ropes they had thrown over the side. They told us not to use our hands, but just get the loop around us, and they'd pull us up. At the time, my stomach was growling from hunger and my body was numb from the cold. I wondered whether I would have the strength to put the loop around my body. I managed to grab a line. I thought I was saved at last. But a group of panic-stricken sailors climbed all over me to seize the line and pushed me under the surface. I went down about a meter or more but found the strength to fight my way back to the surface. I had swallowed a lot of water and coughed and sneezed to get rid of it. I spotted another free line and grabbed it. No legs for me. I put the loop under my arm and waved to the destroyer men. I was quickly hauled aboard, freed from the line, and handed a glass of whiskey. It warmed me immediately. It was *good!*[15]

Aboard *Shinano,* after Captain Abe had bid his farewell to his staff, Ensign Shoda, the chief quartermaster, suggested to Captain Nakamura that it was time they took their leave of the ship. He asked the chief navigator whether he had any preference regarding a good site from which they could jump off the ship. He noted that the sea appeared to be very rough over the port side.

The navigator, however, had no intention of jumping from *Shinano* and said, "I intend to stay with Captain Abe until the end. Please leave the ship by yourself."

The junior officer, respecting the veteran officer's wishes, turned about and crawled toward the bow. Many seamen, hesitant to plunge into the cold water were huddled there in a mass.

Ensign Shoda[16] shouted: "Any people from steering here? Go over the side now. If you don't, you'll probably be sucked under when she goes down. Come on, men. Follow me."

Very few of the sailors moved. They were paralyzed with fear. The ensign pointed to one young seaman clinging to a deck handrail. "C'mon, son, you can go down with me."

The youth blurted out, "I can't swim, sir."

"Don't worry about it. Here, I'll toss down a piece of lum-

199

ber and you can hold on to it and float. I'll pull you after me."

Realizing that the youth was too terrified to move, Ensign Shoda tore his hands from the handrail and pushed him overboard. He then shifted quickly about and threw four more young sailors into the sea in this manner. Then he leaped in after them. A strong swimmer, he ignored the chilling effect of the sea and pushed one young sailor after another to the large section of lumber and ordered them to hold tightly. He began pushing it, kicking his feet.

"C'mon, men. We can make it. Hold on and kick your legs. All together now. We'll make it."

The small party of *Shinano* men moved slowly away from the dying ship, passing through similar groups and lone seamen who were trying to make it to safety. Ensign Shoda's group had propelled themselves almost 200 yards from the ship when the officer heard a tremendous hissing sound. The incredible sound reminded him of an animal's dying breath. He looked about to see *Shinano*'s red hull standing almost straight up, with the bow pointing skyward.

All about him the sailors in the sea were staring back wide-eyed for a final glimpse of their ship and hundreds of their desperate comrades still clutching the rails and decks, awaiting their end in a resigned and benign fashion. In almost one voice, the officer and his rescued seamen called out: *"Shinano, banzai!"*[16]

Commander Miura,[17] nobody's fool when it came to survival and living to fight another day, was swimming away from *Shinano* when he heard a loud, shrill cry. Later he would describe it as a "devil-like cry." He stopped swimming momentarily and treaded water to turn about and watch the ship's final moments. He decided that the drawn-out cry resulted from the sea rushing into the carrier's series of fireroom smoke stacks. They had been empty volcanoes. Now they were receiving their share of the flood waters. They reacted angrily at the impact of the cold sea.

Commander Miura allowed his eyes to sweep along the capsized length of *Shinano*. She was going down by the stern; the great bulbous-nose bow rising higher toward the sky until the ship reared up almost perpendicular to the horizon. He thought that her two bow-anchor chain hawse pipes resembled the gaping eyes of a wounded whale, casting beseeching looks about for assistance. He was surprised at the number of men who were still clinging to her hull, fearful of taking their chances with the Pacific. Others clung to the bilge keel. He knew instinctively that most of them were doomed.

Then, on the very tip of the bow, Commander Miura spotted Captain Abe and young Yasuda. Damn fools, what were they up to? *Komatta na!* They should get their backsides off the fool ship before she took them down into the depths with her. Oh well, life was too sweet for him. He turned away a final time and swam toward a destroyer.

At 1055, as Captain Abe and Ensign Yasuda clung to the railing at the bow, *Shinano* gave another sudden lurch to starboard. The two officers were higher above the surface of the sea as the stern sank lower under the ocean. They were nearly deafened by the hissing noises when the seawater streamed into the ship's funnels. They knew that this cacophony signaled her final plunge to the bottom.

Captain Abe turned to the ensign. "It's time you were away. You've more than done your duty. You have my compliments, young sir. You have the log?"

Ensign Yasuda, his demeanor as serene as his skipper's, replied, "I've got it, sir, securely tied to my waist. If I can't swim away, I'll quickly untie it. It should surface with the flotation device attached."

Captain Abe nodded his understanding. What did it all mean now in any case? The young man's karma was of his own choosing.

Shinano's stern dipped deeper into the ocean, raising the bow in a final salute to the sky. Like a harpoon, she was preparing herself to be launched into the depths. She would hang for a moment as the seawater pounded through her to flood the remaining space, then give one loud, plaintive roar before plunging 4,000 meters to the floor of the Pacific.

When the decisive moment arrived, *Shinano,* shuddering with lost promises, went beneath the surface in a series of explosions, roars of released steam, rending bulkheads, and imploding compartments. Down with her, their hands outstretched to each other, went Captain Abe and Ensign Yasuda. The stricken carrier's suction took them, the entombed living and dying, and hundreds of the men clutching helplessly to her hull and decks, to their deaths.

About a half mile away, Ensign Shoda still bobbed about awaiting rescue. For several hours since abandoning the ship, the ensign had suffered the ravages of the cold sea and fatigue, the loss, one by one, of his young sailors, and the shock of witnessing the demise of his ship. Finally he was spotted by a destroyer that threw him a line. He slipped the loop over his head and under his arms. As the voices of his rescuers shouted their encouragement, he passed out. He was brought aboard and revived.

At 1400, when *Shinano* had been lying for more than three hours in a rush of massive bubbles on the bottom, all rescue attempts of survivors ceased. The division commander, Captain Shintani, directed that the following message be transmitted to Imperial Japanese Navy Headquarters, Yokosuka Naval Shipyard, and to the base at Kure:

"OUT OF 2,515 PERSONNEL ABOARD SHINANO, MISSING, 1,435; SURVIVORS, 1,080. SURVIVING OFFICERS, 55; COMMON SEAMEN AND NONCOMMISSIONED OFFICERS, 993; CIVILIANS, 32. THE EMPEROR'S PORTRAIT IS SECURE ABOARD HAMAKAZE. ALL SECRET DOCUMENTS SANK WITH THE SHIP IN A LOCKED SAFE IN 4,000 METERS OF WATER."[18]

Shinano, the world's greatest aircraft carrier, sank 17 hours into her maiden voyage on Wednesday, November 29, 1944, at 33 degrees, 07 minutes north and 137 degrees, 04 minutes east —or 65 miles southeast of the nearest land.

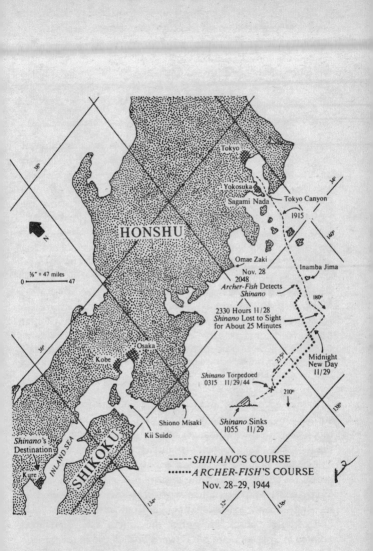

N

3/8" = 47 miles
0 ——————— 47

Tokyo

Yokosuka
Sagami Nada

Tokyo Canyon
1915

HONSHU

Inamba Jima

Omae Zaki
Nov. 28
2048
Archer-Fish Detects
Shinano

180°

2330 Hours 11/28
Shinano Lost to Sight
for About 25 Minutes

Osaka

Kobe

275°

Midnight
New Day
11/29

Shinano Torpedoed
0315 11/29/44

210°

138°

Shiono Misaki

Kii Suido

Shinano Sinks
1055 11/29

Shinano's
Destination

INLAND SEA

SHIKOKU

Kure

----- *SHINANO*'S COURSE
•••••• *ARCHER-FISH*'S COURSE
Nov. 28-29, 1944

203

14. Victory

Confidential
Subject: U.S.S. *Archer-Fish* (SS-311)—Report of
Fifth War Patrol

November 29, 1944
2000 Notified [B-29] strike is on for tonight.

November 30, 1944 (Thanksgiving Day)
0551 Quick dive.
1718 Surfaced.

December 1, 1944
0554 Made quick dive in vicinity of attack.
0650 Sighted one trawler and one sub chaser.
      Probably looking for survivors, which is
      our intent. Ship contact No. 5.

Archer-Fish passed an uneventful evening patrolling on the surface on Wednesday, November 29, 1944. The nearly full moon cast a resplendent silver hue across the sea and provided the lookouts with excellent visibility. It was a scene of remarkable beauty and gave us the sense that we were on a moonlight cruise rather than a wartime mission.

By then I had determined why torpedo No. 5 had fired on its eight-second schedule although Commander Bobczynski had ordered "check fire" after the fourth fish. The finger pointed at Torpedomate 2/c Edward F. Zielinski in the torpedo room. He was assigned the responsibility of hand-firing the forward torpedoes in the event any failed to leave the tubes when fired electrically by Chief Carnahan in the conning tower.

Zielinski was concentrating so intently on the fact that all six torpedoes in the forward tubes were set to fire every eight seconds that the order to check fire didn't register in his mind until after he had pushed the firing valve at his station. After the attack he was deeply apologetic, but we assured him that no harm had been done. All six torpedoes had hit the target—or so we believed at the time. In fact, "Ski's" torpedo was the fourth, and last, to hit *Shinano*.

Thursday, November 30, 1944, was a peaceful Thanksgiving Day. We were back on our lifeguard station, but no B-29 raids were scheduled. We patrolled Area No. 5 at periscope depth. Through the scope I could distinctly observe the Japanese sacred Mount Fuji, its snowcapped peak crisply outlined against the blue sky.

Our cooks had provisioned well before we left on patrol in anticipation of preparing a memorable holiday dinner. They literally served us everything from soup to nuts. I carved the turkey for *Archer-Fish*'s officers at the table in the wardroom. We also had dressing, yams, creamed onions, and peas. Our baker had made fresh rolls and pies. We also had frozen strawberry shortcake with whipped cream. There were the usual ice cubes for our drinking water and linen napkins in the wardroom.

During the day I gave some thought—and I'm sure everyone else on board did also—to the hundreds of thousands of our fellow Americans and Allies in the Pacific, fighting a horrible war in swamps and jungles. We shared their hatred of the war and the earnest hope that the fighting and dying would soon be over.

Nothing of significance occurred during the remainder of *Archer-Fish*'s fifth war patrol. On December 15 we returned to Guam for our ship's refit. We moored alongside the submarine tender *Sperry* to receive a hero's welcome. The senior submarine officers on Guam were on hand to welcome us and offer their congratulations. Ray Anthony's band was there to provide us with some upbeat musical renditions. Crates of fruit were ready to be pounced upon by men who seldom saw such treats on patrol. Best of all, on the pier there were bags of mail from home. We looked forward to some pleasant reading.

Commander John Corbus, a longtime friend and the former skipper of the submarine *Bowfin,* was the first to come aboard. We welcomed each other warmly, and he offered his compliments to the crew for their victory. John, who was the operations officer for the local Subordinate Command, got me off to the side after a while and asked how sure I was that our target had been a carrier. I told him that there was absolutely no doubt. I was positive it had been a carrier but did not know which one because it was different from any included in the *Recognition Manual.*

Then came the shocker.

"I'm sorry, Joe, but Navy Intelligence won't support your claim that you sank a carrier. They're saying there wasn't any carrier in Tokyo Bay, so how could you have sunk one?"

For a moment I looked at him in disbelief. Our moment of glory now seemed very fleeting.

"Will you settle for a cruiser?" John said. "There was some indication of a new enemy cruiser being at sea."

Irritated, I said, "Hell no, John." I repeated my earlier claim and told John how I had got a clear view of the warship in my scope. "I know it was a carrier." I mentioned the rough sketches I had made of the ship's island, bow, and stern during the approach to help my fire-control party identify her. Hell, I wouldn't make up something like that.

I reiterated, "It was a bright, moonlit night, John. I could see it clearly."

"What about the sketches, Joe?" he inquired with a flicker of interest. "Do you have them? I could attach them to your patrol report. They could help us get this matter straightened out."

"I'm not sure, John. I mean they were rough as hell. I'm no Michelangelo. I did them in just a few seconds between periscope observations. Hell, I just don't know. Like I said, they weren't any help to us in identifying the son-of-a-bitch."

John shook his head in obvious disappointment. "They would've been a big help, Joe."

Talk about timing, I had a sudden brainstorm and requested Quartermaster Ed Mantzey to join us. "Mantzey," I said as he came up and reported, "do you have any idea what happened to those rough drawings I made of the Japanese carrier?"

"Yes, sir," he responded. "I have them. I took them out of the trash can where you threw them. They're with the charts in the conning tower. Do you want me to get them?"

Good old Ed Mantzey. God bless him. He was back in a few minutes with the sketches, which I handed over to Commander Corbus. John studied them while I explained their meaning.

"These are great, Joe," he said. "I'll forward them with your patrol report. Let's see what happens."

That was the last I saw of them. They were never reproduced. Later I asked Mantzey how he had happened to save them. "Easy, skipper. When I joined the Navy I was told never to throw anything away. You never know when it might come in handy."

The silhouettes helped to confirm our claim. When Naval Intelligence saw them, they forgot about the cruiser. With the exaggerated clipper bow, it was determined that our target was the "missing" third battleship of the *Yamato* class. On the day she sank, our people had intercepted an enemy radio message reporting: "*Shinano* sunk." At the time they thought she was a cruiser named for the Shinano River rather than a converted battleship named for the Shinano prefecture of old Japan.

Eventually *Archer-Fish* was given credit for sinking a carrier of 28,000 tons in our patrol report endorsement. I thought the carrier was larger than that, based on comparisons to the size of the destroyers escorting her. However, my estimate fell short of the kind of factual evidence needed to justify a revised assessment. I was happy enough about the outcome: 28,000 tons put our carrier at about the size of such big U.S. carriers as *Essex* and *Yorktown*. [1]

Archer-Fish remained in Guam for refitting until January 10, 1945, when we sailed on her sixth war patrol to the Luzon Straits and the South China Sea. On this patrol, I was in command of a small wolf pack of three submarines: *Archer-Fish*, *Batfish*, and *Blackfish*. Commanders Jake Fyfe and Mike Sellars were the skippers of *Batfish* and *Blackfish*, respectively. In a period of three nights, *Batfish* sank a trio of surfaced enemy submarines and *Archer-Fish*, following a two-day hiatus, got another one, identified many years later as a 277-ton, army-built in secret from their navy to avoid its appropriation. The Japanese army operated it as a logistic sub used to feed troops on bypassed islands. We completed this patrol on February 19, 1945, at Saipan.

My ship was then ordered to San Francisco via Pearl, and we arrived on March 13, 1945. *Archer-Fish* was at Hunter's Point Naval Drydock for a major overhaul until June 14, when we departed for Pearl, arriving on June 22. Many of our old hands had left and were replaced by new men. *Archer-Fish* sailed on her seventh and last war patrol on July 10. She returned to her old hunting grounds in the waters off the main Japanese island of Honshu. There were many moments during that patrol when I thought of the broken hulk of *Shinano*. Now and again we passed over the approximate site where she lay, thousands of feet below, on the bottom. I still thought of her as only a target, and not about the men who had perished when she sank.

We were on a lifeguard station for Admiral Halsey's third fleet when the first atom bomb was dropped on Hiroshima on August 6 and the second one on Nagasaki two days later. We heard the radio reports but didn't comprehend the full significance of their impact until later. I decided at the time, with the information available, that they had been a necessary evil because of the much greater loss of lives both sides would have suffered if the war had continued.

Early on the morning of August 11 *Archer-Fish* had her last contact with the enemy. Sonar pinging was detected by us, probably from a submerged Japanese submarine. At that stage of hostilities, with surrender expected momentarily, I had no desire to take either offensive or defensive action. Let someone else fire the last shot of the war; I wanted to bring *Archer-Fish* and her crew safely home. We dived and evaded the confrontation.

On August 16, two days after Japan surrendered, I enthusiastically complied with Admiral Halsey's message to the fleet to "splice the main brace." Of course, liquor is not permitted aboard fighting ships. But the intent of the admiral's message was very clear and quickly comprehended, and *Archer-Fish* complied smartly.

Accordingly, I broke out a part of the supply of medicinal bourbon in its miniature bottles. As each of the watch sections came off duty at 1200, 1600, and 2000, I greeted the men in the crew's mess and offered them a toast: "To victory, a speedy return home, and lasting peace!"

No toast was ever more welcome.

EPILOGUE

Commander Enright and the crewmen of *Archer-Fish* had an opportunity at the time of the Japanese surrender to view the huge graving dock No. 6 at Yokosuka Naval Shipyard in which *Shinano* had been built. Their ship was one of 12 submarines assigned to enter Tokyo Bay with the United States Fleet for the surrender ceremonies aboard the U.S. battleship *Missouri* on September 2, 1945.

Arriving 48 hours early, Commander Enright received permission for his party to go ashore and visit the town of Yokosuka and the adjacent shipyard. There were few Japanese about, so the Americans were unable to confirm their suspicions that the largest drydock was their victim's building berth. Confirmation of this did not come until considerably later.

Following the memorable entrance of the fleet into the Bay, *Archer-Fish* moored with her sister submarines next to the tender *Proteus,* about a mile from the anchored *Missouri.* Vice Admiral Lockwood, COMSUBPAC, was the only SUB-FORCE official invited aboard the battleship for the surrender. Once General Douglas MacArthur signed the documents, an armada of U.S. carrier-borne planes swept over the fleet at low levels and with an exuberant roar of victory.

As a restored member of the first team, Commander Enright joined the other sub skippers and their officers as the guests of Admiral Lockwood in the recently expropriated and renamed U.S. Submarine Officers Club at Yokosuka. The admiral had pulled out all stops to provide entertainment, food, and drink for his officers. In a brief talk he reminded them that the drinks were the ones he had been promising his people for years—"just as soon as we whipped the Japanese."

The war was over, but Commander Enright would remain in the United States Navy for another 18 years. He was promoted to the rank of captain on January 1, 1952. Whenever possible, he sought assignments with the submarine service, serving successively in a series of more responsible posts. His final submarine billet was as chief of staff to Rear Admiral F. B. Warder, commander, Submarines, Atlantic Fleet.

At other times Captain Enright served in the Office of the Chief of Naval Operations and assisted the U.S. delegation as the naval adviser at the signing of the Japanese Peace Treaty. At the direction of Vice Admiral Arleigh Burke, he obtained congressional approval for the transfer of 16 landing craft in reserve to Japan as patrol craft in its new Maritime Defense Force. On July 21, 1959 he was given command of U.S.S. *Boston* (CAG 1), the world's first missile cruiser. One year later Captain Enright reported for another tour of duty with the chief of Naval Operations. His 30-year career ended on July 1, 1963, when he was released from active duty and placed on the Retired List.

With warm memories of New England and the many friends they had in the region, the Enrights purchased a spacious home adjacent to an eight-acre pond in Dover, Massachusetts. Shortly afterward, Captain Enright was employed by the Navigation Department of Northrop Corporation in the neighboring town of Needham. Until 1970 he was primarily involved with the development of the Omega Long-Range Navigation System.

The Enrights' only child, Joe Jr., graduated from the U.S. Military Academy at West Point and became a career officer. He served in the professional Army for 20 years, including two tours of duty in Vietnam, where he won numerous decorations. Colonel Enright's only son, Lieutenant Michael Enright, earned an Annapolis degree and is today a flying officer aboard the aircraft carrier *Nimitz*.

After the war the Joint Army-Navy Assessment Committee reviewed the Japanese records and determined that *Shinano* was the largest ship sunk by a submarine. The Japanese listed her at 69,000 tons, and the committee confirmed her at 62,000 tons.

The initial information Captain Enright received of *Shinano*'s great size was a copy of a message reporting the foregoing details, mailed to him in January 1946 by his friend and classmate Bob Keating, who was on submarine duty in the Pacific. At the time, Captain Enright was assigned to the Naval Academy as a marine engineering instructor.

In that same year, the United States Technical Mission to Japan gathered information from surviving Japanese naval personnel and listed *Shinano*'s full-load displacement at 70,755 tons. For the pursuit and sinking of *Shinano,* Commander Enright was awarded the Navy Cross by Secretary of the Navy James Forrestal. In the accompanying citation *Shinano*'s tonnage was listed at 72,000 tons, making it the biggest warship in history to be sunk by a submarine. *Archer-Fish* was awarded a Presidential Unit Citation.

Any attempt to record the history of *Shinano,* as well as her two sister ships, *Yamato* and *Musashi,* was hindered by the fact that the official documents relating to their construction and filed in the Imperial Naval Technical Bureau at Ofuna were destroyed prior to the surrender. Details are derived from the memory of surviving naval personnel.

The material on *Shinano* that is most readily available and appears to be most authentic is contained in "*Shinano:* The Jinx Carrier," an article researched and written by Lynn Lucius Moore, Journalist 2/c, U.S. Navy. It was published in the February 1953 issue of *Naval Institute Proceedings.*

In his article Mr. Moore states that *Shinano*'s armored flight deck made her "the heaviest warship ever constructed." This supports information in "The Imperial Japanese Navy" by A. J. Watts and B. G. Gordon, which lists *Shinano*'s full-load displacement at 70,755 tons and *Musashi*'s and *Yamato*'s at 69,988 tons. The conflicting data regarding the trio's individual tonnage probably resulted from the fact that both *Musashi* and *Yamato,* after being damaged in separate submarine attacks, were outfitted with further interior protective armor. Thus, depending on the war year, these ships displaced different tonnages.

Shinano's survivors were taken by Captain Shintani's destroyers to Mitsuko Island in Kure Harbor. Landing at about 1700, November 30, 1944, they were confined to barracks that had been previously used as a quarantine station to isolate bearers of infectious diseases. Similarly, no shore leave was granted the crews of the destroyers. The Japanese Navy intended to keep *Shinano*'s existence and loss from the general public.

On December 28, 1944 a group of about 30 surviving officers and chief petty officers were ordered to proceed to the Imperial Navy Ministry in Tokyo to testify in a top-secret investigation into the reasons for *Shinano*'s loss. It was referred to only as the "S Investigation"—"S" for *Shinano.* Vice Admiral Gunichi Mikawa and 12 other high-ranking officers comprised the investigating board.

It was later learned that the officers of *Shinano* resented the tone of the board's questions. The manner of the interrogating officer gave them the impression that they had been prejudged and found responsible for the sinking.

Ensign Shoda,[1] for one, when called to testify, said later that he felt like a defendant under indictment. He was hit with a barrage of questions and hardly given time to reply to one before another was thrown at him. Listening to the interrogation of his fellow officers, his resentment of the bureaucracy became so great that his fists trembled and he had to hold them tightly against his thighs. He disclosed that his one burning thought was that "those who are truly responsible for *Shinano*'s being attacked and sunk are trying us here today."

Admiral Mikawa's board prepared only five copies of a highly classified and voluminous report of its proceedings and findings. One copy was made available to Commander M. Chihaya, who was a staff officer, Operations, Imperial Japanese

Combined Fleet Headquarters, and a veteran combatant. Thirty-six years later, Commander Chihaya would recall that the report apportioned the blame for *Shinano*'s loss widely among "the builder, her crew, and the Yokosuka Naval Station Headquarters, which had been in charge of her steaming operation."[2]

Inasmuch as so many parties were considered at fault in the disaster, none received any further punishment. The report, with its mass of testimony and wealth of details about *Shinano*'s construction and final hours, was never to be scrutinized by the triumphant Americans. In the brief interval between the war's end and U.S. occupation, the Imperial Japanese High Command ordered all official documents destroyed. Among them were the five copies of the "S" board's report. Included, too, was Ensign Yasuda's salvaged log of the *Shinano*.

As for *Shinano*'s officers, it was recalled, their one serious error resulted from the engineers' belief that the pumping valves had malfunctioned, causing the inability to correct the carrier's list. In fact, *Shinano*'s list to starboard made the port Kingston Valves rise above sea level, making it impossible for them to draw the water necessary to counterflood and balance the ship. Even with perfectly functioning pumping valves, the engineers could not have righted the ship. The water was just not available.

Meanwhile, the majority of *Shinano*'s survivors wintering on Mitsuko Island near Kure, the initial destination of their ship, had received new orders. Many were dispatched to the Philippines and to Okinawa to assist in last-ditch battles. Others were sent as replacements to aircraft carriers still with the fleet. A sizable group was transferred to the superbattleship *Yamato*.

Yamato was then the last of the surviving sister ships after the loss of *Musashi* in the battle for Leyte Gulf on October 24, 1944, and of *Shinano* by *Archer-Fish* on November 29, 1944. Both *Yamato* and *Musashi* had been units of the Imperial Navy's Center Force, which had been sighted on October 23 in Palawan Passage approaching Leyte Gulf. Admiral William F.

Halsey, informed of the sighting by the submarines *Darter* and *Dace,* launched his counterattack the next day.

Hundreds of U.S. aircraft from the carriers *Intrepid, Cabot, Essex, Lexington, Franklin,* and *Enterprise* had assailed *Musashi* beginning at 0810 and continuing through 1600 on October 24. At least 19 torpedoes and 17 bombs hit *Musashi,* which flooded and capsized at 1935. Rear Admiral Toshihira Inoguchi, *Musashi*'s commanding officer, and more than 1,000 seamen, went to the bottom with her. *Yamato* had fled north to fight another day.

In April 1945 the Japanese formed a "Special Surface Attack Force" to assault and destroy U.S. task forces and convoys in the waters around Okinawa.[3] The force consisted of the battleship *Yamato;* a cruiser, *Yahagi;* and eight destroyers, including the late *Shinano*'s escorts, *Isokaze, Hamakaze,* and *Yukikaze,* which were still under the command of Captain K. Shintani. If they reached Okinawa they were to use their guns to help the Imperial Army troops battling the American GIs and Marines ashore.

No air cover was available to protect this force. Japan's remaining air squadrons and kamikaze pilots had already been sent ahead to attack the U.S. invasion fleet. The personnel aboard the force's ships had few illusions about the likelihood of their reaching Okinawa. There were reports that a massive American battle fleet had encircled the embattled island, eagerly anticipating the force's arrival. Yet the Japanese seamen were in full agreement that their brothers-in-arms ashore deserved every possible assistance. It would be unconscionable for ships of the Imperial Fleet to lie at anchor in the Inland Sea when there was so much need for their guns. (For some years after the war, there were reports that the ships of this force, particularly *Yamato,* were provided with only enough fuel for a one-way trip to Okinawa. Such reports were erroneous; *Yamato* had been fueled to 63 percent of capacity before her departure.)[4]

The superbattleship was loaded with a full supply of all types of ammunition, including fused antiaircraft projectiles for the

18.1-inch guns of her main battery. *Yamato* was almost to her full-load displacement when she sortied through the Bungo-Suido Channel from the Inland Sea into the Pacific on the evening of April 6, 1945. Aboard were 3,332 officers and men.

The departure of the force was sighted and reported by Captains Jack Foote and Fred Janney of the U.S. submarines *Threadfin* and *Hackleback*. Neither was positioned to attack *Yamato*, but their reports were received by Admiral Spruance of the Fifth Fleet. His command consisted of Vice Admiral Morton L. Deyo's Task Force 54, Gunfire and Covering Force, and Vice Admiral Marc A. Mitscher's Task Force 58, Fast Carrier Force. When Admiral Mitscher, aboard the carrier *Lexington*, made the initial contact, Admiral Spruance granted him the honor of commencing the attack.

It was no contest, yet the Japanese ships died hard. Coordinated swarms of some 400 aircraft flying from six carriers launched their initial assault at 1230 on April 7, loaded to capacity with bombs and torpedoes. The torpedo-armed planes concentrated on *Yamato*, specifically on the port side in an effort to make her capsize. Seven torpedoes hit home; two others struck on her starboard side. There were also two or three "probable" hits on the port side. The exact figure is unknown because of the conflicting reports provided by four surviving Japanese naval officers and the attacking aircraft. *Yamato* was fatally holed. The ocean surged into the hull, and she capsized at 0225. When she plunged to the bottom, all but 269 of her crew died with her.

The cruiser *Yahagi* and three destroyers were also sunk in the U.S. aerial onslaught, among them two of *Shinano*'s escorts, *Isokaze* and *Hamakaze*. The dead included Captain Shintani. The few surviving Japanese ships included the *Yukikaze*, skippered by Commander Terauchi. With a reputation throughout the fleet for her invincibility, *Yukikaze* was still afloat at the surrender. She was turned over to the Nationalist Chinese as a war reparation and remained on active duty with the Chinese Navy until 1971.

Mrs. Toshio Abe had just returned from shopping and was alone in her home at Kamakura when a messenger arrived from the Navy Ministry on December 14, 1944.[5] As she peered out through the doorway at the officer standing on the porch, she knew the news could only be bad. The messenger was wearing white gloves. Mrs. Abe recalled that an admiral's wife had once told her that when such a messenger arrived, he had the duty to present the Empire's condolences.

After she had brought the officer into her small living room, he informed her with great formality: "It is with the deepest sympathy that I must tell you that our Captain Abe died in action on 29 November 1944. Please keep this information secret until the government publicly announces what has happened."

After being informed of her husband's death, Mrs. Abe sold her home in Kamakura and moved with her son, Toshihiko, to the Tokyo suburb of Koganei. To support herself and the boy she found employment in a factory and later as a maid. She never told anyone that she was the widow of an admiral. (Japanese officers were promoted to the next highest rank when killed in combat.) The general public, following the surrender, blamed the officer caste for leading Japan into disaster.

There was no money to finance a college education for Toshihiko, but he remembered his father's last words—relayed to Mrs. Abe by Commander Araki and other surviving officers of the war—and worked diligently for years with a German trading firm. Later he was employed by a Japanese electronics company. He now lives in London with his wife and their three children.

By 1981 Mrs. Abe was leading a quiet life in retirement in Koganei. Each year she attends a reunion in Nagano Prefecture of the families who lost relatives aboard *Shinano*. She also sets aside time to make an annual pilgrimage she has never failed to keep—to the Temple in Yasukuni, where the spirits of fighting men lost in battle are enshrined. There she pays her respects to the dead and prays for the soul of the lost skipper of *Shinano*.

No white-gloved messenger brought the news of Ensign

Yasuda's death to his parents until February 27, 1945, and then they were left to mourn without any details. (None was forthcoming until after the surrender.) The ensign's superior officer, Navigator Nakamura, faithful to his vow, was also listed among the dead.

The U.S. Submarine *Archer-Fish*, which had been launched on May 28, 1943, and commissioned on September 4, 1943, at Portsmouth, New Hampshire, Navy Yard, had lengthy periods of service following World War II. However, she was first decommissioned from June 12, 1946, until March 7, 1952, and again from August 1952 until July 1957. (Ships of the U.S. Navy are placed in reserve status when there is no current need for them, but they are capable of future active service. All machinery and equipment are placed in first-class condition, and spare parts are brought up to inventory specificiations. The flag is lowered, the crew detached, and the ship assigned to a shore-based unit. Silicon gel, an absorbent material, is used throughout the interior to reduce humidity and retard rusting, and then the ship is sealed airtight. As a result of this "mothballing" procedure, these ships can be returned to active duty in a very brief time.)

Ironically, in 1963 *Archer-Fish* was berthed for three weeks at the U.S. Navy Shipyard in Yokosuka, *Shinano*'s birthplace, to undergo an upkeep. At the time, she was participating in a two-year hydrographic survey called "Operation Sea Scan," which took her to seaports throughout the Far East and Australia. Because of her extended cruises all of her crew were bachelors. She was decommissioned for the last time on May 1, 1968. Later that year the Navy decided that the nuclear submarine *Snook* (SSN-592) should test an advanced torpedo by attacking a realistic target. *Archer-Fish* won the toss and was taken into the waters off San Diego, California. *Snook* fired, and the direct hit broke *Archer-Fish* in two. The gallant submarine, which had been awarded the Presidential Unit Citation for her fifth patrol, sank to the ocean floor. Her end seemed somehow more fitting than the scrap heap to which so many of her World War II sister submarines had been consigned.

As for the huge adversary *Archer-Fish* now joined at the bottom of the Pacific, the report of the U.S. Technical Mission to Japan in 1946 recorded that *Shinano*'s torpedo protection system had been inadequate. Specifically, the report contended that the joint between the eight-inch-thick antiprojectile armor on the hull and the antitorpedo armor on the underwater body of the hull was of poor design. *Archer-Fish*'s four torpedoes, set to run at a depth of ten feet, exploded with deadly consequences along this joint.

In addition, the report noted that horizontal transverse H-beams had been installed near the overhead in the firerooms to provide support for the fore and aft bulkheads. The force of the torpedo explosions on the starboard side turned the H-beam in the No. 3 boiler room into a battering ram that punched massive holes into the attached bulkhead and flooded the No. 1 boiler room.

The Mission's report includes this observation: "Of all naval catastrophes, from the Japanese point of view, the loss of *Shinano* was most depressing. The third and last of the super warships, she was sunk on the second day of her maiden cruise, by only four submarine torpedoes. The shock which went through the Japanese Naval Ministry is better imagined than described."

NOTES

Foreword

1. Admiral Clarey's last assignment while on active duty was Commander in Chief, United States Pacific Fleet. While commanding officer of the U.S. Submarine *Pintado,* then Commander Clarey sank the 19,262-ton *Tonan Maru No. 2* on August 6, 1944. She had previously been a whale factory ship and was later converted to an oil tanker. She was the largest merchant ship in history to be sunk by a U.S. submarine (Theodore Roscoe, *U.S. Submarine Operations in World War II,* 356).

2. Ibid., 491.

3. Naval History Division, Office of Chief of Naval Operations, *U.S. Submarine Losses, World War II,* Introduction, 1.

4. Commander John D. Alden, *The Fleet Submarine in the U.S. Navy,* 261. Early in the construction period, the Navy Department inserted a hyphen in *Archer-Fish.* The crew continued this practice, in spite of a later change, as a matter of distinction.

5. Ibid., 105. *Archer-Fish* (SS-311) was a fleet submarine of the *Balao* class. Her length was 311 feet 9 inches, and her beam was 27 feet 3 inches.
   Displacement: Surfaced 1,525 tons standard. 2,010–2,075 tons normal. Submerged 2,415 tons.
   Operating depth: 400 feet
   Torpedo load: 24 max.
   Cruising range: 11,000 miles at ten knots
   Fuel capacity: 116,000 gallons diesel oil.
   Patrol endurance: 75 days

6. Roscoe, *U.S. Submarine Operations,* 250–260.

7. All Japanese names are given in the Western manner: that is, given name and then family name, rather than the Japanese style of family name first.

8. Jack Sweetman, *American Naval History: An Illustrated Chronology,* 202.

Prologue

1. A. J. Watts and B. G. Gordon, *The Imperial Japanese Navy,* 68–72.

2. James C. Fahey, *The Ships and Aircraft of the United States Fleet,* Victory Edition, 4.

3. Baron Burkard von Mullenheim-Rechberg, *Battleship Bismarck: A Survivor's Story,* 21.

4. Watts and Gordon, *The Imperial Japanese Navy,* 68.

5. John Deane Potter, *Yamamoto: The Man Who Menaced America,* 29.

6. Watts and Gordon, *The Imperial Japanese Navy,* 68.

7. Ibid., 69.

8. Ibid., 72.

9. Ibid., 70.

10. Potter, *Yamamoto,* 5.

11. Tom Tompkins, *Yokosuka: Base of an Empire,* 32.

12. Joint Army-Navy Assessment Committee, *Japanese Naval and Merchant Ship Losses During World War II by All Causes,* Table II, page vii.

13. Masataka Chihaya, Letter to author, 25 June 1980.

14. William H. Garzke and Robert O. Dulin, Jr., *Battleships: Axis and Neutral Battleships in World War II,* 99.

15. Norris McWhirter, *Guinness Book of World Records 1986,* 334.

16. Lieutenant Commander (medical) Takamasa Yasuma, "Shinano Sunk on Her Maiden Voyage," trans. Masataka Chihaya, *Maru* Special Supplement on *Taiho* and *Shinano*, November 1960.

17. Walter Lord, *Incredible Victory*, 240.

18. Mitsuo Fuchida and Masatke Okumiya, *Midway: The Battle That Doomed Japan*, 172.

19. Ibid.

20. Ibid., 173.

21. Ibid.

22. Ibid.

23. Ibid.

24. Ibid., 174.

25. Anthony Cave Brown, *Bodyguard of Lies*, 39–44. Extracts indicate the British authorities' difficult and drastic decisions to protect the security of ULTRA.

26. Tompkins, *Yokosuka*, 18.

27. Lynn Lucius Moore, "Shinano: The Jinx Carrier," *U.S. Naval Institute Proceedings*, 147.

28. U.S. Naval Technical Mission to Japan, *Reports of Damage to Japanese Warships*, Article 2: *Yamato* (BB), *Musashi* (BB), *Taiho* (CV), *Shinano* (CV), 25.

29. Moore, "Shinano: The Jinx Carrier," 147.

30. Ensign Singo Shoda, Chief Quartermaster, "I Witnessed the End of *Shinano*," and Lieutenant Commander Tatsuo Miura, Machinery Division Officer, "Why Was the Invincible *Shinano* Sunk?" *Maru* Special Supplement on *Taiho* and *Shinano*, November 1960.

31. Ibid.

32. Ibid.

33. Ibid.

34. Major Gene Burney, USAF, *Journey of the Giants*, 64.

35. Chester Nimitz and E. B. Potter, *The Great Sea War of Naval Action in World War II*, 374. "Ozawa sortied with enough carriers to make an attractive bait [Author's note: Japanese Northern Force prior to the battle for Leyte Gulf] but left behind his less expendable carriers in Japan for future use. Left behind were four large new carriers, the *Shinano, Amagi, Unryu, Katsuragi,* and two older 28,000-ton carriers, the *Junyo* and *Ryuko.*"

36. Masataka Chihaya, Letter to author, 25 June 1980.

37. Roscoe, *U.S. Submarine Operations,* 426. "Burt's Brooms."

38. Naval Operations Archives Branch, Naval Historical Center, "*Scabbardfish* (SS-397) Report of Second War Patrol." "November 29, 1944. Sank Japanese submarine I-365. A captured survivor stated they had been on patrol off Guam for 50 days."

39. Jo Toyoda, Conversation with author, 30 October 1979.

40. Shoda, "I Witnessed the End of the *Shinano.*"

41. Jo Toyoda, *The Life of the Shinano,* trans. Mieko Negishi Greene, chapter 16.

42. Garzke and Dulin, *Battleships,* 78.

Chapter 1: Contact

1. Capt. Kitaro Matsumoto, IJN, and Commander Masataka Chihaya, IJN, "Design and Construction of the *Yamato* and *Musashi,*" *U.S. Naval Institute Proceedings,* October 1963.

2. Vice Admiral (shipbuilding) Keiji Fukuda, "Secrets of CV *Shinano,* Which I Designed," trans. Masataka Chihaya, *Maru* Special Supplement on *Taiho* and *Shinano,* November 1960.

3. Yasuma, "*Shinano* Sunk on Her Maiden Voyage."

4. Jo Toyoda, Conversation with author.

5. Fukuda, "Secrets of CV *Shinano.*"

6. Masataka Chihaya, Letter to author, 25 June 1980.

7. U.S. Naval Technical Mission to Japan, *Reports of Damage to Japanese Warships,* Section V: The loss of *Shinano,* page 26.

8. Yasuma, "*Shinano* Sunk on Her Maiden Voyage."

9. Shoda, "I Witnessed the End of *Shinano.*"

10. Ibid.

Chapter 2: Target

1. This prayer, composed by Colonel James H. O'Neill during the Battle of the Bulge, was distributed on printed cards:

   Almighty and merciful Father, we humbly beseech Thee, of Thy great goodness, to restrain these immoderate rains with which we have to contend. Grant us fair weather for Battle. Graciously hearken to us as soldiers who call upon Thee, that armed with Thy power, we may advance from victory to victory, and crush the oppression and wickedness of our enemies, and establish Thy justice among men and nations.
   Amen.

   On the reverse side:

   To each officer and soldier in the Third United States Army, I wish a Merry Christmas. I have full confidence in your courage, devotion to duty, and skill in battle. We march in our might to complete victory. May God's blessing rest upon each of you on this Christmas Day.
   G. S. Patton, Jr.
   Lieutenant General
   Commanding, Third United
       States Army

   On December 23, the day after the prayer was issued, the weather cleared and remained perfect for about six days, enough to allow the Allies to break the backbone of the Von Runstedt offensive and turn a temporary setback into a crushing defeat for the enemy.

2. Zielinski is one of five survivors of the ill-fated U.S. submarine *R-12,* which sank off Key West, Florida, on June 12, 1943, because of an operational accident.

1. The commanding officer of *Shinano*, Toshio Abe, held the rank and title of captain. He had been selected for rear admiral and would have assumed that rank and title when *Shinano* joined the fighting forces. Four other officers holding the rank of captain were assigned duties normally filled by commanders: the executive officer, Captain Mikami (referred to in the third person as "the commander"); the navigator, Captain Nakamura; the gunnery officer, Captain Yokote; and the chief engineer, Captain Kōno.

2. The Joint Army-Navy Assessment Committee credits *Scabbardfish* in Area 4, immediately to the east of *Archer-Fish*, with sinking *Kisaragi Maru*, an 875-ton merchantman, at 28 degrees 56 minutes north, 141 degrees 59 minutes east on November 16. At 0700 local time the same day, *Scabbardfish* reported the sinking to COMSUBPAC by radio.

3. *Archer-Fish* sent a weather report to the B-29 command in Guam, and Captain Enright was in the radio shack during the transmission and personally heard the Japanese operator request a repeat by sending "IMI AA" and the date-time group.

4. *Scabbardfish* submerged and torpedoed a surfaced Japanese submarine mid-morning on November 29. Commander F. A. "Pop" Gunn, the skipper, then surfaced and sighted five survivors swimming. Only one permitted himself to be rescued. He was a torpedoman who told Pop by sign language and the use of a chart that his submarine was the I-365 and they were returning home after a 50-day patrol off Guam.

5. Two of the executive officers of the destroyers to escort *Shinano* were classmates of Toyoda at the Japanese Naval Academy. After the war, when Toyoda returned home from the prisoner-of-war camp in Wisconsin, where he had been since the battle of the Coral Sea, he met them. He interviewed them for information on his book, *The Life of the Shinano*, and learned of the "heated" discussions at the presailing conference with Captain Abe.

6. Roscoe, *U.S. Submarine Operations*, 39.

7. James Leutze, *A Different Kind of Victory: A Biography of Admi-*

ral Thomas C. Hart, 245. Admiral Hart was not informed until 0900 on December 24, 1941 that General MacArthur would clear all military and declare Manila an open city on Christmas Day.

8. The radio transmission was from *Archer-Fish*.

9. Toyoda, *The Life of the Shinano*, Chapter 15. Toyoda's research included data from the diary of *Shinano* signalman Umenda. It was recorded that an unidentified submarine was sighted on the starboard bow at 0245 on 29 November at a range of between 5,000 and 7,000 meters. At that time *Archer-Fish* was nine miles on the port beam (to the southwest) of *Shinano*. It was at 2245 on November 28 that *Archer-Fish* was sighted on the starboard bow. The error probably came from faulty memory after many years or, possibly, poor penmanship.

Chapter 4: Frustration

1. Not until after the war did Commander Enright learn that there was no Japanese ship named *Hayataka*, nor *Hitaka*. The explanation is found in Admiral Samuel Eliot Morison's *History of United States Naval Operations in World War II, Volume VIII, New Guinea and the Marianas, March 1944 to August 1944*. A portion of the footnote on page 295 is quoted: "This carrier . . . is called *Hitaka*, which is another reading of the characters for *Hiyo*. There was no Japanese ship named *Hitaka*. A similar confusion arose from misreading *Junyo* characters as *Hayataka*."

Chapter 5: Flight

1. Roscoe, *U.S. Submarine Operations*, 365. On March 29, 1944 the submarine *Tunny*, Commander John A. Scott commanding, was operating in the vicinity of U.S. Task Force 58, and in the general area of the western Caroline Islands. *Musashi* was sighted and *Tunny* made an excellent submerged approach on her and fired six torpedoes, but an alert escort sighted the approaching steam torpedoes and the battleship turned to avoid. Two hits were obtained on *Musashi*, and she was able to escape to Japan for repairs.

2. Ibid., 289. *Skate*, commanded by Commander Eugene McKinney, was on patrol north of Turk when he received ULTRA information on *Yamato*. He sighted her and made a submerged attack on the battleship on Christmas Day, 1943. According to Japanese records, only one torpedo hit; however, the damage was much greater than the Japanese expected. *Yamato* was able to return to Japan for repairs.

In November 1982, Gene McKinney wrote to Captain Enright providing more information on the attack. The ULTRA warned him not to be caught on the surface within 30,000 yards of *Yamato* because of the excellent new radar the escorting destroyers had installed. He therefore submerged after detecting the battleship at 35,000 yards and used high speed to close. Just prior to firing his six-bow tubes, the target zigged, requiring McKinney to fire the four after tubes. He believes he got two hits, and the ship returned to Japan for lengthy repairs.

3. Miura, "Why Was the Invincible *Shinano* Sunk?"

4. Toyoda, *The Life of the Shinano*, verbal trans. by Hatsue Akagi for author.

5. Toyoda, *The Life of the Shinano*, trans. by Mieko Negishi Greene.

Chapter 7: Optimism

1. Nimitz and Potter, *The Great Sea War*, 374.

Chapter 8: Fulfillment

1. Alden, *The Fleet Submarine in the U.S. Navy*, 261. "Archerfish (Originally Archer-Fish)."

Chapter 9: Zigzag

1. Toyoda, *The Life of the Shinano*, trans. by Mieko Negishi Greene. Lieutenant Shibata, the executive officer of the port escort, *Yukikaze*, stated that his ship had detected a radio transmission not long before torpedoes hit the carrier. There is no report

in Toyoda's book that it was also detected aboard *Shinano*, but circumstantial evidence points to this.

Chapter 10: Onslaught

1. It was not until many years later, when Captain Enright learned that the stacks were in fact constructed with a 26-degree slope to starboard, that this illusion was clarified. As *Archer-Fish* went deep and its periscope dipped below the surface, Enright had a clear view from astern *Shinano*. The 26-degree angle of the stacks made the actual list of 9–10 degrees seem much more severe.

Chapter 11: Gutted

1. U.S. Naval Technical Mission to Japan, *Reports of Damage to Japanese Warships*, Article 2, narrative, paragraphs 1–15.

2. Ibid.

3. Ibid.

4. Ibid.

5. Ibid.

6. Ibid.

7. Toyoda, *The Life of the Shinano*, trans. by Mieko Negishi Greene, Chapter 15.

8. Ibid.

9. Toyoda, *The Life of the Shinano*, trans. by Hatsue Akagi, 197.

10. Ibid., trans. by Mieko Negishi Greene.

11. Ibid.

12. Ibid.

13. Yasuma, "*Shinano* Sunk on Her Maiden Voyage."

14. Ibid.

15. Ibid.

16. Ibid.

17. Shoda, "I Witnessed the End of the *Shinano.*"

18. Toyoda, *The Life of the Shinano,* trans. by Mieko Negishi Greene, Chapter 15.

19. Ibid.

20. Ibid.

21. Miura, "Why Was the Invincible *Shinano* Sunk?"

22. Toyoda, *The Life of the Shinano,* trans. by Mieko Negishi Greene, Chapter 15.

23. Ibid. These are the recollections of Murano Ueno as related to Jo Toyoda.

24. Ibid.

25. Ibid.

26. Ibid.

27. Ibid. These are the recollections of Seaman Kanenari as related to Jo Toyoda.

28. Ibid.

29. Ibid. This information is from the diary of Seaman Kobari as related to Jo Toyoda.

30. Ibid. This information is from the diary of Seaman Ishii as related to Jo Toyoda.

31. Ibid.

32. Ibid.

33. Ibid.

34. Ibid. Lieutenant Shibata and Jo Toyoda were classmates at the Japanese Naval Academy at Etajima. Toyoda received this information during an interview with Shibata.

35. Toyoda, *The Life of the Shinano,* trans. by Hatsue Akagi, Chapter 15.

36. U.S. Naval Technical Mission to Japan, *Reports of Damage to Japanese Warships,* narrative, paragraph 11.

1. Toyoda, *The Life of the Shinano*, trans. by Mieko Negishi Greene. Toyoda obtained this transcript many years after the war from the official communication log of Commander Destroyer Division 17.

2. Miura, "Why Was the Invincible *Shinano* Sunk?"

3. U.S. Naval Technical Mission to Japan, *Reports of Damage to Japanese Warships*, narrative, paragraph 12.

4. Toyoda, *The Life of the Shinano*, trans. by Mieko Negishi Greene. These entries are from Yamagishi's diary, which was made available to Toyoda.

5. Ibid. Toyoda's interview with Ueno.

6. Shoda, "I Witnessed the End of the *Shinano.*"

7. U.S. Naval Technical Mission to Japan, *Reports of Damage to Japanese Warships*, narrative, paragraph 13.

8. Toyoda, *The Life of the Shinano*, trans. by Mieko Negishi Greene.

9. Ibid. Also Shoda, "I Witnessed the End of the *Shinano.*"

10. Toyoda, *The Life of the Shinano*, trans. by Hatsui Akagi, 229.

11. Toyoda, *The Life of the Shinano*, trans. by Mieko Negishi Greene.

12. Ibid.

13. Ibid.

14. Ibid.

15. Ibid. This account is from Seaman Sua's diary, made available to Toyoda.

16. Ibid. Shoda provided this information to Toyoda in an interview.

17. Miura, "Why Was the Invincible *Shinano* Sunk?"

18. Toyoda, *The Life of the Shinano*, trans. by Mieko Negishi Greene. Toyoda read the file copy of the message in the communication log of Commander Destroyer Division 17 while gathering material for his book.

1. An entry in Enright's patrol report submitted on December 15, 1944 suggested that the Army Air Corps Bomber Command planes seen by *Archer-Fish* from her lifeguard station as they flew toward Tokyo, might be helpful in identifying her aircraft carrier victim. But no help was forthcoming. (In 1983, when Enright learned that a Boston friend, Richard H. "Dick" O'Connell, had been on duty at the Joint Intelligence Center, Pacific Ocean Area, Enright asked about this. Dick said that a shortage of photo interpreters was to blame for the lack of coordination.)

   For many years, it appeared that no photograph of *Shinano* existed anywhere. But in April 1986, two photographs of *Shinano* appeared in *Battleships: Axis and Neutral Battleships in World War II*, a book by William H. Garzke and Robert O. Dulin, Jr. With their assistance, Enright contacted the holder of the first picture, Mr. W. G. Somerville of London, who kindly granted permission to include it in this book. This photograph had been taken by a B-29 reconnaissance aircraft flying over Tokyo at 32,000 feet on November 1, 1944. It appears that this photo never reached Commander Submarines Pacific for distribution to submarines.

   Dulin and Garzke also put Enright in touch with the holder of the second picture, Mr. Walter Chesneau of London, who granted permission to use it. This photograph was taken on November 11, 1944, when *Shinano* was in Tokyo Bay conducting builder's trials. A new tug owned by a large heavy industry company was also undergoing trials in the bay. A photographic technician, Mr. Hiroshi Arakawa, was aboard the tug and surreptitiously took a picture with *Shinano* in the distance. He destroyed all but one print, which he gave to the president of the company, who in turn sent it to Shizuo Fukui. After the war, it was given to Mr. Chesneau.

Epilogue

1. Toyoda, *The Life of the Shinano*, trans. by Mieko Negishi Greene.

2. Miura, "Why Was the Invincible *Shinano* Sunk?" Footnote by the translator, Commander Masataka Chihaya.

3. Admiral Samuel Eliot Morison, *The Two-Ocean War*, 538.

4. Russell Spurr, *A Glorious Way to Die*, 164. *Yamato* fueled at the Tokuyama fuel depot. A directive from the Combined Fleet limited her on-board oil to only what was needed for a one-way trip to Okinawa. However, the supply officer at the depot refused to limit fighting ships in that manner. He provided the Special Attack Force with 8,000 tons of fuel oil rather than the authorized 2,000 tons. Men with hand pumps in the bottom of the storage tanks rendered the difference.

5. Toyoda, *The Life of the Shinano*, trans. by Mieko Negishi Greene. Toyoda informed Captain Enright that he had visited Mrs. Toshio Abe for an interview during his research.

Sailing List—U.S.S. ARCHER-FISH (SS311) FIFTH WAR PATROL

(Obtained from the National Archives–Washington, D.C.)

Departed: Saipan, Marianas Islands
November 11, 1944

Returned: Guam, Marianas Islands
December 15, 1944

Name	Rank or Rate	Hometown or Residence of next of kin
Joseph Francis Enright	Commander	Bismarck, N.D.
Sigmund Albert Bobczynski	Lt. Commander	Portsmouth, N.H.
Davis Eli Bunting	Lieutenant	Corfu, N.Y.
Romolo Cousins	Lieutenant	Fallbrook, Cal.
John Kneeland Andrews	Lieutenant(jg)	Fennville, Mich.
Joseph Jasper Bosza	Lieutenant(jg)	Pittsburgh, Pa.
Gordon Eugene Crosby, Jr.	Ensign	Versailles, Missouri
Justin Clark Dygert	Ensign	Albany, Cal.
Daniel Webster Ellzey	Boatswain	New London, Conn.
Adams, John Calvin	RT1c	Warrenton, Ore.
August, John Frederick	S1c	Arvada, Colo.
Baird, Willie Benjamin	EM2c	Savedge, Va.
Baroody, Joseph James	SC2c	Patterson, N.J.
Barton, Harvey Buell	EM1c	Los Angeles, Cal.
Becker, Robert Clayton	TM3c	Buffalo, N.Y.

233

Name	Rank or Rate	Hometown or Residence of next of kin
Biorn, Kopel Sidney	RM3c	Baltimore, Md.
Bjorgan, Clifford Ordell	SM3c	Mount Vernon, Wash.
Bovard, James Chester	S1c	Calais, Maine
Brown, Paul Tappan	F1c	Dayton, Ohio
Brown, William Allen	STM2c	Ridgewood, N.J.
Buntain, Finley Cline Monroe	TM1c	Tulare, Cal.
Burke, James Anthony	MoMM1c	Astoria, N.Y.
Carnahan, Eugene Earl	CY	Gary, Ind.
Carnifax, Thomas Henry	EM3c	Miami Springs, Fla.
Cichon, John Joseph	MoMM1c	Chicago, Ill.
Conk, Gerald James	EM3c	Brooklyn, N.Y.
Cousins, Thomas Earle	CEM	Portland, Ore.
Cousins, Richard Merton	RT2c	Bath, Maine
Craft, Robert Charles	QM3c	Omaha, Neb.
Deiss, Donald Albert	S1c	Salinas, Cal.
DeSola, Ben Hoeb	EM3c	Houston, Tex.
Dolan, James Carl	S1c	Kayser, W. Va.
Dretke, William David	S1c	Clintonville, Wisc.
Ford, Garland Thomas	TM1c	Ozark, Ark.
Freepartner, John Joseph	S2c	Seattle, Wash.
Fuller, Marteen William	TM3c	Fort Smith, Ark.
Fuller, William Marlin	S1c	Detroit, Mich.
Gibbons, Bernard Thomas	MoMM3c	Charlestown, Mass.
Gravatt, Albert Carlisle	MoMM3c	Traer, Iowa
Healey, John Patrick	Bkr3c	Scranton, Pa.
Hoffman, Lambert Dall	CMoMM	Aurora, Ill.
Hughes, William Douglas	CPhM	Eugene, Ore.
Keast, Edwin Paul	Sc2c	Skowhegan, Maine
Kenney, Richard Albert	FCS1c	San Francisco, Cal.

Name	Rank or Rate	Hometown or Residence of next of kin
Kramer, Dwight Francis	EM3c	Fresno, Cal.
Lefebvre, Gerald Alfred	RM3c	Iron Mountain, Mich.
Lighter, Hershel Arthur	MoMM1c	Dodge City, Kan.
Lippacher, Robert Frank	RM3c	Utica, N.Y.
Lubeck, Ernest Howard	MoMM2c	N. Hollywood, Cal.
Mackin, William Andrew	Y2c	Baltimore, Md.
Mantzey, Edward Minnis	QM1c	Hale, Missouri
McKearin, Paul Gordon	TM3c	Ansonia, Conn.
McLaughlin, Charles Francis, Jr.	MoMM1c	Lowell, Mass.
McMahon, Edward Charles	EM3c	Clinton, Ill.
Myers, Earl Edgar	RT3c	Bowling Green, Ohio
Nelson, Billy George	S1c	Kansas City, Md.
Noroos, Olaf	EM2c	Brooklyn, N.Y.
Peterson, Orville Orby	TM3c	Salem, Neb.
Pierce, Evans John	S1c	Caraway, Ark.
Potanovic, John Francis	MoMM2c	Yonkers, N.Y.
Scanlan, Richard Cullen	RM1c	Chattanooga, Tenn.
Scott, Levi Frank	StM1c	Charleston, S.C.
Spriet, Edwin Albert	F1c	St. Charles, Ill.
Steullet, Frederick Thomas	MoMM1c	Rockville, Conn.
Stewart, Irwin Grant	S1c	Sabetha, Kan.
Sykes, William Lewis	QM2c	Arlington, Mass.
Valentine, Elgin Richard	EM2c	Cambridge, Ohio
Verzwyvelt, Anthony Everest	MoMM3c	Long Leaf, La.
Ward, Emory Dan	S1c	Sullivan, W. Va.

Name	Rank or Rate	Hometown or Residence of next of kin
Wells, Charles Neal	MoMM2c	Detroit, Mich.
Wells, Lowell Earnest	TM2c	Yerdon, Neb.
Whalen, Thomas William	MoMM1c	Altamont, Ill.
Wharton, Wade Lemuel	BM1c	Laredo, Tex.
Wheeler, George Dewey, Jr.	TM3c	Portsmouth, N.H.
White, Robert	EM2c	Indianapolis, Ind.
Wilken, Carl Anthony	MoMM2c	Sandusky, Ohio
Will, Alfred Irving	MoMM2c	Ft. Oglethorpe, Fla.
Wilson, Norman Jay	FCS3c	Sedan, Kan.
Winkle, Norman William	GM3c	Harbor Beach, Mich.
Yotter, Carl Norman	TM2c	Kenmore, N.Y.
Zielinski, Edward Felix	TM2c	Plainville, Conn.
Zych, Henry Joseph	MoMM2c	Milwaukee, Wisc.

BIBLIOGRAPHY

Books

Adams, Henry H. *Witness to Power: The Life of Fleet Admiral William D. Leahy.* Annapolis: Naval Institute Press, 1985.

Agawa, Hiroyuki. *The Reluctant Admiral: Yamamoto and the Imperial Navy.* Tokyo, New York: Kodansha International, Inc., 1979.

Alden, Commander John D., USN. *The Fleet Submarine in the U.S. Navy.* Annapolis: Naval Institute Press, 1979.

Bagnasco, Ermino. *Submarines of World War II.* Annapolis: Naval Institute Press, 1977.

Barnes, Robert H. *United States Submarines.* New Haven: H. F. Morse Associates, 1944.

Beach, Commander Edward L., USN. *Submarine.* New York: Henry Holt and Company, 1952.

Blair, Clay Jr. *Silent Victory: The U.S. Submarine War Against Japan.* Philadelphia, New York: J. B. Lippincott and Company, 1975.

Brown, Anthony Cave. *Bodyguard of Lies.* New York: Bantam Books, 1976.

Buell, Thomas B. *Master of Sea Power: Biography of Fleet Admiral Ernest J. King.* Boston: Little, Brown and Co.; Annapolis: Naval Institute Press, 1980.

————. *The Quiet Warrior: A Biography of Admiral Raymond A. Spruance.* Boston: Little, Brown and Co., 1974.

Compton-Hall, Commander Richard, MBE, RN. *The Underwater War, 1939–1945.* Poole: Blandford Press, 1982.

Deacon, Richard. *Kempei Tai: A History of the Japanese Secret Service.* New York: Beaufort Books, Inc., 1983.

Fahey, James C. *The Ships and Aircraft of the United States Fleet,* Victory Edition. New York: Ships and Aircraft, Inc. 1976.

Forrestal, Vice Admiral E. P., USN. *Admiral Raymond A. Spruance, USN: A Study in Command.* Washington, D.C.: U.S. Government Printing Office, 1966.

Fuchida, Mitsuo, and Masatake Okumiya. *Midway! The Battle That Doomed Japan.* New York: Ballantine Books, 1955.

Garzke, William H. and Robert O. Dulin, Jr. *Battleships: Axis and Neutral Battleships in World War II.* Annapolis: Naval Institute Press, 1985.

Grider, George, as told to Lydel Sims. *War Fish.* Boston: Little, Brown and Company, 1958.

Gurney, Maj. Gene, USAF. *Journey of the Giants.* New York: Coward-McCann, 1961.

Halsey, William F. and J. Bryan III. *Admiral Halsey's Story.* New York: McGraw-Hill, 1947.

Holmes, W. J. "Jasper." *Double-Edged Secrets.* Annapolis: Naval Institute Press, 1979.

———. *Undersea Victory.* Garden City, NY: Doubleday and Company, Inc., 1966.

Ito, Masanori with Roger Pineau. *The End of the Imperial Japanese Navy.* New York: The Berkley Publishing Group, 1984.

Jentschura, Hansgeorg, Jung Dieter, and Peter Mickel. *Warships of the Imperial Japanese Navy, 1869–1945.* Annapolis: Naval Institute Press, 1977.

Kase, Toshikazu. *Journey to the Missouri.* New Haven, CT: Yale University Press, 1950.

Leutze, James. *A Different Kind of Victory: A Biography of Admiral Thomas C. Hart.* Annapolis: Naval Institute Press, 1981.

Karig, Walter. *Battle Report: The End of an Empire.* New York: Rinehart and Company, Inc., 1947.

———. *Battle Report: Victory in the Pacific.* New York: Rinehart and Company, Inc., 1948.

Lockwood, Vice Admiral Charles A., USN, and Colonel H. C. Adamson, USAF. *Zoomies, Subs, and Zeros.* Philadelphia, New York: Chilton Co., 1956.

Lord, Walter. *Incredible Victory.* New York: Harper and Row, 1967.

Lowder, Hughston E. and Jack Scott. *Batfish: The Champion "Submarine Killer" Submarine of World War II.* Englewood Cliffs, NJ: Prentice-Hall, 1980.

Mars, Alaster. *British Submarines at War 1939–1945.* Annapolis: Naval Institute Press, 1971.

McWhirter, Morris. *Guinness Book of World Records*. New York: Sterling Publishing Co., 1986.

Middleton, Drew. *Submarine: The Ultimate Weapon: Its Past, Present, and Future*. Chicago: Playboy Press, 1976.

Miller, Nathan. *U.S. Navy: An Illustrated History*. New York: American Heritage Publishing Co.; Annapolis: Naval Institute Press, 1977.

Mitsuru, Yoshida. *Requiem for Battleship Yamato*. Seattle: University of Washington Press, 1985.

Morison, Admiral Samuel Eliot. *History of the United States Naval Operations in World War II*, Volume VIII. Boston: Atlantic-Little, Brown and Co., 1975.

————. *History of the United States Naval Operations in World War II*, Volume XIV. Boston: Little, Brown and Co., 1960.

————. *The Two-Ocean War*. Boston: Little, Brown and Co.

Naval History Division, Office of the Chief of Naval Operations. *U.S. Submarine Losses, World War II*. Washington, D.C.: U.S. Government Printing Office, 1963.

Nimitz, Chester and E. B. Potter. *The Great Sea War of Naval Action in World War II*. Englewood, NJ: Prentice-Hall, 1960.

O'Neill, Richard. *Suicide Squads: Divine Wind*. New York: Random House, Ballantine Books, 1984.

Orita, Zenji with Joseph D. Harrington. *I Boat Captain*. Canoga Park, CA: Major Books, 1976.

Polmar, Norman. *The Ships and Aircraft of the U.S. Fleet*. Annapolis: Naval Institute Press, 1978.

————. *The American Submarine*. Annapolis: The Nautical and Aviation Publishing Company of America, 1981.

Potter, E. B. *Nimitz*. Annapolis: Naval Institute Press, 1976.

————. *Bull Halsey: A Biography*. Annapolis: Naval Institute Press, 1985.

Potter, John Deane. *Yamamoto: The Man Who Menaced America*. New York: The Viking Press, 1965.

Prange, Gordon W. *Miracle at Midway*. New York: McGraw-Hill Book Co., 1982.

Roscoe, Theodore. *U.S. Submarine Operations in World War II*. Annapolis: Naval Institute Press, 1949.

Simmons, Jacques. *Warships*. New York: Grosset and Dunlap, 1971.

Spurr, Russell. *A Glorious Way to Die*. New York: Newmarket Press, 1981.

Stewart, Adrian. *The Battle of Leyte Gulf.* New York: Charles Scribner's Sons, 1980.

Sweetman, Jack. *American Naval History: An Illustrated Chronology.* Annapolis: Naval Institute Press, 1984.

Toland, John. *The Rising Sun.* New York: Bantam Books, Random House, 1970.

Tompkins, Tom. *Yokosuka: Base of an Empire.* Novato, CA: Presidio Press, 1981.

Toyoda, Jo. *The Life of the Shinano.* Tokyo: Shūeisha, 1980. Partial translation by Hatsue Akagi, Wellesley College 1980; Partial translation by Mieko Negishi Greene, Whitestone, New York, 1986.

von Mullenheim-Rechberg, Baron Burkard. *Battleship Bismarck: A Survivor's Story.* Annapolis: Naval Institute Press, 1980.

Warner, Oliver et al. *The Encyclopedia of Sea Warfare from the First Ironclads to the Present Day.* New York: Thomas Y. Crowell Co., 1975.

Watts, A. J. *Japanese Warships of World War II.* Shepperton, Surrey: Ian Allan, Ltd., 1966.

Watts, A. J. and B. G. Gordon. *The Imperial Japanese Navy.* Garden City, NY: Doubleday and Company, Inc., 1971.

Wheeler, Keith. *War Under the Pacific.* Chicago: Time-Life Books Inc., 1977.

Winton, John. *War in the Pacific.* New York: Mayflower Books, 1977.

Magazines and Articles

Beach, Commander Edward L., USN. "Jackpot!" *Reader's Digest,* February 1953.

Fukuda, Vice Admiral Keiji, IJN (shipbuilding). "Secrets of CV Shinano, Which I Designed," trans. M. Chihaya. *Maru* Special Supplement on *Taiho* and *Shinano,* November 1960.

Herzog, Bodo and Allison Saville. "Top Submarines in Two World Wars." *Naval Institute Proceedings,* September 1961.

Joint Army-Navy Assessment Committee. *Japanese Naval and Merchant Ship Losses During World War II by All Causes.* Washington: U.S. Government Printing Office, February 1947.

MacDonald, Scot. "The End of the 'Bokubokan' in World War II." *Naval Aviation News,* April 1963.

Maeda, Captain Tatsuo, IJN (engineering). "A Doomed Destiny for Shinano," trans. M. Chihaya. *Maru* Special Supplement on *Taiho* and *Shinano,* November 1960.

Matsumoto, Kitaro and Masataka Chihaya. "Design and Construction of the *Yamato* and *Musashi.*" *U.S. Naval Institute Proceedings*, October 1953.

Miura, Lieutenant Commander Tatsuo, Machinery Division Officer, IJN. "Why Was the Invincible *Shinano* Sunk?" trans. M. Chihaya. *Maru* Special Supplement on *Taiho* and *Shinano*, November 1960.

Moore, Lynn Lucius. "*Shinano*: The Jinx Carrier." *U.S. Naval Institute Proceedings*, February 1953.

Naval Operations Archives Branch, Naval Historical Center. "*Archer-Fish*: Report on Fifth War Patrol." December 15, 1944.

———. "*Scabbardfish* (SS-397): Report of Second War Patrol."

U.S. Naval Technical Mission to Japan. *Reports of Damage to Japanese Warships*, Index No. S-06-2, January 1946.

Office of Naval Intelligence. "The *Yamato* and the *Musashi.*" *The ONI Review*, July 1946.

———. "The *Taiho* and the *Shinano.*" *The ONI Review*, August 1946.

Shoda, Ensign Singo, Chief Quartermaster. "I Witnessed the End of *Shinano*," trans. M. Chihaya. *Maru* Special Supplement on *Taiho* and *Shinano*, November 1960.

Suddath, Captain Thomas H., USN. "All Tubes Ready—But Were the Torpedoes?" *Shipmate* (U.S. Naval Academy Alumni Association), January–February 1980.

Tachikawa, Yoshiharu, Naval Engineering Officer, IJN. "Conversion of BB *Shinano* Into CV," trans. M. Chihaya. *Maru* Special Supplement on *Taiho* and *Shinano*, November 1960.

Yasuma, Lieutenant Commander (medical) Takamasa, IJN. "*Shinano* Sunk on Her Maiden Voyage," trans. M. Chihaya. *Maru* Special Supplement on *Taiho* and *Shinano*, November 1960.

INDEX

242

EYEWITNESS ACCOUNTS...
POWERFUL HISTORY

FORTRESS WITHOUT A ROOF: THE ALLIED BOMBING OF THE THIRD REICH
by Wilber H. Morrison
The vivid account of the sky-high offensive that ended Hitler's dream.
_____ 90179-8 $4.95 U.S.   _____ 90180-1 $5.95 Can.

THE LAST BATTLE STATION: THE SAGA OF THE U.S.S. HOUSTON
by Duane Shultz
The riveting story of the doomed ship and her crew as captives of the Japanese.
_____ 90222-0 $4.95 U.S.   _____ 90223-9 $6.25 Can.

STORMING HITLER'S RHINE—THE ALLIED ASSAULT: February-March 1945
by William B. Breuer
The story of the largest single airborne operation in history.
_____ 90335-9 $4.95 U.S.   _____ 90336-7 $5.95 Can.

KOMMANDO: GERMAN SPECIAL FORCES OF WORLD WAR TWO
by James Lucas
Inside Hitler's special elite forces—land, sea and air.
_____ 90497-5 $4.95 U.S.

All include authentic photos!

CLASSIC
TRUE WAR ACCOUNTS
OF ACTION AND ADVENTURE

THE LAST ENEMY by Richard Hillary
The devastating memoir of a dashing pilot who, after he is shot down and horribly burned, learns the true meaning of courage.
_____ 90215-8 $3.95 U.S.

BOLDNESS BE MY FRIEND by Richard Pape
The all-time adventure classic of World War II in the tradition of *The Great Escape* with newly declassified accounts of espionage inside Hitler's Third Reich.
_____ 90515-7 $4.50 U.S.

MY SECRET WAR by Richard Drury
A combat pilot's gunsight view of America's "unofficial" war in Laos and Vietnam.
_____ 90503-3 $3.95 U.S.   _____ 90527-0 $4.95 Can.

TUMULT IN THE CLOUDS by Lt. Col. James A. Goodson
The first-hand story of the Eagle Squadron, the American air aces who flew with the RAF against the Germans. With 16 pages of photos.
_____ 90477-0 $4.95 U.S.